Microsoft® Data Mining

Related Titles From Digital Press

Rhonda Delmater and Monte Hancock, *Data Mining Explained:
A Manager's Guide to Customer-Centric Business Intelligence*,
ISBN 1-55558-231-1, 352pp, 2001

Thomas C. Redman, *Data Quality: The Field Guide*,
ISBN 1-55558-251-6, 240pp, 2001

Jesus Mena, *Data Mining Your Website*,
ISBN 1-55558-222-2, 384pp, 1999

Lilian Hobbs and Susan Hillson, *Oracle8i Data Warehousing*,
ISBN 1-55558-205-2, 400pp, 1999

Lilian Hobbs, *Oracle8 on Windows NT*, ISBN 1-55558-190-0, 384pp, 1998

Tony Redmond, *Microsoft® Exchange Server for Windows 2000: Planning,
Design, and Implementation*, ISBN 1-55558-224-9, 1072pp, 2000

Jerry Cochran, *Mission-Critical Microsoft® Exchange 2000:
Building Highly Available Messaging and Knowledge Management Systems*,
ISBN 1-55558-233-8, 352pp, 2000

**For more information or to order these and other Digital Press
titles please visit our website at www.bhusa.com/digitalpress!**

At www.bhusa.com/digitalpress you can:

- Join the Digital Press Email Service and have news about
  our books delivered right to your desktop

- Read the latest news on titles

- Sample chapters on featured titles for free

- Question our expert authors and editors

- Download free software to accompany select texts

Microsoft® Data Mining

Integrated Business Intelligence for e-Commerce and Knowledge Management

Barry de Ville

Digital Press
An imprint of Butterworth-Heinemann

Boston • Oxford • Auckland • Johannesburg • Melbourne • New Delhi

Library of Congress Cataloging-in-Publication Data

de Ville, Barry.
   Microsoft® data mining : integrated business intelligence for e-commerce and knowledge
management / by Barry de Ville.
      p. cm.
   Includes index.
   ISBN 1-55558-242-7 (pbk. : alk. paper)
   1. Data mining. 2. OLE (Computer file) 3. SQL server. I. Title.

   QA76.9.D343 D43 2000
   006.3--dc21

                    00-047514

British Library Cataloging-in-Publication Data

A catalogue record for this book is available from the British Library.

The publisher offers special discounts on bulk orders of this book.
For information, please contact:

Manager of Special Sales
Butterworth–Heinemann
225 Wildwood Avenue
Woburn, MA 01801-2041
Tel: 781-904-2500
Fax: 781-904-2620

For information on all Butterworth–Heinemann publications available, contact our
World Wide Web home page at: http://www.bh.com.

10 9 8 7 6 5 4 3 2 1

Printed in the United States of America

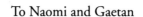

To Naomi and Gaetan

Contents

Foreword

The year 1989 seems so long ago! Back in those heady days of the software industry, a chap named Barry de Ville approached me with a view to having my organization license a rudimentary software tool for data mining. At the time, I worked in a large multinational software firm and was responsible for the business side of several mission-critical R&D projects aimed at changing the paradigm of software tools for knowledge workers. Each project involved data modeling and data mining. In the end, after spending many millions of dollars, these projects were either dropped or significantly altered. However, one piece that survived this purge was the software licensed from de Ville. In fact, it went on to become part of the product that changed the company and established a market for desktop analytics.

The business decision to terminate or severely curtail what were once corporate priorities had its roots in the realization that the marketplace, and in particular the high-end business customer in large corporations, was not yet ready for large-scale data mining. Two reasons for this dominated, and both related to the past and not the present. First, there were no generally accepted standards to link nascent mining tools to various data models, and there certainly were no widely used data mining frameworks. Second, there was a general lack of know-how and a poor understanding of analytics in the target user community.

Today, the advent of de facto standards such as OLAP databases and tools such as OLE DB for DM, along with the emergence of data mining frameworks, have firmly established data mining as a viable and important use of computing in business. For example, this capability has been honed into powerful applications such as customer relationship management. This application domain is becoming all the more important with the advent of large-scale databases underpinning e-commerce and e-business.

The second reason for the earlier failure had much more to do with the receptor capacity of the marketplace than with the vendor community's ability to deliver appropriate tools. With the vast majority of organizations seeing the database only in terms of a relational model, the concept of applying multidimensional analytics to corporate data was little more than a dream. Consequently, the second key to opening the data mining market has been the spread of know-how. In the workplace this know-how is primarily supplied through widely available information in the trade press and commercial computer-related publications.

The decision by Microsoft Corporation, as early as 1998, to become a major player in the data mining arena set the stage for things to come. Today's coupling of the latest data mining capabilities with SQL Server 2000 has created a clear and present need to capture and consolidate in one place the principles of data mining and multidimensional analytics with a practical description of the Microsoft data mining architecture and tool set. This book does just that.

Recognizing the receptor problem and the power and ease of use of the new Microsoft data mining solution has afforded Barry de Ville with the opportunity to help redress receptor capacity by writing this practical guidebook, which contains illustrative and illuminating examples from business, science, and society. Moreover, he has taken an approach that compartmentalizes concepts and relationships so that the reader can more readily assimilate the content in terms of his or her own general knowledge and work experience, rather than dig through the more classical formalisms of an academic treatise.

Peter K. MacKinnon
Managing Director
Synergy Technology Management
e-mail: petemac@istar.ca
telephone: (613) 241-1264

Preface

Data mining exploits the knowledge that is held in the enterprise data store by examining the data to reveal patterns that suggest better ways to produce profit, savings, higher-quality products, and greater customer satisfaction. Just as the lines on our faces reveal a history of laughter and frowns, the patterns embedded in data reveal a history of, for example, profits and losses. The retrieval of these patterns from data and the implementation of the lessons learned from the patterns are what data mining and knowledge discovery are all about.

This book will appeal to people who have come to depend upon Microsoft to provide a high-performance and economical point of entry for an ever-increasing range of computer applications and who sense the potential value of pursuing data mining approaches to support business intelligence initiatives in their enterprises. Traditional producers and consumers of business intelligence products and processes, especially OLAP (On-Line Analytical Processing), will also be attracted by this information. Most business intelligence vendors, especially Microsoft, recognize that business intelligence and data mining are different facets of the same process of turning data into knowledge. SQL Server 7, released late in 1998, introduced SQL Server 7 OLAP services, thus providing a built-in OLAP reporting facility for the database. In the same manner, SQL Server 2000 provides built-in data mining services as a fundamental part of the database. Now, both these important forms of business reporting will be available as core components of the database functionality; further, by providing both sets of facilities in a common interface and platform, Microsoft has taken the first step in providing a seamless integration of the various methods and metaphors of business reporting so that one simple, unified interface to the knowledge contained in data is provided. Whether that knowledge was delivered on the basis of an OLAP technique or data mining technique is irrelevant to most users, and now it will be irrelevant in a unified SQL 2000 framework.

This book will emphasize the data mining aspects of business intelligence in order to explain and illustrate data mining techniques and best practices, particularly with respect to the data mining functionality that is available in the new generation of Microsoft business intelligence tools: the new OLE DB for DM (data mining) and SQL Server functions. Both OLAP and data mining are complex technologies. OLAP, however, is intuitively easier to grasp, since the reporting dimensions are almost always business terms and concepts and are organized as such. Data mining is more flexible than OLAP, however, and the patterns that are sought out in data through data mining are often counter-intuitive from a business standpoint. So, initially, it can be more difficult to conceptualize data mining. A core goal of this book is to help all users to move through this conceptualizational task in order to reap the benefits of an integrated OLAP and data mining framework.

Discovering successful patterns that are contained in data, but that are normally hidden, can be a formidable challenge. For example, take gross margins in a retail sales data store. Here we see that the margins fluctuate over the course of a year. A plot of the values held in the gross margin field in the data store might reveal a 10 percent increase in gross margin between summer and fall. We might be tempted to conclude that sales margins increase as we move from summer to fall. In this case we would say that the increase in gross margin depends upon the season.

But there are many other potential dependencies, which could influence gross margin, that are locked in the data store. Along with the field *season* are other fields of data—for example, quantity sold, discount rate, commission paid, customer location, other purchases made, length of time as a customer, and so on. What if the discount rate is greater in the summer than in the fall? Then, possibly, the increase in gross margin that we see in the fall is simply a result of a lower discount rate. In this case gross margin does not vary by season at all—it varies according to the discount rate! In this case the apparent relationship, or dependency, that we observed between season and discount rate is a spurious one. If we adjust our view of gross margins to remove the effect of discount rate, then maybe we would find that, actually, gross margins would be higher in the summer. So, in order to do a thorough job of data mining and knowledge discovery it is essential to look at all potential explanatory factors and associated data elements to ensure that the very best pattern is retrieved from the data and that no spurious, and potentially misleading, effects are introduced into the patterns that we select.

What if the data store could be manipulated so that all of the dependencies that affect the questions we are looking at (e.g., gross margin) could be considered together? What if we could search through all the combinations of dependencies and find a unique combination, or pattern, that isolates a particular combination of events that maximizes the gross margin? Then, instead of simply showing the effect of one condition, say season, on gross margin, we could show the combined effect of a pattern, say a particular time, location, and discount rate, that produces the maximum gross margin. Once we have isolated this optimal pattern, we have a particular gem of wisdom, since, if we can reproduce that pattern more often in the future, we can establish a strategy that will systematically increase our gross margin and associated profitability over time.

There is no lack of data in the modern enterprise. So the raw material for data mining and knowledge discovery is abundantly available. The data store contains records that have the potential to reveal patterns of dependencies that can enrich a wide variety of enterprise goals, missions, and objectives. Retail sales can benefit from the examination of sales records to reveal highly profitable retail sales patterns. Financial analysts can examine the records of financial transactions to reveal patterns of successful transactions. An engineering enterprise can search through its records surrounding the engineering process—manufacturing time, lot size, assembly parameters, and operator number—to determine the combination of data conditions that relate to the quality measure of the device coming off the assembly line. Marketing analysts can look at the marketing data store to detect patterns that are associated with market growth or customer responsiveness.

The data are freely available and the pay-offs are enormous: the ability to decrease inventory, increase customer buying propensity, drive product defects detection closer to the assembly line, and so on by as little as 1 percent represents a truly staggering, Midas-like fortune in the billion-dollar-a-day industries of finance, manufacturing, retail services, and high technology. The key to reaping the rewards of data mining is to have a cost-effective set of tools and body of knowledge to undertake the knowledge discovery.

Until recently the tools that were available to accomplish this task were relatively rare and relatively expensive. Business intelligence OLAP facilities have become much more commonplace but, as demonstrated above, business intelligence OLAP tools may not find all the patterns and dependencies that lie in data. For this, a data mining tool is required.

Microsoft recognized this requirement after the release of SQL Server 7 and began a development program to migrate data mining and knowledge discovery capabilities into the SQL Server 2000 release. This release, and the associated data mining and knowledge discovery tools, techniques, concepts, and best practices, are reviewed here. The primary task will be to explain data mining and the Microsoft data mining framework. The chapters are as follows:

1.   Introduction to Data Mining: its relevance and utility to 2000-era enterprises and the role of Microsoft architecture and technologies. This chapter provides a big-picture view of data mining: what it is, why it is useful, and how it works. What are the barriers to the adoption of data mining and what is Microsoft doing about these barriers? This covers the Microsoft Socrates project and the directions that Microsoft will pursue in data mining in the future.

2.   The Data Mining Process: This chapter discusses the process of using data to model and reflect real-world events and activity: the interoperation of measurement, data and business models, and conceptual paradigms to reflect real-world phenomena. Testing and refining the models—patterns, structure, relationships, explanation, and prediction—are also discussed. Best practices in executing the data mining mission, such as business goal, ROI outcome identification, the conceptual model, operational measures, data elements, data transformation, data exploration, model development, model exploration, model verification, and performance measurement, are addressed in depth.

      Chapter 2 also discusses the following topics:

   ▪ ROI and the choice of an appropriate business objective

   ▪ Creating a seamless business process for data mining

   ▪ Closed-loop processes

      You can't manage what you can't measure—the role of performance measurement and campaign management for continuous improvement in data mining is explained in this chapter.

3.   Data Mining Tools and Techniques (and the associated Microsoft data mining architecture): revealing structure in data—profiling and segmentation approaches, and predictive modeling—applications and their lifetime value optimization through profitable customer acquisition. Data mining query languages and the integration with OLAP, OLE DB for DM, and scaling to large databases are explained in detail. Leveraging the Microsoft architecture—how developers and users can leverage the Microsoft

technology and architecture and how Microsoft's strategy plays to the broadened focus of data mining, the Web, and the desktop— is discussed in this chapter.

4.   Managing the Data Mining Project: assembling the data mart; best practices in preparing data for analysis (includes best practices in data assembly for data mining). Techniques for integrating data preparation with Microsoft database management tools: Access and SQL.

5.   Modeling Data: best practices for producing models (includes a discussion of best practices for producing both descriptive and predictive models); techniques for using OLE DB DM extensions; best practices for testing models, including validation and sanity checks.

6.   Deploying the Data Mining Project Results: best practices for deploying the model results; predictive models. This includes managing the deployment results by implementing a closed-loop campaign management and performance measurement system.

7.   Managing Knowledge about the Project: knowledge management in data mining. A framework for conceptualizing and capturing an integrated view of profitability drivers in the business and associated Microsoft technologies.

Acknowledgments

This book would never have been produced without input from several talented and supportive people at various stages along the way. Rolf Schliewen and Jacques deVerteuil were the first to introduce me to decision trees and sent me down a path toward data mining from which I have never returned. Doug Laurie Lean, Ed Suen, David Biggs, Rob Rose, Tim Eastland, Mike Faulkner, and Andy Burans provided invaluable assistance on this path.

I never would have written this book without the advice, assistance, support, and urging of my long time friend, Peter Neville. Another Neville, Padraic, urged me on, and two dear business associates, Ken Ono and Eric Apps, provided a safe, supportive, and stimulating environment in which to hatch the plan.

Lorna Palmer is a seasoned hand in the area of knowledge management and has helped me over the years come to an understanding and appreciation of the relationship between it and data mining. She contributed the outline and much of the content in the chapter on knowledge management and I simply could not have written it without her.

Jesus Mena, a fellow data mining traveler for over ten years, introduced me to the publishing family that has continued to move this project forward: Phil Sutherland, who started the project, and Theron Shreve, Pam Chester, Katherine Antonsen, Lauralee Reinke, and Alan Rose who, together, finished it.

Peter MacKinnon, who wrote the Foreword, has been a constant inspiration, as has Stan Matwin. Greg James and Sergei Anayan have provided many detailed notes and comments to help shape the text you see today.

I received constant support and encouragement as the product you see here took its sometimes-torturous route to completion from Laurie O'Neil. Writing tends to be a solitary activity and Laurie chose to support me rather than regret my absence or chafe at not being with me; for that, I am both thankful and mindful that—thanks to this support—better results are reflected in the pages to follow.

Introduction to Data Mining

The thirst for knowledge is an innate human characteristic.

—Aristotle

People have been recording and extracting knowledge from data since the beginning of time. The cave drawings of Arles, the cuneiform tablets documenting shipboard loading manifests of ancient Babylon, and the Rosetta Stone are examples of the defining human characteristic to make sense of the world through data constructs recorded in symbolic—frequently numeric—form. The cave drawings capture the experience of the day—the life and death dramas of the hunt, the harvest, the feasting, and the fertility; the cuneiform tablets record the minutiae of early trade—counting the weight, cut, and number of precious stones or the number and volume of amphorae filled with olive oil; and the Rosetta Stone provides a key to Egyptian hieroglyphics.

Everywhere and always people reflect and record their reality in data laid down in various recording media. The earliest data miners reconstructed life styles from cave drawings so as to describe and predict human activity in those circumstances. They could describe and predict trading patterns and the effect of variables on the olive tree harvest in the ancient Mediterranean Sea area. Indeed, even today archeologists and anthropologists can infer effects on current-day trading patterns based on early trading models built from examining the data contained in these and other tablets. These tablets, of course, are "little tables"—the precursors of modern database systems.

So data mining has its roots in one of the oldest of human activities: the desire to summarize experience in some numeric or symbolic form so as to describe it better and preserve both meaning and experience. As soon as we describe and preserve experience through data and symbolic traces, we inevitably begin the process of disentangling the meanings through some kind of data mining process. Regardless of the source of the record, it seems inevitable that someone will come along to interpret it so as to make better predictions about the experience that has been recorded. Often the description seems out of idle curiosity, but inevitably the motivation turns toward extracting some kind of knowledge for profit or knowledge that can potentially be translated into another kind of spiritual or material return.

Although data mining, or knowledge discovery as it is sometimes called, seems to be a very recent and novel invention, the origins of data mining and knowledge discovery are as old as the record of civilization. Nowadays, as our ability to record data increases—astronomically it seems—so too does our ingenuity turn to develop more powerful data mining (data disentangling) methods to keep up with the interpretation of the constant, and growing, accumulation of data. This leads us to a definition of data mining: Data mining is a current-day term for the computer implementation of a timeless human activity. It is the process of using automated methods to uncover meaning—in the form of trends, patterns, and relationships—from accumulated electronic traces of data.

It is normal to use data mining for a purpose—typically to gain insight and improvements in business functions. The utility of data is unquestioned. But how does the utility present itself? Utility presents itself in the form of a model. If I can describe the operation of natural phenomena with a few well-chosen data elements, then I can present a simple data summarization—a model built from data—that is easy to grasp and conceptualize. Knowing my minimal monthly average in my savings account provides me with a simple and readily understandable indicator of many aspects of my financial well-being. The average is a conceptual construct—built from data. It is a model of the world and, by manipulating the model in my mind, I can make intelligence guesses, or inferences, about the real world that is reflected in my model. For example, if I can plot an upward or downward trend in my account earnings rate, then I can predict with greater certainty the likely rate of return in the next period. If I double (or halve) my average savings rate, then I can make some important inferences about the state of my earning power that is behind this doubling or halving.

We use symbolic models to reflect real-world events in an ever-broadening range of areas. By manipulating the models we find out more about the real world. We can translate model manipulations, carried out conceptually (and safely) into real-world manipulations, often at a profit. This is the power of knowledge; specifically, this is the power of knowledge discovery or data mining.

Data are exploding all around us: We leave daily electronic traces of our activity in almost everything we do. As computer power, storage capacity, and broadband networking continue to expand, so too do our data traces broaden and deepen. It can be interesting to imagine what future anthropologists, armed with data detection devices, will make of our current civilization. It is easy to believe that the archeological digs of tomorrow will be data mining workstations that can detect, extract, summarize, and apply meaning to the data traces we leave in this vast, interconnected computer and communications network we inhabit.

In fact, in this age of the Web, the data mining workstations of tomorrow are being built today. What do these workstations look like? How do they work? What can we do with them? Specifically, what is Microsoft up to in this area? Will organizations such as Microsoft tap into something like a basic human instinct to extract meaning from data? Does data mining have the same intuitive appeal as the graphical user interface? Does it have the same appeal as word processing, spreadsheets, e-mail, and database software? Does data mining belong on the desktops of computer users everywhere? Data mining is certainly here. It is not going to go away. Let's see where current technology appears to be taking data mining and where it is likely to go.

1.1   Something old, something new

As suggested previously, civilization has always tapped data to uncover meaning and to make intellectual, economic, and technical progress. Until the late 1990s, most of the data tapping and disentangling of meaning took place in a specialized research and development–oriented environment and took specialized skills to produce results. Data mining techniques were developed in scientific settings and, originally, had scientific goals and objectives in mind. The computer algorithms to perform data mining tasks were developed by statisticians and artificial intelligence researchers.

However, by the turn of the century, computer technology—and associated computer networks—had become commodity items. Just as a spreadsheet program provides sophisticated business planning functions on the desktop, so too could tools be designed to provide sophisticated statistical and artificial intelligence functions on the desktop. If statistical and numerical algorithms could be harnessed to design buildings, bridges, and even nuclear weapons, so too could these same algorithms be used to build new products, better customer relationships, and, quite possibly, new forms of businesses based on intelligent and automated data mining algorithms.

To mine data you need to have access to data. It is no coincidence that data mining grew at the same time that data warehousing developed. As computer power and database capability grew through the late 1900s, it became increasingly clear that data were not simply passive receptacles, useful in performing billing or order-entry functions, but data could also be used in a more proactive role so as to provide predictive value that would be useful in guiding a business forward. This concept led to the development of computer decision support, or executive information systems (EIS). The idea was to harness growing computing power and improved graphical interfaces in order to slice and dice data in novel ways to blow away old, static reporting concepts. Slicing and dicing data—drilling down into many detailed reports or zooming up to a 10,000-foot "big-picture" view— required special ways of organizing data for decision making. This gave rise to the concept of the data warehouse.

Decision support systems and associated data warehousing created an environment that integrated data from disparate business systems. This extended traditional business reporting to support consolidated reporting across multiple sources of data, usually in an interactive, graphically-enhanced mode.

The term *data warehousing* was virtually unknown in 1990. Ten years later data warehousing had become a $10+ billion business annually—a business that was devoted to capturing and organizing data so as to provide a proactive analytical (versus operational) environment in which to deploy data in the service of defining and guiding business activity.

Business caught on to the same thing that science caught on to: Data capture experience and, appropriately treated, can provide lots of ammunition to win competitive battles. Data warehousing, by organizing data for analysis, provides the raw material of data organized for analysis and decision making.

The field of decision support and executive information systems continued to evolve in line with the growth of data warehousing. Decision support and executive information systems gave way to the more general concept of business intelligence (coined in 1996 by IT trend watcher, Howard Dresner of the Gartner Group). Dresner's insight suggested that as data moved from supporting operational purposes to include analytical purposes, the analytical user community would expand beyond specialists to include business analysts and managers. By the turn of the century, business intelligence, as distinct from data warehousing, had become a $5 billion business worldwide.

The general term *business intelligence* involved the concept of organizing data along various potential dimensions of analysis so that any one view of data—for example, sales results—could be cross-referenced and displayed from within any number of other potential dimensions—for example, region or product line. The ability to move up and down dimensions involved the concept of drilling down into detail or zooming up for a more general view. The ability to show variations in data along several dimensions involved the concept of slicing and dicing data along various dimensional views. This general approach became known as on-line analytical processing—that is, processing data for analytical purposes (as opposed to operational purposes). The on-line concept referred to the idea of having the analytical data continuously available. This on-line analytical processing, or OLAP, required, therefore, the existence of a data warehouse so that data were continuously available and available in a form that would support analytical, decision support tasks.

While OLAP certainly represented a major step forward, particularly when compared with old-style, static batch reports and difficult to execute ad hoc queries, the approach ran into significant limitations when faced with the multiple fields and dimensions of data that were accumulating on mainframes and servers at the turn of the century. To display four products, in five sales regions, at three discount rates, over four quarters is a $4 \times 5 \times 3 \times 4$ combinatorial problem—that is, 240 combinations of data. Add another dimension—for example, channel (direct, mail order, regional, and national distributor)—and the combinations increase to 960. Modern databases and information collection mechanisms can deliver hundreds of potential dimensions of analysis—enough to provide significant conceptual obstacles to effective OLAP processing.

The OLAP dimensional data representation is constructed so as to contain all relevant dimensions of analysis and associated summaries in easy to retrieve, preprocessed form. This preprocessing of data means that the results of a query can be presented almost instantaneously—if the dimensional combination the end users want has been reflected in the construction of the dimensional representation. What is missing in OLAP is the ability to sort through all the potential dimensions of analysis and quickly identify only the meaningful ones. A dimension is meaningful if it displays data in a fashion that leads to better business decisions—for example, in a

Figure 1.1
*The origins of
data mining*

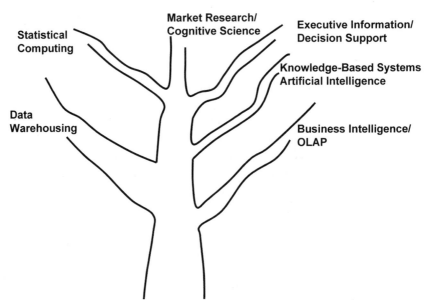

regional sales report, only some regions might be under or over projected sales. So the end user might only want to look at certain regions. In order to understand the deviations of the actual figures compared with planned figures, only a few other factors in the data—for example, discount rate, product line—might turn out to be influential in explaining the sales figure deviations. In an OLAP environment, it is possible to spend a lot of time in a fruitless search for meaningful dimensions of analysis in order to correctly identify the patterns in data that can make or break a good sales analysis. Often, the relevant dimensions are not presented in the dimensional representation, because the relevancy only becomes obvious when presented in combination with other dimensions. If this is not known ahead of time, the combination is not built.

Figure 1.1 illustrates the origins of data mining.

A cohesive approach to looking through many combinations of data dimensions in order to identify useful patterns in data would be very helpful and would complement OLAP styles of analysis very well. Weeding through hundreds of competing and potentially useful dimensions of analysis and associated combinations is a job that is custom-crafted for data mining solutions: All data mining algorithms have built-in mechanisms to examine huge numbers of potential patterns in data in order to reduce the results to a simple summary report.

The most common techniques employed in data mining are decision trees, neural networks, cluster analysis, and regression. The results are typically used to describe relationships in data or to make predictions. OLAP cubes are appropriate for a limited amount of data exploration, in order to explore major variations according to critical and known business dimensions. But when the dimensions change—as the business changes—or when novel situations are being explored, data mining turns out to be an extremely flexible and powerful complement to OLAP. The two approaches to reporting on data belong together and are synergistic when presented and deployed together.

By the late 1990s OLAP had become almost routine, and data mining was well on its way toward integration with the evolving business reporting paradigm of using data to drive the business as well as run it. Microsoft released SQL Server 7 in the fall of 1998 in order to provide OLAP access as standard components of the desktop. At the same time, the company announced a data mining initiative, which would also introduce data mining functions, as a complement (and supplement) to the OLAP functions as part of its SQL Server 2000 release.

1.2   Microsoft's approach to developing the right set of tools

Doing knowledge discovery by browsing through the enterprise data store is a bit like working an archaeological dig. You know that the evidence that could yield a brilliant insight on the significant drivers of the enterprise is there, but it is deeply buried, concealed by a lot of noisy data, and, if you are not careful, are impatient, or simply not on your toes, you are going to miss it.

Welcome to the dig. Given the fortunes to be made in knowledge discovery, the intrepid knowledge discovery agent would be wise to assemble a comprehensive, effective, easy to use, and efficient tool kit to execute the knowledge discovery mission. What are the components of this tool kit?

1.2.1   Discovery of relationships

One of the key features of a knowledge discovery tool is the ability to unearth relationships. These are the dependencies that are captured in the data and that reveal the patterns characterizing the operation of the phenomenon under investigation. Relationships may be subtle and multifaceted or they may be in your face and brutally simple. An effective knowledge discovery tool has to be tuned to detect either kind of pattern—from the deeply complex to the most straightforward. In either case the evidence to support the relationship may be captured by the data store. Therefore, the knowledge discovery tool has to be able to unearth both simple and complex relationships when searching through the data store.

As shown previously (in the Preface), the most obvious relationship (e.g., the relationship between season and gross margin) may not be the operative relationship at all (the gross margin may be a combined effect of quantity sold, discount rate, and type of product). The knowledge discovery tool has to be smart enough not to leap on the most readily apparent dependency in the data, since this relationship (often referred to as a spurious relationship), as with the relationship between gross margin and season, may be more apparent than real. Since these types of spurious relationships are very common in the examination of dependencies in a data store, the knowledge discovery tool must have a method to detect spurious relationships—that is, relationships that are the result of the operation of another dependency in the data. This will prevent the knowledge discovery tool from presenting a distorted view of the dynamics of the question being examined.

1.2.2   Defining the model of the world

There is a Catch-22 to knowledge discovery. The end user, acting as a discovery agent, cannot know in advance whether the relationships to be discovered are simple or complex. Ahead of time it is difficult to assess which dependencies are spurious (i.e., spring from the operation of another dependency in the data) and which dependencies are fundamental patterns that characterize the operation of the question under investigation. To escape from this Catch-22, users of the discovery tool need to employ their knowledge of the area under investigation and need to incorporate that knowledge into the search for data patterns so as to guide the search engine to identify fundamental relationships and ignore the spurious ones. Briefly, this means that the knowledge discovery agent needs to speculate on the form of the data pattern and associated data dependencies by forming a mental model of the operation of the data pattern in terms of how data elements interact to produce the effect that characterizes the question being investigated.

The mental model formed by the knowledge discovery agent will have components that match the contents of the fields of data contained in the data store. The knowledge discovery agent has to determine how the components of the mental model relate to the contents of the data store. The fields of data in the data store contain measurements that form a trace of the phenomenon that the data store is meant to reflect. Thus, discount rate becomes a measure of purchase practice and, possibly, supply and demand. Purchase practice and supply and demand may be components of the mental model formed by the knowledge discovery agent.

The knowledge discovery tool needs to illuminate the relationship between the data store and the mental model. It needs to facilitate the construction of a mental model the data patterns can fit into. In this manner not only will the data patterns show strong effects, but these effects will support the viewpoint and understanding of the knowledge discovery agent, as revealed by the model of the phenomenon that is being employed. This, in turn, will contribute to a greater understanding of the theory of operation that is used to explain the question under examination. It will ensure that the dependencies that are revealed will be fundamental ones, not spurious ones.

1.2.3   Dealing with data quality

The tools need to be robust to deal with the reality of real-world data. The data store may not be fully suited to capture the essence of the model construct, simple or complex, that eventually is constructed. The data store may contain missing data, so the data discovery tool has to make provisions for this.

Most certainly, the data store will contain data that are measured in various ways—for example, discount rate may be captured as a percentage or it may be captured as a range (e.g., 5 percent to 15 percent). So the data discovery tool has to deal with data, like percentage, that are quantitative (i.e., range from 1 to 100 in continuous increments) or qualitative (i.e., more than 50 percent, less than 25 percent). It needs to deal with data that are very simple, such as the qualitative type of data—M for male and F for female—and data that are very complex, such as the quantitative data refractive index, which is used in the manufacturing of optical components.

The data discovery tool also has to deal with data that are stored in a variety of formats—for example, alphabetic formats (as seen in the M and F, above), numeric formats (like, percentage), and even specialized data formats, such as time and date stamps (e.g., day, month, year codes).

1.2.4   Consolidated data mining tool requirements

This perspective on data mining and knowledge discovery provides a number of criteria on the requirements for a robust, pragmatic, real-world knowledge discovery tool. These requirements can be summarized as follows:

- The tool should be able to dig into the data set to identify effects within effects; it should not automatically assume that the strongest effect is the best effect, since this effect may be spurious—that is, it may be the result of a more fundamental relationship contained within the data.

- To help develop a mental model of the phenomenon under study, the tool should provide features that enable the association of data values, and groups of data values, with corresponding components of the mental model used by the knowledge discovery agent to model and explain the theory of operation under investigation.

- The tool needs to deal with missing values in the data elements of fields of the data store.

- The tool should be able to support both qualitative measurements of concepts as well as quantitative measurements and should be able to describe the relationships between any two or more concepts regardless of whether the measurement is qualitative or quantitative.

1.3   Benefits of data mining

Data mining offers three major advantages to the enterprise:

1.   It provides information about business processes, the customer, and market behavior.

2.   It takes advantage of data that may already be available in operational data collections, data marts, and the data warehouse.

3.   It provides patterns of behavior, reflected in data, that can drive the accumulation of business knowledge and the ability to foresee and shape future events.

Data mining, by providing more information about the market, goes to the heart of the competitive advantage enjoyed by the enterprise. In this view, the benefit that can be delivered by data mining is only constrained by the amount of novel, useful information it can deliver as a result of its analysis of the data store.

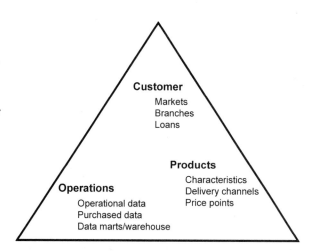

Figure 1.2
Role of data mining and knowledge discovery in the three areas of enterprise excellence (Treacy and Wiersma model)

Data mining allows for additional leverage of operational data and associated data collections in data marts and data warehouses. There is no shortage of raw data in today's networked, computer-mediated world. Data mining turns this accelerating accumulation of data into an inexhaustible supply of raw materials for the generation of business advantage.

Since the range of data, and associated, revealed trends and patterns, is very large and includes marketing, sales, engineering, finance, and human resource information, the potential application of data mining, and its associated reach into all key areas of business, is broad. According to a model developed by Treacy and Wiersma,[1] operational excellence, customer excellence, and product excellence distinguish businesses (see Figure 1.2). Since data mining can tap into data sources that reflect upon any of these three areas, it can provide business advantage in these areas.

Various data mining groups routinely deploy data mining in these three areas, as shown in the following examples:

- *Customer excellence.* Bank of America used data mining to identify the characteristics of customers for their high-margin home equity loan product to find likely new prospects for the offering. The associated targeting profile was so effective that it ended up identifying some new equity loan prospects who were already in the preliminary application phases of the loan.

- *Operational excellence.* American Express uses a worldwide operation data repository to negotiate volume discounts from suppliers and to

1.   *Harvard Business Review*, January–February 1993.

pinpoint—and eliminate—high-cost activities (and, conversely, to identify and promote high-margin operational practices).

- *Product excellence.* Bell Canada is one of the many providers in the area of telecommunications that is using business intelligence and customer relationship management tools to ensure that it gets the right products to the right customers at the right time. "Delivering products to customers becomes more complicated all the time," says Bill Comeau, senior director of database marketing services for Bell Canada International Inc. in Toronto (as quoted in the March 13, 2000, issue of *Information Week*). The goal is to create a unified system that can discover patterns in information and support development and marketing of products to customers.

1.3.1 Enterprise applications of data mining

A review of the applications of data mining shows that indeed, if data can be found to capture and record the operation of a given phenomenon, then the meaning of the phenomenon can be described, modeled, and predicted using data mining approaches. This means that data mining can be used to work toward customer, operational, and product excellence in both business-to-business and business-to-customer situations.

Here are just a few examples, drawn from media reports, that describe how data mining is being used today. As shown in the following list, data mining applies to the entire customer life cycle—from product conceptualization through customer acquisition, servicing, retention, and lifetime value optimization—and to many business-to-business life-cycle activities as well. In any area where we can collect data, we can use data mining to extract knowledge for competitive advantage. This clearly involves creating advantage in the three areas of enterprise excellence: products, customers, and operations (according to Treacy and Wiersma). These examples are shown in greater detail in Table 1.1.

- Customer acquisition and customer targeting
- Profitability and risk reduction
- Loyalty management and cross-selling
- Operational analysis and optimization
- Relationship marketing
- Customer attrition and churn reduction

- Fraud detection

- Campaign management

- Business-to-business/channel, inventory, and supply chain management

- Market research, product conceptualization

- Product development, engineering and quality control

- Sales and sales management

Table 1.1   *Illustrative Data Mining Best Practices Drawn from Media Reports*

Customer acquisition and customer targeting	Data mining can reveal the trends and patterns that characterize the best customers. Data mining can also show what unique combination of characteristics tends to be associated with customer use of specific products. Knowledge of these characteristics can be used to target specific groups of people for acquisition or for specific product promotions.
	Firstar Bank of Milwaukee is a typical user of this kind of data mining approach to direct marketing. Firstar uses information gained from data mining to rank order customers into different groups according to propensity to purchase home equity loans, charge cards, CDs, savings, or investments. This ranking is then used to target offers to the most likely prospects.
	The payoff for Firstar is a fourfold improvement in response to promotions—a substantial improvement in the cost/return ratio of direct marketing campaigns.
	FirstUnion is the sixth largest banking company in the United States. FirstUnion now also ranks among the country's largest credit card issuers and has climbed to the number six slot of top debit card issuers. In one series of data mining–driven acquisition campaigns, the Card Products Division nearly tripled the size of its managed credit card portfolio to more than $6.5 billion in receivables. FirstUnion also developed techniques for acquisitions and prospect targeting and employs a market test strategy prior to rollout and data mining techniques to target prospects.
	Capital One Financial Corp., one of the largest credit card issuers in the United States, uses data mining to help sell the most appropriate of its 3,000 financial products—including secured, joint, cobranded, and college student cards—to 150 million potential prospects in its data warehouse.
	Capital One's data mining techniques, which use actuarial and behavioral principles, not only track the success of various mailings but also the ongoing profitability and other characteristics of the 8.6 million customers who have signed up. These capabilities helped the company pioneer a "balance transfer" strategy—offering prospects a temporarily low interest rate to move balances from competing cards—that is now a common industry feature. Data mining and other information-based strategies not only helped the firm expand from $1 billion to $12.8 billion in managed loans from 1988 to 1996 but also to win the 1996 Excellence in Technology Award from the Gartner Group.

Table 1.1   *Illustrative Data Mining Best Practices Drawn from Media Reports (continued)*

Profitability and risk reduction	Profitability and risk reduction use data mining to identify the attributes of the best customers—to characterize customer characteristics through time so as to target the appropriate customer with the appropriate product at the appropriate time. Risk reduction approaches match the discovery of poor risk characteristics against customer loan applications. This may suggest that some risk management procedures are not necessary with certain customers—a profit maximization move. It may also suggest which customers require special processing.
	As can be expected, financial companies are heavy users of data mining to improve profitability and reduce risk. Home Savings of America FSB, Irwindale, CA, the nation's largest savings and loan company, analyzes mortgage delinquencies, foreclosures, sales activity, and even geological trends over five years to drive risk pricing.
	According to Susan Osterfeldt, senior vice president of strategic technologies at NationsBank Services Co., "We've been able to use a neural network to build models that reduce the time it takes to process loan approvals. The neural networks speed processing. A human has to do almost nothing to approve it once it goes through the model."
Loyalty management and cross-selling	Cross-selling relies on identifying new prospects based on a match of their characteristics with known characteristics of existing customers who have been and still are satisfied with a given product. *Reader's Digest* does analysis of cross-selling opportunities to see if a promotional activity in one area is likely to respond to needs in another area so as to meet as many customer needs as possible.
	This is a cross-sell application that involves assessing the profile of likely purchasers of a product and matching that profile to other products to find similarities in the portfolio. Cross-selling and customer relationship management are treated extensively in *Mastering Data Mining* (Berry and Linoff, 2000) and *Building Data Mining Applications for CRM* (Berson, Smith, and Thearling).
Operational analysis and optimization	Operational analysis encompasses the ability to merge corporate purchasing systems to review and manage global expenditures and to detect spending anomalies. It also includes the ability to capture and analyze operational patterns in successful branch locations, so as to compare and apply lessons learned to other branches.
	American Express is using a data warehouse and data mining technique to reduce unnecessary spending, leverage its global purchasing power, and standardize equipment and services in its offices worldwide. In the late 1990s, American Express began merging its worldwide purchasing system, corporate purchasing card, and corporate card databases into a single Microsoft SQL Server database. The system allows American Express to pinpoint, for example, employees who purchase computers or other capital equipment with corporate credit cards meant for travel and entertainment. It also eliminates what American Express calls "contract bypass"—purchases from vendors other than those the company has negotiated with for discounts in return for guaranteed purchase levels.

Table 1.1 *Illustrative Data Mining Best Practices Drawn from Media Reports (continued)*

Operational analysis and optimization *(cont'd)*	American Express uses Quest, from New York–based Information Builders, to score the best suppliers according to 24 criteria, allowing managers to perform best-fit analyses and trade-off analyses that balance competing requirements. By monitoring purchases and vendor performance, American Express can address quality, reliability, and other issues with IBM, Eastman Kodak Co., and various worldwide vendors. According to an American Express senior vice president, "Many of the paybacks from data mining, even at this early stage, will result from our increased buying power, fewer uncontrolled expenses, and improved supplier responsiveness."
Relationship marketing	Relationship marketing includes the ability to consolidate customer data records so as to form a high-level composite view of the customer. This enables the production of individualized newsletters. This is sometimes called "relationship billing."
	American Express has invested in a massively parallel processor, which allows it to vastly expand the profile of every customer. The company can now store every transaction. Seventy workstations at the American Express Decision Sciences Center in Phoenix, AZ, look at data about millions of AmEx card members—the stores they shop in, the places they travel to, the restaurants they've eaten in, and even economic conditions and weather in the areas where they live. Every month, AmEx uses that information to send out precisely aimed offers. AmEx has seen an increase of 15 percent to 20 percent in year over year card member spending in its test market and attributes much of the increase to this approach.
Customer attrition and churn reduction	Churn reduction aims to reduce the attrition of valuable customers. It also aims to reduce the attraction and subsequent loss of customers through low-cost, low-margin recruitment campaigns, which, over the life cycle of the affected customer, may cost more to manage than the income produced by the customer.
	Mellon Bank of Pittsburgh is using Intelligent Miner to analyze data on the bank's existing credit card customers to characterize their behavior and predict, for example, which customers are most likely to take their business elsewhere. "We decided it was important for us to generate and manage our own attrition models," said Peter Johnson, vice president of the Advanced Technology Group at Mellon Bank.
Fraud detection	Fraud detection is the analysis of fraudulent transactions in order to identify the significant characteristics that identify a potentially fraudulent activity from a normal activity.
	Another strategic benefit of Capital One's data mining capabilities is fraud detection. In 1995, for instance, Visa and MasterCard's U.S. losses from fraud totaled $702 million. Although Capital One will not discuss its fraud detection efforts specifically, it noted that its losses from fraud declined more than 50 percent last year, in part due to its proprietary data mining tools and San Diego–based HNC Software Inc.'s Falcon, a neural network–based credit card fraud detection system.

Table 1.1   *Illustrative Data Mining Best Practices Drawn from Media Reports (continued)*

Campaign management	IBM's DecisionEdge campaign management module is designed to help businesses personalize marketing messages and pass them to clients through direct mail, tele-marketing, and face to face interactions. The product works with IBM's Intelligent Miner for Relationship Marketing.
	Among the software's features is a load-management tool, which lets companies give more lucrative campaigns priority status. "If I can only put out so many calls from my call center today, I want to make sure I make the most profitable ones," said David Raab at the analyst firm Raab Associates. "This feature isn't present in many competing products," he said.
	IBM's DecisionEdge campaign management module is designed to help businesses personalize marketing messages and pass them to clients through direct mail, tele-marketing, and face to face interactions. The product works with IBM's Intelligent Miner for Relationship Marketing.
	Among the software's features is a load-management tool, which lets companies give more lucrative campaigns priority status. "If I can only put out so many calls from my call center today, I want to make sure I make the most profitable ones," said David Raab at the analyst firm Raab Associates. "This feature isn't present in many competing products," he said.
Business-to-business/ channel, inventory, and supply chain management	The Zurich Insurance Group, a global, Swiss-based insurer, uses data mining to analyze broker performance in order to increase the efficiency and effectiveness of its business-to-business channel. Its primary utility is to look at broker performance relative to past performance and to predict future performance.
	Supply chains and inventory management are expensive operational overheads. In terms of sales and sales forecasting price is only one differentiator. Others include product range and image, as well as the ability to identify trends and patterns ahead of the competition. A large European retailer, using a data warehouse and data mining tools, spotted an unexpected downturn in sales of computer games. This was before Christmas. The retailer canceled a large order and watched the competition stockpile unsold computer games before Christmas.
	Superbrugsen, a leading Danish supermarket chain, uses data mining to optimize every single product area, and product managers must therefore have as much relevant information as possible to assist them when negotiating with suppliers to obtain the best prices.
	Marks and Spencer use customer profiling to determine what messages to send to certain customers. In the financial services area, for example, data mining is used to determine the characteristics of customers who are most likely to respond to a credit offer.

Table 1.1   *Illustrative Data Mining Best Practices Drawn from Media Reports (continued)*

Market research, product conceptualization	Blue Cross/Blue Shield is one of the largest health care providers in the United States. The organization provides analysts financial, enrollment, market penetration, and provider network information. This yields enrollment, new product development, sales, market segment, and group size estimates for marketing and sales support.
	Located in Dallas, TX, Rapp Collins is the second largest market research organization in the United States. It provides a wide range of marketing-related services. One involves applications that measure the effectiveness of reward incentive programs. Data mining is a core technology used to identify the many factors that influence attraction to incentives.
	J. D. Power and Associates, located in Augora Hills, CA, produce a monthly forecast of car and truck sales for about 300 different vehicles. Their specialty is polling the customer after the sale regarding the purchase experience and the product itself. Forecasts are driven by sales data, economic data, and data about the industry. Data mining is used to sort through these various classes of data to produce effective forecasting models.
Product development, engineering and quality control	Quality management is a significant application area for data mining. In the manufacturing area the closer that a defect is detected to the source of the defect the easier—and less costly—it is to fix. So there is a strong emphasis on measuring progress through the various steps of manufacturing in order to find problems sooner rather than later. Of course, this means huge amounts of data are generated on many, many measurement points. This is an ideal area for data mining:
	▪ Hewlett-Packard has used data mining to sort out a perplexing problem with a color printer that periodically produced fuzzy images. It turned out the problem was in the alignment of the lenses that blended the three primary colors to produce the output. The problem was caused by variability in the glue curing process that only affected one of the lens. Data mining was used to find which lens, under what curing circumstances, produced the fuzzy printing resolution.
	▪ R. R. Donnelley and Sons is the largest printing company in the United States. Their printing presses include rollers that weigh several tons and spit out results at the rate of 1,000 feet per minute. The plant experienced an occasional problem with the print quality, caused by a collection of ink on the rollers called "banding." A task force was struck to find the cause of the problem. One of the task force members, Bob Evans, used data mining to sort through thousands of fields of data related to press performance in order to find a small subset of variables that, in combination, could be used to predict the banding problem. His work is published in the February 1994 issues of *IEEE Expert* and the April 1997 issue of *Database Programming & Design*.

1.4   Microsoft's entry into data mining

Obviously, data mining is not just a back-room, scientific type of activity anymore. Just as document preparation software and row/column–oriented workbooks make publishers and business planners of us all, so too are we sitting on the threshold of a movement that will bring data mining—integrated with OLAP—to the desktop. What is the Microsoft strategy to achieve this?

Microsoft is setting out to solve three perceived problems:

1.   Data mining tools are too expensive.

2.   Data mining tools are not integrated with the underlying database.

3.   Data mining algorithms, in general, reflect their scientific roots and, while they work well with small collections of data, do not scale well with the large gigabyte- and terabyte-size databases of today's business environment.

Microsoft's strategy to address these problems revolves around three thrusts:

1.   *Accessibility.* Make complex data operations accessible and available to nonprofessionals, by generalizing the accessibility and lowering the cost.

2.   *Seamless reporting.* Promote access and usability by providing a common data reporting paradigm through simple to complex business queries.

3.   *Scalability.* To ensure access to data operations across increasingly large collections of data, provide an integration layer between the data mining algorithms and the underlying database.

Integration with the database engine occurs in three ways:

1.   Preprocessing functionality is done in the database, thus providing native database access to sophisticated and heretofore specialized data cleaning, transforming, and preparation facilities.

2.   Provide a core set of data mining algorithms directly in the database and provide a broadly accessible application programming interface (API) to ensure easy integration of external data mining algorithms.

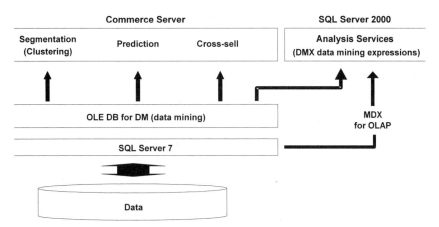

Figure 1.3
SQL Server development path for data mining

3.   Provide a deployment mechanism to ensure that modeling results can be readily built into other applications—both on the server and on the desktop—and to break down business process barriers to effective data mining results utilization.

Figure 1.3 shows the development of the current Microsoft architectural approach to data mining, as Microsoft migrated from the SQL Server 7 release to the SQL Server 2000 release.

One message from this figure is that data mining, as with OLAP and ad hoc reports before it, is just another query function—albeit a rather super query. Whereas in the past an end user might ask for a sales by region report, in the Microsoft world of data mining the query now becomes: Show me the main factors that were driving my sales results last period. In this way, one query can trigger millions—even trillions—of pattern matching and search operations to find the optimal results. Often many results will be produced for the reader to view. However, before long, many reader models of the world will be solicited and presented—all in template style— so that more and more preprocessing will take place to ensure that the appropriate results are presented for display (and to cut down on the amount of pattern searching and time required to respond to a query).

1.5   Concept of operations

As can be seen in Figure 1.3, the data mining component belongs to the DB query engine (DMX expressions). With the growth—depth and breadth— of data sources, it is clear that data mining algorithmic work belongs on the server (shown in the figure as Commerce Server). We can also see that the core data mining algorithms include segmentation capabilities and associated description and prediction facilities and cross-selling components. This particular thrust has a decidedly e-commerce orientation, since cross-sell, prediction, and segmentation are important e-commerce customer relationship management functions.

Whatever algorithms are not provided on board will be provided through a common API, which extends the OLE DB for data access convention to include data mining extensions.

The Socrates project, formed to develop the Microsoft approach to data mining, is a successor to the Plato Group (the group that built the Microsoft OLAP services SQL Server 7 functionality). Together with the Database Research Group, they are working on data mining concepts for the future. Current projects this group is looking at include the following:

- It is normal to view the database or data warehouse as a data snapshot, frozen in time (the last quarter, last reporting period, and so on). Data change through time, however, and this change requires the mining algorithms to look at sequential data and patterns.

- Most of the world's data are not contained as structured data but as relatively unstructured text. In order to harvest the knowledge contained in this source of data, text mining is required.

- There are many alternative ways of producing segmentations. One of the most popular is K-means clustering. Microsoft is also exploring other methods—based on expectation maximization—that will provide more reliable clusters than the popular K-means algorithms.

- The problem of scaling algorithms to apply data mining to large databases is a continuing effort. One area—sufficiency statistics—seeks to find optimal ways of computing the necessary pattern-matching rules so that the rules that are discovered are reliable across the entire large collection of data.

- Research is underway on a general data mining query language (DMQL). This is to devise general methods within the DBMS query language to form data mining queries. Current development efforts focus on SQL operators Unipivot and DataCube.

- There are continuing efforts regarding OLAP refinements in the direction of data mining to continue integration of OLAP and data mining.

■ A promising area of data mining is to define methods and procedures to continue to automate more and more of the searching that is undertaken automatically. This area of metarule-guided mining is a continuing effort in the Socrates project.

2

The Data Mining Process

We are drowning in information but starving for knowledge.
—John Naisbett

In the area of data mining, we could say we are drowning in algorithms but too often lack the ability to use them to their full potential. This is an understandable situation, given the recent introduction of data mining into the broader marketplace (also bearing in mind the underlying complexity of data mining processes and associated algorithms). But how do we manage all this complexity in order to reap the benefits of facilitated extraction of patterns, trends, and relationships in data? In the modern enterprise, the job of managing complexity and identifying, documenting, preserving, and deploying expertise is addressed in the discipline of knowledge management. The area of knowledge management is addressed in greater detail in Chapter 7. The goal of this chapter is to present both the scientific and the practical, profit-driven sides of data mining so as to form a general picture of the knowledge management issues regarding data mining that can bridge and synergize these two key components to the overall data mining project delivery framework.

In the context of data mining, knowledge management is the collection, organization, and utilization of various methods, processes, and procedures that are useful in turning data mining technology into business, social, and economic value. Data miners began to recognize a role for knowledge management in data mining as early as 1995, when, at a conference in Montreal, they coined the term *Knowledge Discovery in Databases* (KDD) to describe the process of providing guidance, methods, and procedures to extract information and knowledge from data. This development provides us with an understanding of an important distinction: the distinction between data mining—the specific algorithms and algorithmic approaches that are used to detect trends, patterns, and relationships in data—and Knowledge Discovery in Databases (KDD)—the set of skills, techniques, approaches, processes, and procedures (best practices) that provides the process management context for the data mining engagement.

Knowledge discovery methods are often very general and include processes and procedures that apply regardless of the specific form of the data and regardless of the particular algorithm that is applied in the data mining engagement. Data mining tools, techniques, and approaches are much more specific in nature and are often related to specific algorithms, forms of data, and data validation techniques. Both approaches are necessary for a successful data mining engagement.

2.1 Best practices in knowledge discovery in databases

Since its conception in 1995, KDD has continued to serve as a conduit for the identification and dissemination of best practices in the adaptation and deployment of algorithms and approaches to data mining tasks. KDD is thought of as a scientific discipline, and the KDD conferences themselves are thought of as academic and scientific exchanges. So access to much of what the KDD has to offer assumes a knowledge and understanding of academic and scientific methods, and this, of course, is not always present in business settings (e.g., scientific progress depends on the free, objective, and open sharing of knowledge—the antithesis of competitive advantage in business). On the other hand, business realities are often missing in academic gatherings. So a full understanding of the knowledge management context surrounding data mining requires an appreciation of the scientific methods that data mining and knowledge discovery are based on, as well as an understanding of the applied characteristics of data mining engagements in the competitive marketplace.

As a knowledge management discipline, what does KDD consist of? KDD is strongly rooted in the scientific tradition and incorporates state-of-the-art knowledge developed through a series of KDD conferences and industry working groups that have been wrestling with the knowledge management issues in this area over the last decade. KDD conference participants, as well as KDD vendors, propose similar knowledge management approaches to describe the KDD process. Two of the most widely known (and well-documented) KDD processes are the SEMMA process, developed and promoted by the SAS Institute (http://sas.com), and the CRISP-DM process, developed and promoted by a consortium of data mining consumers and vendors that includes such well-known companies as Mercedes-Benz and NRC Corporation (http://www.crisp-dm.org/).

At this point Microsoft does not appear to have developed a KDD process, nor have they endorsed a given approach. Much of their thinking on this is reflected in the various position papers contained on their data mining Web site (http://www.microsoft.com/data). In addition, quite a bit of thinking is also captured in the commentary surrounding the OLE DB for data mining standards. All approaches to data mining depend heavily on a knowledge of the scientific method, which embodies one of the oldest, best documented, and useful practices available today. An understanding of the scientific method, particularly the concepts of sampling, measurement, theories, hypotheses and paradigms, and, most certainly, statistics, is implied in all data mining and knowledge discovery methodologies. A general, high-level treatment of the scientific method, as a data mining best practice, follows. A discussion of the specific statistical techniques that are most popularly used in data mining applications is taken up in later chapters, which review the application of these methods to business problem solving.

2.2   The scientific method and the paradigms that come with it

I'd wager that very few people who are undertaking a data mining engagement for the first time think of themselves as scientists approaching a scientific study. It is useful, possibly essential, to bring a scientific approach into data mining, however, since whenever we look at data and how data can be used to reflect and model real-world events we are implicitly adopting a scientific approach (with an associated rule book that we are well advised to become familiar with).

The scientific method contains a wide, well-developed, and well-documented system of best practices, which have performed a central role in the evolution of the current scientific and technological civilization as we know it. While we may take much of science and engineering for granted, we know either explicitly or intuitively that these developments would not have been possible without a scientific discipline to drive the process. This discipline, which reserves a central place for the role of data in order to measure, test, and promote an understanding of real-world events, operates under the covers of any data mining and KDD system. The scientific method plays such a central role—either explicitly or implicitly—that needs to be recognized and understood in order to fully appreciate the development of KDD and data mining solutions.

An excellent introduction to the scientific method is given in Abraham Kaplan's *The Conduct of Enquiry*. In a world where *paradigm shift* has entered the popular lexicon, it is also certainly worth noting the work of Thomas Kuhn, author of *The Structure of Scientific Revolutions*. Kaplan describes the concept of theory advancement through tests of hypotheses. He shows that you never really prove a hypothesis, you just build ever-increasing evidence and detailed associated explanations, which provide support for questions or hypotheses and which, eventually, provide an overall theory.

The lesson for data miners is this: we never actually "prove" anything in a data mining engagement—all we do is build evidence for a prevailing view of the world and how it operates and this evidence is constrained to the view of the world that we maintain for purposes of engaging in the data mining task. This means that facts gain certainty over time, since they show themselves to be resistant to dis-proof. So you need to build a knowledge store of facts and you need to take them out and exercise them with new bits of data from time to time in order to improve their fitness. Data mining—like science itself—is fundamentally cumulative and iterative, so store and document your results.

There is another lesson: Facts, or evidence, have relevance only within the context of the view of the world—or business model—in which they are contained. This leads us to Thomas Kuhn.

Kuhn is the originator of the term *paradigm shift*. As Kaplan indicates, a set of hypotheses, when constructed together, forms a theory. Kuhn suggests that this theory, as well as associated hypotheses, is based on a particular model, which serves as a descriptive or explanatory paradigm for the theory. When the paradigm changes, so too does everything else: hypotheses, theory, and associated evidence. For example, a mechanistic and deterministic description of the universe gave way to a new relativistic, quantum concept of the universe when Einstein introduced a new paradigm to account for Newton's descriptions of the operations of the universe. In a Newtonian world, a falling object is taken as evidence for the operation of gravity. In Einstein's world, there is no gravity—only relative motion in a universe that is bent back upon itself. Just as Newton's paradigm gave way to Einstein's, so too did Keplar's paradigm (the sun as the center of the universe) give way to Newton's.

What does this have to do with data mining and knowledge discovery? Today we are moving into a new business paradigm. In the old paradigm, business was organized into functional areas—marketing, finance, engineering—and a command and control system moved parts or services for manufacture through the various functional areas in order to produce an output for distribution or consumption. This paradigm has changed to a new, customer-centric paradigm. Here the customer is the center of the business, and the business processes to service customer needs are woven seamlessly around the customer to perceive and respond to needs in a coordinated, multidisciplinary and timely manner with a network of process feedback and control mechanisms. The data mining models need to reflect this business paradigm in order to provide value. So just as experimental methods and associated explanatory and descriptive models changed in the scientific world to support Einstein's view of the universe, so too do knowledge discovery methods and associated explanatory and descriptive models need to change to support a customer-centric view of business processes.

2.2.1   Creating an operational model of the paradigm in the data mining engagement

At the start of the data mining engagement it is important to be clear about the business process that is being modeled as well as the underlying paradigm. Our paradigm will serve as a world view, or business model. How does this work?

Say we have a hunch, or hypothesis, that customers develop loyalty over time. We may not know what the factors are that create loyalty, but, as firm believers of the scientific method, we intuitively understand that if we can get the data in place we can construct a scientific experiment and use data mining techniques to find the important factors. We might draw inspiration from some early work conducted by pioneers in the field of science—for example, tests to verify and validate a somewhat revolutionary concept at the time or the concept that air has mass (i.e., it is not colorless, weightless, etc.). To test the concept that air has mass we form a hypothesis.

Figure 2.1 illustrates the process of testing a hypothesis. This hypothesis is based on an "air has mass" paradigm. So, if air has mass, then it has weight, which, at sea level, would press down on a column of mercury (liquid poured into a glass tube with a bottom on it). If air has mass, then, as I move away from sea level by walking up a mountain, for example, the weight of air should be less and less. I can test this hypothesis, empirically, by using data points (measurements of the height of mercury as I move up

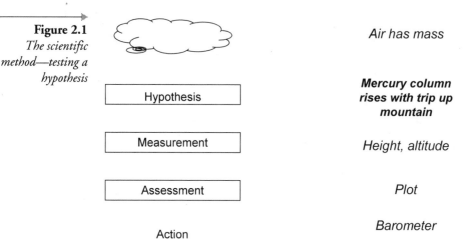

Figure 2.1
*The scientific
method—testing a
hypothesis*

the mountain). Of course, at the end of this experiment, having measured the height of the column of mercury as I walk up the mountain, I will have collected evidence to support my theory. If this were applied science (and try to see how it is), then I would have a report, support for the theory, and an action plan ready for executive approval based on the findings that are supported by data and a solid experimental process based on the scientific method.

In the case of customer loyalty, my paradigm is based on the concept that customers interact with the business provider. Over time, some interactions lead to loyalty while other interactions lead to the opposite—call it disloyalty. Call this an interaction-based paradigm for customer relationship modeling.

So what is the associated hypothesis? Well, if I am right—and the data can confirm this—then long-time customers will behave differently from short-term customers. A "poor" customer interaction, which will lead short-term customers to defect, will not have the same outcome with a long-term customer.

How do I test this hypothesis? As with the mountain climbing measurements for the air mass experiment, I need to begin with a model. We might begin with a napkin drawing, as illustrated in Figure 2.2. From the model I will form hypotheses—some, such as customer recruitment will lead to customer interaction, are trivial. Others, such as customer interactions may lead to loyalty or defections and that this outcome may depend on the time of the interaction, are rich in possibilities. To test a hypothesis I need data. In this case I will need to assemble a data set that has customer time of

Figure 2.2
*A model as
hypothesis—
customer loyalty*

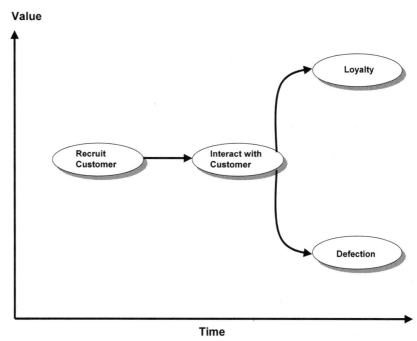

service measurements (tenure, or length of time, as a customer). I will also need some indicator of interactions (e.g., number of calls at the call center, type of call, service requests, overdue payments, and so on). I will also need to construct an indicator of defection on the data set. This means that I need customer observations through time and I need an indicator of defection. Once I do this, I will have an indicator of tenure, an interaction indicator, and a defection indicator on my data set.

The test of my hypothesis is simple: All things considered, I expect that a complaint indicator for newer customers will be associated with more defections than would be the case with long-term customers. The business advice in this simple explanation is correspondingly simple: Pay more attention to particular kinds of customer complaints if the customer is a new-comer! As with the scientific experiment discussed previously, we are now in a position to file a report with a recommendation that is based on fact, as illustrated through empirical evidence collected from data and exploited using peerless techniques based on the scientific method. Not bad. In the process we have used the idea of forming a paradigm and associated hypotheses and tests as a way to provide guidance on what kind of data we need, how we need to reformat or manipulate the data, and even how we need to guide the data mining engine in its search for relevant trends and patterns.

All this adds up to a considerable amount of time saved in carrying out the knowledge discovery mission and lends considerable credibility in the reporting and execution of the associated results. These are benefits that are well worth the effort. (See Figure 2.2.)

2.3   How to develop your paradigm

All scientific, engineering, and business disciplines promote and propose conceptual models that describe the operation of phenomena from a given point of view. Nowadays, in addition to the napkin, it seems that the universal tool for visualizing these models is the whiteboard or a Powerpoint slide. But what are the universal mechanisms for collecting the key conceptual drivers that form the model in the first place?

A number of interesting and promising model development techniques have emerged out of the discipline of the *Balanced Scorecard* (Robert S. Kaplan and David P. Norton). Other techniques, originally inspired by W. Edwards Deming, have emerged from the field of quality management.

The search for quality, initially in manufacturing processes and now in business processes in general, has led to the development of a number of effective, scientifically based, and time-saving techniques, which are exceptionally useful for the data mining and knowledge discovery practitioner. Many best practices have been developed in the area of quality management to help people—and teams of people—to better conceptualize the problem space they are working in. It is interesting to note that W. Edwards Deming is universally acknowledged as the father of quality management. Deming was a statistician who, after World War II, transformed manufacturing processes forever through the introduction of the scientific method and associated statistical testing procedures in the service of improving the manufacturing process. Quality management best practices are discussed in many sources. One useful discussion and summary is found in *Management for Quality Improvement: The 7 New QC Tools* by Mizuno.

One such best practice is a team brainstorming practice, which results in the development of an issues and drivers relations diagram, as illustrated in Figure 2.3. This diagram is a facilitating mechanism, useful to tap the group memory—and any available documented evidence—in order to develop a preliminary concept of all the relevant factors that could drive the understanding and explanation of a particular data mining solution.

The issues and drivers diagram shows which drivers are likely to be associated with a given issue and—importantly—it shows, in a preliminary

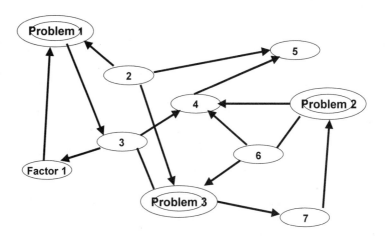

Figure 2.3
Developing the paradigm—issues and drivers relationship diagram

manner, what the relationships between the drivers and issues appear to be. The arrows and connections show not only relationships but the direction of the presumed relationships.

The issues and drivers diagram is an important tool, especially when it is used to tap into the group memory and problem-solving ability. It provides the knowledge that is relevant in constructing the conceptual model or paradigm, which will later serve to drive the selection of data for the data mining solution as well as the search for relationships in data to characterize data mining trends, patterns, and statistical associations displayed in the construction of the data mining solution.

One other useful diagram, once again drawn from the area of quality assurance, is the "fish bone," or Ishikawa diagram (so named in honor of its original developer, Kaoru Ishikawa, a Japanese disciple of W. Edwards Deming) (see Figure 2.4).

In outlining the issues and drivers diagram it will usually become apparent that many of the drivers can be classified together in line with some

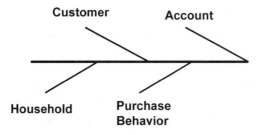

Figure 2.4
An example of the Ishikawa diagram

conceptual similarity. In the examination of customer purchasing behavior, for example, we may find that purchases depend upon such issues as discount rate, timing, frequency, and channel of the offer, credit instrument, and so on. Drivers may include such considerations as customer status (e.g., new, elite), customer attributes (e.g., gender, occupation, home owner), purchase behavior (e.g., quantity and frequency of purchase), and so on. The Ishikawa diagram is very useful in grouping these drivers together—as a common class or driving factor—as one of the unique branches (or main "bone," if using the fish bone metaphor) drawn at an angle from the main "spine" of the diagram.

2.3.1   Operationalization—turning concepts into measurements

All empirical techniques begin with decidedly nonempirical components: The analysis will end up sitting in an area with a numerical (empirical) basis, but it will be guided by a theoretical model or paradigm of some kind. Darwin's Theory of Natural Selection, for example, serves as an orienting framework to understand the adaptation of various new forms of life to various ecosystems. Economists would have similar theories to understand currency shifts and product success and failure. The trick is to convert thoughts or concepts—analytical constraints—into operational measures that can be manipulated symbolically by the data mining engine embedded in software.

Analytical constructs become empirically rooted when a specific database measurement of the construct is adopted. For example, dollars spent, as measured on the data set, can serve as an operational measure of the

Figure 2.5
Relationship between concepts (analytical constructs) and data (operational measures)

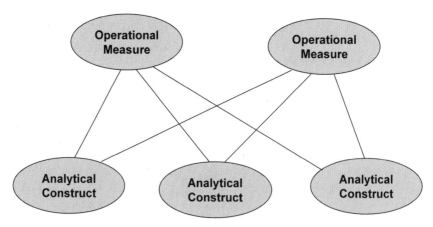

"price" construct in our economic model. (See Figure 2.5.) Our biological model could use "number of offspring" as a measure of fitness for survival.

Within the theoretical framework we need to narrow in on a manageable research question to serve as a specific case in point within the overall theory. Some questions will be amenable to empirical testing and some won't (this depends heavily on what data are available and how well the data can serve as an empirical measurement of the question under consideration—for example, does dollars spent serve as a good measure of price?). The final analytical model will be that set of testable hypotheses set up for empirical verification that can be examined in order to move the exploration of the research question forward.

To take Darwin's "survival of the fittest" paradigm, as shown in Figure 2.6, we would need to begin with the conceptual pieces of the paradigm, such as "gene pool candidates," "stressors," and "mating and species propagation." These processes, taken as components of a generalized process of "natural selection," would show that the "survival of the fittest" paradigm produces a better "adapted, improved species." The terms in quotes represent objects or actions. We can put them together to construct the conceptual description of the operation of the paradigm. In examining the interoperation of these constructs, through a process of analysis, we can generate and test hypotheses that relate to the presumed operation of the paradigm. These "analytical constructs" then become central to our ability to test and refine our paradigm so as to shed more light on the operation of the process (in this case natural selection).

Figure 2.6
Example paradigm

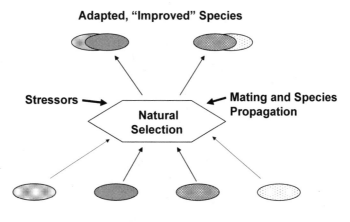

Adapted, "Improved" Species

Stressors →

Natural Selection

← Mating and Species Propagation

Gene Pool Candidates

Since modern science is an empirical science, we need real, objectively verifiable measurements to represent our analytical constructs, and, eventually, when we form a hypothesis, we will test the hypothesis, using scientific tests of significance, on the data points, or measurements, that we have taken to represent the analytical constructs.

So, for "gene pool candidates" and "adapted, improved species" we will have such relevant measurements as average lifetime, running speed, resistance to disease, and, for example, adaptability to various diets. We will have stressors, such as attacks by predators, feast/famine cycles, weather variations, and so on. For mating, propagation measures will have mating episodes and number of offspring.

A simple hypothesis would be that the more the stress, the more the mating–offspring episodes that better the base capability of life indicators over successive generations. We expect, for example, that successor generations will run faster than earlier generations (assuming, in this simple example, that fleeing from a predator was a stressor response). If we can confirm this finding—in this case by reference to empirical measurements of running speed—then we take this as evidence in support of our paradigm.

2.3.2 Beyond hypotheses—developing the analytical model

Now we have seen how a general conceptual paradigm can help in the development of the data mining question, or hypothesis. The examination of the flow and direction of the relationships taken from the issues and drivers diagram can help us look at the direction, sequence, and timing of the drivers and classes of drivers, or factors, in the issues and drivers analysis. The sequence of events is critically important in building an analytical model of behavior. Not all relationships in data make sense from a sequential point of view. For example, in the data mining analysis you may want to explore the relationship between age and amount purchased. You will probably find that as age increases so too does the purchase amount (if for no other reason than, in general, as age increases so too do earning power and disposable income). So the sequence of the analysis would be age → income → purchase amount. Unless your analytical model explicitly supports this type of sequential view, you may find yourself in the uncomfortable position of building a model like this: purchase amount → income → age or even, income → purchase amount → age. We can see how increases in age lead to increases in income and this, in turn, leads to increases in purchases. But we will never be successful in showing how increases in purchase

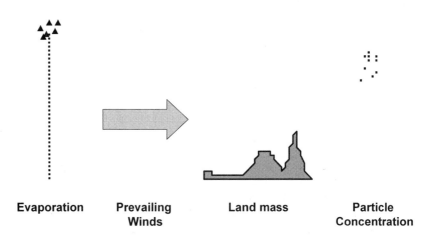

Figure 2.7
*An example model
showing the
direction of effects*

Evaporation   **Prevailing**   **Land mass**   **Particle**
                       Winds   **Concentration**

amounts lead to increases in income, which, in turn, lead to increases in age. So the examination of sequence is central to the construction of a good analytical model to reflect the business behavior that you are looking at and is essential to identifying the correct questions or hypotheses to explore.

To consider a more complex example, examine the construction of a model that predicts precipitation. As shown Figure 2.7, rainfall on the western coast depends upon a variety of factors: from evaporation rate over the ocean, to prevailing winds, to the land mass on the coast (particularly variations caused by mountain ranges, for example), and such local factors as particle concentration in the atmosphere. It only makes sense to look at the relationship between evaporation rate and precipitation if you consider, in appropriate sequence, the intervening effects of prevailing wind, land mass, and particle concentration. The examination of intervening effects (factors that appear between two related elements in a model) and predisposing effects (prior factors that act on the related elements) is essential in identifying the appropriate relationships to examine in an analysis.

The sequence A → intervening effect → B is a legitimate analysis path. Beware, however, of looking at the relationship between A and B without looking at the intervening effects. This could lead to a misspecified model that asserts, for example, that low evaporation leads to precipitation on the coast by failing to take into consideration the lagged effects of the intervening variables.

Looking at a relationship without examining intervening and predisposing effects can lead to the identification of spurious relationships—that is, the relationships may be strong but incorrect (you may find a strong relationship between low evaporation and high precipitation but only because this ignores the intervening operation—through time—of prevailing winds that contain the water-logged atmosphere that actually fueled the precipitation at the time the measurements were taken).

The sequence A (predisposing effect) → B → C provides an example of the operation of a spurious relationship. You may observe a relationship between elevation and precipitation. Simplistically, you may assert that elevation "causes" precipitation, as if water leaked out of rocks as air mass decreases. This is a tenable hypothesis, but the empirical validation is flawed because you have neglected to include the predisposing (earlier sequence) affect of evaporation rate over the true source of water (the ocean).

The Ishikawa diagram, originally shown in Figure 2.4, can help us in defining sequences of relationships. Say, for example, that the issue or outcome we are looking at is a determinant of customer purchases. Our issues and drivers diagram may have suggested an Ishikawa diagram. Here, drivers tend to group in customer, household, account, and behavior groupings. Customer groupings include such data as age, gender, marital status, and, typically, when other data sources can be tapped, indicators of income, and even educational or occupational attributes. Household indicators may include such measurements as type of household, own or rent status, and, potentially, number of children in the household and even kind and number of appliances (electronic or otherwise). Account status may include type of account, number of accounts, account payment indicators, activation date, and length of service. Behavior may include such indicators as date of purchase, purchase time or location, and such information as quantity of purchase, price, and, possibly, discount rate.

In developing the Ishikawa diagram it is useful to arrange the general concepts and specific data points that belong to the factors in order, moving from left to right on the diagram. This results in another diagram, shown in

Figure 2.8
Example Ishikawa diagram illustrating the flow of effect and components of the descriptive model of purchase behavior

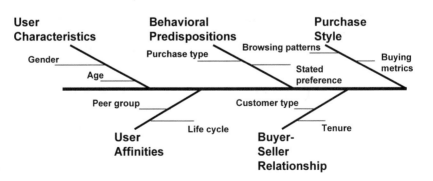

Figure 2.8. Here you can readily see why these diagrams are sometimes referred to as "fish bone diagrams."

2.4   The data mining process methodology

A number of best practice methodologies have emerged to provide guidance on carrying out a data mining undertaking. Two of the most widely known methodologies are the CRISP-DM methodology and the SEMMA methodology. CRISP-DM stands for Cross-Industry Standard Practice for Data Mining. It has been promoted as an open, cross-industry standard and has been developed and promoted by a variety of interests and data mining vendors, including Mercedes-Benz and NCR Corporation. SEMMA is a proprietary methodology, which was developed by the SAS Institute. SEMMA stands for Sample, Explore, Modify, Model, and Assess. There are many other methodologies that have been proposed and promoted; many of them are contained in the various books that have been written about data mining. (See, for example, *Data Mining Techniques* [Berry and Linoff].) Most can be seen to be themes and variations of the CRISP-DM methodology.

2.4.1   CRISP-DM Process

The CRISP-DM methodology is a multinational, standards-based approach to describe, document, and continuously improve data mining (and associated data warehousing, business intelligence) processes. The CRISP-DM framework identifies six steps in the data mining process, as shown in the following list. I have added a seventh step—performance measurement—to capture the closed-loop characteristic of a virtuous cycle of continuous process improvement through successive plan, analyze, implement, measure iterations of data mining projects.

1.   Business understanding

2.   Data understanding

3.   Data preparation

4.   Modeling

5.   Evaluation

6.   Deployment

7.   Performance measurement

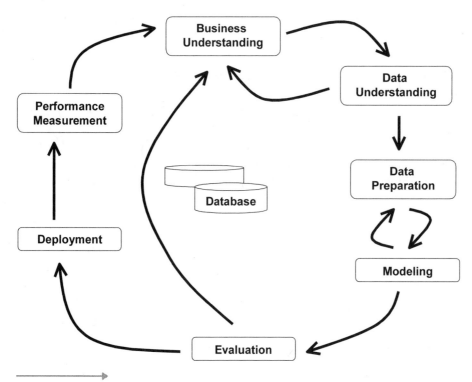

Figure 2.9   *An example of the CRISP-DM framework*

The process is illustrated in Figure 2.9, which illustrates a number of important characteristics of data mining:

1.   It is, at its core, a top-down, goal-driven process: Everything hinges on the definition of the business goal to be accomplished.

2.   It is a closed-loop process: everything flows into an assessment step, which, in turn, flows back into the redefinition (and reexecution) of the goal-setting phase. This closed-loop nature of the process has been dubbed "the virtuous cycle" by many observers (prominently, Michael Berry and Gordon Linoff in their popular treatment of data mining: *Data Mining Techniques*). The closed-loop cycle tells us that there is no virtue in a one-off, "quick hits" approach to data mining. True value comes over time with successive refinements to the data mining goal execution task.

3.   The methodology is not a linear process: There are many feedback loops where successive, top-down refinements are interwoven in the successful closed-loop engagement.

These "phases," as they are called in the CRISP-DM methodology, are sufficiently robust to accommodate most tasks that can be imagined for a data mining engagement.

2.5   Business understanding

Data mining is so flexible in its application, and the range of data that is available to support data mining is so diverse, that business applications and associated business understanding can occur in a variety of areas. According to a model developed by Treacy and Wiersma,[1] operational excellence, customer excellence, and product excellence can be used to distinguish and classify businesses in terms of primary area of excellence. This view was previously illustrated in Figure 1.2.

This model provides a convenient way of looking at the range and types of possible data mining projects, shown in the following classification of different forms of data mining (see Figure 2.10).

In any of these areas an understanding of the associated business will drive the analysis. This implies the development of an issues and drivers perspective in any of the three areas of potential application (see Figure 2.11).

An understanding of the business will drive the identification of one or more key issues—and associated return on investment goals—that need to be addressed in the analysis. Once the issue and the associated drivers have been identified—possibly through the use of the issues and drivers dia-

Figure 2.10
Defining best practices in line with Treacy and Wiersma

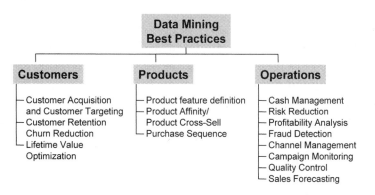

1.   *Harvard Business Review,* January–February 1993.

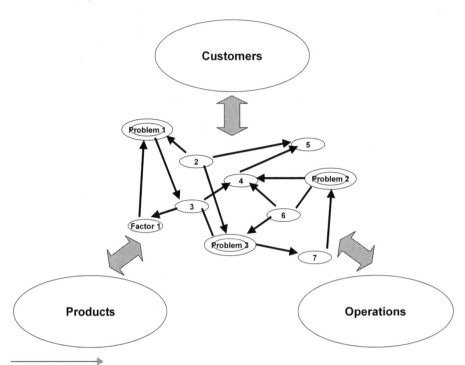

Figure 2.11   *Applying issues and drivers frameworks in the three areas of business excellence*

gram—then it is possible to produce a high-level analytical model for the analysis. For example, an exploration of the weather paradigm, shown in Figure 2.7, may produce an analytical model, as shown in Figure 2.12.

From this graphical representation of the analytical model we can see that the analyst weather paradigm includes the operation of three sets of factors: originating factors (evaporation rate and so on); intermediate or intervening factors (prevailing winds); and immediate factors, which mitigate the other sets of factors and produce a specific prediction of probability of precipitation.

Note that the analytical model implicitly identifies the flow and direction of the presumed relationships. If evaporation rate, taken alone, were assumed to have a direct effect on precipitation, then there would be an arrow flowing from evaporation rate directly to the rain/shine outcome. Since no such arrow exists, then the analyst has specified that evaporation rate is influenced by two levels of intervening factors in determining its ultimate effect on precipitation.

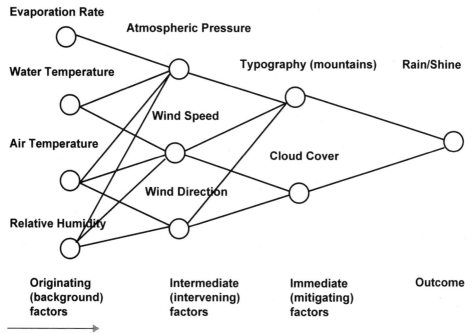

Figure 2.12   *Building layers of relevant explanatory/descriptive factors in the analytical model*

The graphical construction of the analytical model serves to clarify the operation of the underlying paradigm that is being tested and sets the stage for both data preparation and subsequent modeling stages of the analysis. It affects data preparation by clearly indicating which concepts need to have an operational measurement associated with them. It affects modeling by showing which relationships, in which order, need to be examined in order to produce a well-specified model.

2.6   Data understanding

Data understanding relates to developing an understanding about the relationship between raw data and the conceptual components of the analytical model. This involves developing a clear understanding of the following:

1.   Which data elements relate to which conceptual component of the proposed analytical model?

2.   What is the data type or level of measurement?

3.   What metadata are associated with the data?

4.   What is the underlying time dimension or time representation of
      the data?

5.   How are the data stored?

6.   Are the data organized so as to be representative of the phenome-
      non under examination?

2.6.1 Conceptual component

Understanding the conceptual component of data relates to binding data
elements to the various conceptual components of the analytical model.
What conceptual component does PurchaseQuantity refer to, for example?
PurchaseQuantity probably refers to some purchasing behavior model component and, on occasion, may even be the outcome, or issue, that is being
modeled according to the behavior of various drivers that have been identified in the analytical model.

2.6.2 Data type or level of measurement

Typically, data may be character data—for example, alphanumeric strings—
or may be numeric data. Numeric data will usually be categorical, ordinal,
or continuous, and this normally relates to the values that the data element
can assume. Is the data element a categorical data element, which assumes
the value of, for example, 0 or 1 (which might indicate inactive and active),
or does it assume a continuous range of values (as a price field might). Ordinal data assume an ordered range of values such as 1, 2, 3, …, 10 to indicate
quantity purchased. One of the many subtle "gottchas" of data types
includes the fact that most computers order numeric and character data differently, so algorithms that work with order may work differently depending on whether the data is numeric or character.

2.6.3 Metadata

The minimum metadata that must be available include data element name
and meaning. An extended label may also be present. So the field ActivIND
may have an extended label of "Customer active/inactive indicator." Valid
values are 0 ("Inactive") and 1 ("Active").

Recently, the interest in and awareness of the role of metadata in successful enterprise knowledge, data management, and business intelligence has
grown to the point that metadata has become a field of study in its own
right. A good source fo metadata information is http://www.omg.org/.

2.6.4   Time dimension

It is almost always true that a data mining view of the data is constructed in order to feed and analyze various dimensions that are organized according to some time dimension. This mining view may form a picture of the customer base—for example, at a particular point in time (e.g., customer activity up to first quarter). This is a "cross-sectional" view of data (i.e., a cross section at a particular point in time). Customer purchase data will not normally be captured in this time dimension (rather, individual purchases will be captured on a daily basis). Data captured at various time points, or episodes, are sometimes referred to as "time series" data. The analyst needs to know the underlying time dimension of all the data elements so as to be in a position to put all data elements in a common representation required by the construction of the mining view.

2.6.5   Data storage

It is normal for data to come to the mining view from a variety of internal and external sources. On a rare occasion the data will be available from the data mart or data warehouse. Typically, all data are stored in data tables, where the rows typically relate to the units of observations—for example, customers—that make up the analysis, and the columns typically relate to the data elements, or measurements, that are available to describe the attributes that make up the factors that will form the drivers of the analysis. While all data are typically stored in this manner, there are a variety of different representations, file systems, and data access mechanisms that are needed to get at the data. Microsoft has changed the rules of the game with the release of SQL Server 2000 so that the case, or unit of analysis, may be stored in either relational or dimensional form and the case base is assembled "on the fly" as the mining operation begins (this is treated in more detail in Chapter 3). In all events, it is necessary to have a common index— or key—to relate all the tables together at a common unit of analysis. So, if the unit of analysis is the customer, then all tables must have a common value to associate their values with the customer values (e.g., a customer complaints table must have a customer identifier so that number of complaints can be attached to the customer record).

2.6.6   Data representation

If data elements are supposed to serve as empirical, operational measures of the concepts that are included in the analytical model, then it is important that they be representative of the phenomenon being examined. It is normal to look at the relationship between various customer characteristics and purchase behavior, for example. In this case it is important to qualify what purchase behavior is being examined, since, for example, behavior is typically different in winter and summer. So the data need to reflect the season that is being examined.

2.7   Data preparation

The data preparation phase covers all activities to construct a data set that contains empirical, or operational, measures to appropriately reflect the concepts and hypotheses that are captured in the best practices business goal of the mining exercise. In a recent book entitled *Data Preparation for Data Mining* by Dorian Pyle, the author notes that the data preparation stage of a data mining project can consume from 60 percent to 80 percent of the total project duration. This is surely not a very glamorous activity when compared with the excitement of the projected profits that emerge from a "street smart" analytical model and associated implementation plan. It is a necessary part of successful data mining, however, and, if done poorly, can lead to extremes in time and resource consumption; worse, poor data will produce poor results and will probably sabotage the whole project.

Data preparation is covered in greater detail in Chapter 4. The following list identifies important best practices to ensure success in the data preparation phase of data mining:

1.   Anchor the analysis so that, regardless of the time scale or granularity of the units of observation, there is a common unit of analysis (e.g., customer oriented; time-period oriented). In SQL 2000 this is the process of establishing the "case key."

2.   Choose the target or issue/outcome carefully. Have a clear indication of what is being modeled—for example, buy—no buy; lapsed—no lapse; $ spent.

3.   Having determined the drivers and the data elements that operationalize the driver effects in the model, ensure that all driver data points are assembled on the analysis record.

4.   Reformat the data to ensure that all data elements reflect the same time period as well as the same unit of analysis. For example, customer transactions will need to be rolled up and summed so that the final figure relates to one (and only one) customer record for the appropriate time period of the analysis.

5.   Recalculations and derivations. Many data elements will need to be recalculated and transformed to suit the analysis. In addition to aggregation of transactional, episodic, or sequential data, consider, for example, the transformation of gender data into a common representation (1 and 2, Male and Female, M and F; all need to be mapped to the same code).

6.   Look at the data distributions. It is important to have an up-front understanding of the low value, high value, and average of the fields of data that are in the analysis. If the data are categorical— for example, a gender field—then the percentages of the various codes in the data (in this case Male and Female) should be displayed and examined.

Data preparation tasks are likely to be performed multiple times, and not in any prescribed order. Tasks include table, record, and attribute selection manipulations, as well as transformations, computing derivations, and cleaning of data for modeling tools.

2.8   Modeling

This phase begins with a clear understanding of the modeling goals: explanation or prediction are common goals; however, often in the final analysis, profitability (or cost savings) is the ultimate goal. Most often people engage in a data mining exercise because they want to gain a good understanding of the area they are examining. So, in fact, they are looking for an explanation of the issues and drivers that surround a particular outcome they want to examine (e.g., a likely purchase). In line with the modeling approach discussed previously, they are interested in gaining empirical support, through data analysis, of the nature, timing, and sequence of relationships that characterize the interactions of the various factors they include in their analysis. It is this need for explanation that has driven the discussion of the scientific method and associated discussions of paradigms and such modeling approaches as the construction of Ishikawa and issues and drivers diagrams.

In fact, many data mining exercises dead-ended in the task of prediction. If your primary interest is prediction, then the conceptual requirements and the construction of the analytical model and associated empirical tests are much easier to accomplish. Alternatively, if the construction of the analytical model is weak, then, potentially, the best you can hope for is some improvement in prediction. In prediction you are simply interested in how well a set of numbers—data points—predicts the values of another number (or set of numbers). So, rather than seeking an understanding of the factors

Table 2.1   *A Comparison of Predictive and Descriptive Model Attributes and Requirements*

Type of Analysis	Predictive	Descriptive
Goal of the analysis	How well can you predict an outcome?	What factors explain the variations in an outcome?
Conceptual model	Less important	Vitally important
Model set up/restrictions	Relaxed	Potentially complex
Benefit	Ability to predict	Understanding of the phenomenon (including an ability to predict and compute profitability/loss)

that affect the likelihood of purchase, you simply want to know how well potentially relevant factors predict the likelihood of purchase. In terms of the issues and drivers diagram a prediction-only orientation means that you are interested only in the combined effect of the drivers on affecting a particular outcome. In particular, in a prediction-only modeling situation, you have no interest (and no ability) to describe or explain the relationships between the various drivers in the model.

As shown in Table 2.1, the descriptive or predictive goals have a major bearing on both the time and complexity of the supporting analytical model, as well as the choice of the analysis technique, since different techniques are tuned to support different modeling tasks. Neural networks, for example, while very popular, are chronically inadequate in the development and support of explanatory models and so are used almost exclusively for predictive tasks. Various modeling techniques may be selected and applied and need to be calibrated to produce optimal results. Typically, there are several techniques for the same data mining problem type. Some techniques have specific requirements on the form of data.

2.8.1   Outcome and cluster-based methods

Data mining techniques can be broken down into three categories: outcome techniques, cluster techniques, and affinity techniques. In outcome methods there is an outcome, or dependent variable, that is modeled (e.g., income as a function of work, capital, and human resources). In cluster-based methods the goal is to detect similarities among groups of records or observations in the data set based on a set of characteristics (variables) as measured in the data set. The most commonly used methods are decision trees—for outcome modeling—and cluster analysis—for clustering. Both

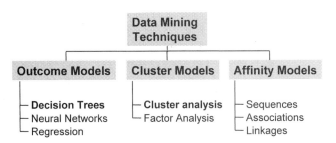

Figure 2.13
Types of data mining techniques (those added in SQL Server 2000 are in bold)

methods are supported in the SQL Server 2000 release. Affinity models are very popular in retail applications. Here the goal is to detect sequences of behavior, various links between activities, and typical components of a shopper's market basket. (See Figure 2.13.)

2.8.2 Decision trees

Decision trees are probably the most commonly used data mining technique. In many respects this is because they combine the power of advanced statistical techniques yet incorporate ease of use features that are closer to typical reporting packages. Decision trees can also be used for both predictive and explanatory goals. Decision trees are well adapted to supporting the hypothesis testing approach of the scientific method and the associated development and testing of conceptual models that are necessary to support an explanatory outcome. Some characteristic advantages of decision trees are as follows:

- They provide a visual representation of the factors and model conceptual development process that is not as well displayed by other techniques.

- It is very easy to interact with the shaping and unfolding of the decision tree. This supports tests and queries of different lines of enquiry, as well as spontaneous development of new ideas in support of hypothesis testing and theory development.

Many data mining techniques are built to take as much advantage as possible of the characteristics of the data in order to find the trends and patterns buried in the data. A feed forward neural network is an example of such an approach. These techniques are not necessarily atheoretical, but they tend to be; moreover, because of their underlying technology and pattern identification approach, it can be very difficult to discern the operation of the underlying theoretical constructs unless you are extremely careful in the construction and use of models using these techniques.

Some data-driven approaches will produce adequate—often superior—predictive models, even in the absence of a theoretical orientation. In this case you might be tempted to employ the maxim "If it ain't broke, don't fix it." In fact, the best predictive models, even if substantially data driven, benefit greatly from a theoretical understanding. The best prediction emerges from a sound, thorough, and well-developed theoretical foundation—knowledge is still the best ingredient to good prediction. The best predictive models available anywhere are probably weather prediction models (although few of us care to believe this or would even admit it). This level of prediction would not be possible without a rich and well-developed science of meteorology and the associated level of understanding of the various factors and interrelationships that characterize variations in weather patterns. The prediction is also good because there is a lot of meterological modeling going on and there is an abundance of empirical data to validate the operation of the models and their outcomes. This is evidence of the value of the interative nature of good modeling regimes (and of good science in general).

2.8.3 Cluster analysis

Cluster analysis can perhaps be best described with reference to the work completed by astronomers to understand the relationship between luminosity and temperatures in stars. As shown in the Hertzsprung-Russell diagram, Figure 2.14, stars can seem to cluster according to their shared similarities in temperature (shown on the horizontal scale) and luminosity (shown on the vertical scale). As can be readily seen from this diagram, stars tend to cluster into one of three groups: white dwarfs, main sequence, and giants/supergiants.

If all our work in cluster analysis involved exploring the relationships between various observations (records of analysis) and two dimensions of analysis (as shown here on the horizontal and vertical axes), then we would be able to conduct a cluster analysis visually (as we have done here). As you can well imagine, it is normally the case in data mining projects that we want to determine clusters or patterns based on more than two axes, or dimensions, and in this case visual techniques for cluster analysis do not work. Therefore, it is much more useful to be able to determine clusters based on the operation of numerical algorithms, since the number of dimensions can be manipulated.

Various types of clustering algorithms exist to help identify clusters of observations in a data set based on similarities in two or more dimensions. It is usual and certainly useful to have ways of visualizing the clusters. It is

What's the difference between Outcome view + scatter plot

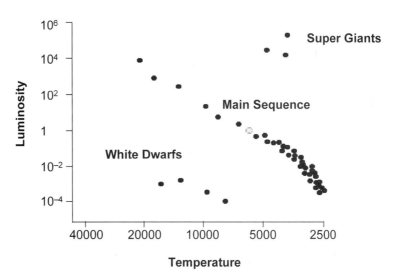

Figure 2.14
Hertzsprung–
Russell diagram of
stars in the solar
neighborhood

also useful to have ways of scoring the effect of each dimension on identify-ing a given cluster. This makes it possible to identity the cluster characteris-tics of an observation that is new to the analysis.

2.9   Evaluation

The evaluation phase of the data mining project is designed to provide feed-back on how good the model you have developed is in terms of its ability to reflect reality. It is an important stage to go through before deployment to ensure that the model properly achieves the business objectives that were set for it at the outset.

There are two aspects in evaluating how well the model of the data we have developed reflects reality: accuracy and reliability. Business phenomena are by nature more difficult to measure than physical phenomena, so it is often difficult to assess the accuracy of our measurements (a thermometer reading is usually taken as an accurate measure of temperature, but do annual purchases provide a good measure of customer loyalty, for exam-ple?). Often, to test accuracy, we rely on face validity; that is, the data mea-surements are assumed to accurately reflect reality because they make sense logically and conceptually.

Reliability is an easier assessment to make in the evaluation phase. Essentially reliability can be assessed by looking at the performance of a model in separate but equally matched data sets. For example, if I wanted to make the statement that "Men, in general, are taller than women," then I could test this hypothesis by taking a room full of a mixture of men and women, measuring them, and comparing the average height of men versus women. As we know, in most likelihood, I would show that men are, indeed, taller than women. However, it is possible that I could have selected a biased room of people. In the room I selected the women might be unusually tall (relative to men). So, it is entirely possible that my experiment could result in a biased result: Women, on average, are taller than men.

The way to evaluate a model is to test its reliability in a number of settings so as to eliminate the possibility that the model results are a function of a poorly selected (biased) set of examples. In most cases, for convenience, two sample data sets are taken: one set of examples (a sample) to be used to learn the characteristics of the model (train the data to reflect the results) and another set of examples to be used to test or validate the results. In general, if the model results that are produced using the learning data set match the model results produced using the testing data set, then the model is said to be valid and the evaluation step is considered a success.

As shown in Figure 2.15, the typical approach to validation is to compare the learning, or training, data set against a test, or validation, data set. A number of specific techniques are used to assess the degree of conformance between the learning data set results and the results generated using the test data set. Many of these techniques are based on statistical tests that test the likelihood that the learning results and testing results are essentially the same (taking account of variations due to selecting examples from different sources). It is not very feasible to estimate whether learning results and testing results are the same based on "eyeballing the data" or "a gut instinct," so statistical tests have a very useful role to play in providing an objective and reproducible measurement which can be used to evaluate whether data mining results are sufficiently reliable to merit deployment.

Figure 2.15
An example showing learn and test comparisons in validation

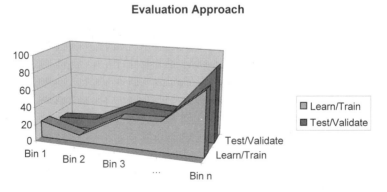

2.10 Deployment

The main task in deployment is to create a seamless process between the discovery of useful information and its application in the enterprise. The information delivery value chain might be similar to that shown in Figure 2.16.

To achieve seamlessness means that results have to be released in a form in which they can be used. The most appropriate form depends on the deployment touch point. Depending on the requirements, the deployment phase can be as simple as generating a report or as complex as implementing an iterative data mining process, which, for example, scores customer visits to Web sites based on real-time data feeds on recent purchases.

The most basic deployment output is a report, typically in written or graphical form. Often the report may be presented in the form of (IF ... THEN) decision rules. These decision rules can be read and applied by a person. For example, a set of decision rules—derived from a data mining analysis—may be used to determine the characteristics of a high-value customer (IF TimeAsCustomer greater than 20 months AND NumberOfPurchasesLastYear greater than $1,000 THEN ProbabilityOfHighValue greater than .65).

As organizations become more computing intense, it is more and more likely that the decision rules will be input to a software application for execution. In this example, the high-value customer probability field may be calculated and applied to a display when, for example, a call comes into the call center as a request for customer service. Obviously, if the decision rule is going to be executed in software, then the rule needs to be expressed in a computer language the software application can understand. In many cases, this will be in a computer language such as C, Java, or Visual BASIC, and, more often, it will be in the form of XML, which is a generalized data description language that has become a universal protocol for describing the attributes of data.

Figure 2.16
Information and business process flow from data input to deployment

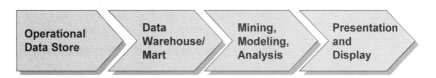

As we will see in later chapters, Microsoft has built a number of deployment environments for analytical results. Business Internet Analytics (BIA) are discussed in Chapter 3. Here we see how Web data are collected, summarized, and made available for dimensional and data mining reports, as well as customer interventions such as segment offer targeting and cross-selling. Microsoft has developed a generalized deployment architecture contained in the Data Transformation Services (DTS) facility. DTS provides the hooks to schedule events or to trigger events, depending on the occurrence of various alternative business rules. Data mining models and predictions can be handled like data elements or data tables in the Microsoft SQL Server environment and, therefore, can be scheduled or triggered to target a segment or to score a customer for propensity to cross-sell in DTS. This approach is discussed in Chapter 6.

As data continue to proliferate, then clearly there will be more and more issues that will occur, more and more data will be available, and the potential relationships and interactions between multiple issues and drivers will lead to increased pressure for the kinds of analytical methods, models, and procedures of data mining in order to bring some discipline to harvesting the knowledge that is contained in the data. So the number of deployments will grow and the need to make deployments quicker will similarly grow.

This phenomenon has been recognized by many observers, notably the Gartner Group, which, in the mid-1990s, identified a "knowledge gap," which relates to the increases in the amount of data, the corresponding increases in business decisions that take advantage of the data, and the associated skills gap due to the relatively slow growth of experienced resources to put the data to effective use through KDD and data mining techniques.

This gap is particularly acute as new business models emerge that are focused on transforming the business from a standard chain of command type of business—with standard marketing, finance, and engineering departments—into a customer-centric organization where the phrase "the customer is the ultimate decision maker" is more than just a whimsical slogan. (See Figure 2.17.)

A customer-centric organization requires the near-instantaneous execution of multiple analytical processes in order to bring the knowledge contained in data to bear on all the customer touch points in the enterprise. These touch points, as well as associated requirements for significant data analysis capabilities, lie at all the potential interaction points characterizing the customer life cycle, as shown in Figure 2.18.

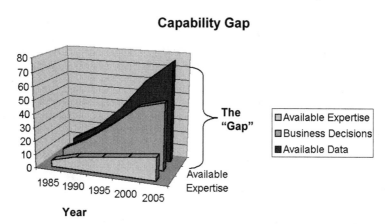

Figure 2.17
The gap between accumulating data, needed decisions, and decision-making skills

Data mining is relevant in sorting through the multiple issues and drivers that characterize the touch points that exist through this life cycle. In terms of data mining deployment, this sets up two major requirements:

1. The data mining application needs to have access to all data that could have an impact on the customer relationship at all the touch points, often in real time or near real time.

2. The dependency of models on data and vice versa needs to be built into the data mining approach.

Figure 2.18
Stages of the customer life cycle

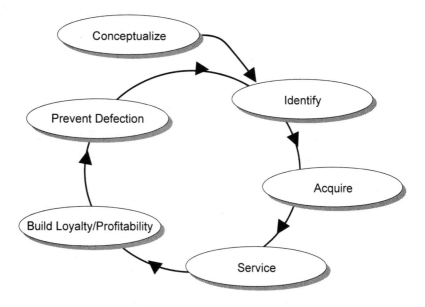

Given a real-time or near-real-time data access requirement, this situation requires the data mining deployment environment to have a very clear idea of which data elements, coming from which touch points, are relevant to carrying out which analysis (e.g., which calls to the call center are relevant to trigger a new acquisition, a new product sale, or, potentially, to prevent a defection). This requires a tight link between the data warehouse, where the data elements are collected and stored, the touch point collectors, and the execution of the associated data mining applications. A description of these relationships and an associated repository model to facilitate deployments in various customer relationship scenarios is shown in http://vitessimo.com/.

2.11   Performance measurement

The key to a closed-loop (virtuous cycle) data mining implementation is the ability to learn over time. This concept is perhaps best described by Berry and Linoff, who propose the approach described in Figure 2.19.

The cycle is virtuous because it is iterative: data mining results—as knowledge management products—are rarely one-off success stories. Rather, as science in general and the quality movement begun by W. Edwards Deming demonstrates, progress is gradual and continuous. The only way to make continuous improvements is to deploy data mining results, measure their impact, and then retool and redeploy based on the knowledge gained through the measurement.

An important component of the virtuous cycle lies in the area of process integration and fast cycle times. As discussed previously, information deliv-

Figure 2.19
Closed-loop data mining—the virtuous cycle

ery is an end-to-end process, which moves through data capture to data staging to analysis and deployment. By providing measurement, the virtuous cycle provides a tool not only for results improvement but also for data mining process improvement. The accumulation of measurements through time brings more information to bear on the elimination of seams and handoffs in the data capture, staging, analysis, and deployment cycle. This leads to faster cycle times and increased competitive advantage in the marketplace.

2.12 Collaborative data mining: the confluence of data mining and knowledge management

As indicated at the beginning of this chapter, knowledge management takes up the task of managing complexity—identifying, documenting, preserving, and deploying expertise and best practices—in the enterprise. Best practices are ways of doing things that individuals and groups have discovered over time. They are techniques, tools, approaches, methods, and methodologies that work. What is knowledge management? According to the American Process and Quality Control (APQC) Society, knowledge management consists of systematic approaches to find, understand, and use knowledge to create value.

According to this definition, data mining itself—especially in the form of KDD—qualifies as a knowledge management discipline. Data warehousing, data mining, and business intelligence lead to the extraction of a lot of information and knowledge from data. At the same time, of course, in a rapidly changing world, with rapidly changing markets, new business, manufacturing, and service delivery methods are evolving constantly. The need for the modern enterprise to keep on top of this knowledge has led to the development of the discipline of knowledge management. Data-derived knowledge, sometimes called explicit knowledge, and knowledge contained in people's heads, sometimes called *tacit knowledge*, form the intellectual capital of the enterprise. More and more, these data are stored in the form of metadata, often as part of the metadata repository provided as a standard component of SQL Server.

The timing, function, and data manipulation processes supported by these different types of functions are shown in Table 2.2.

Current management approaches recognize that there is a hierarchy of maturity in the development of actionable information for the enterprise: data → information → knowledge. This management perspective, com-

Table 2.2   *Evolution of IT Functionality with Respect to Data*

	1970s	1980s	1990s	2000s
IT function	Business reports	Business query tools	Data mining tools	Knowledge management
Type of report	Structured reports	Multidimensional reports and ad hoc queries	Multiple dimensions: analysis, description, and prediction	Knowledge networks: metadata-driven analysis
Role with data	Organization	Analysis	Synthesis	Knowledge capture and dissemination

bined with advances in technology, has driven the acceptance of increasingly sophisticated data manipulation functions in the IT tool kit. As shown in Table 2.2, this has led to the ability to move from organizing data to the analysis and synthesis of data.

The next step in data manipulation maturity is the creation of intellectual capital. The data manipulation maturity model is illustrated in Figure 2.20. The figure illustrates the evolution of data processing capacity within the enterprise and shows the progression from operational data processing, at the bottom of the chain, to the production of information, knowledge, and, finally, intellectual capital. The maturity model suggests that lower steps on the chain are precursors to higher steps on the chain.

As the enterprise becomes more adept at dealing with data, it increases its ability to move from operating the business to driving the business. Sim-

Figure 2.20
Enterprise capability maturity growth path

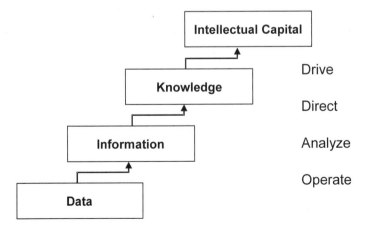

ilarly, as the enterprise becomes increasingly adept at the capture and analysis of business and engineering processes, its ability to operate the business, in a passive and reactive sense, begins to change to an ability to drive the business in a proactive and predictive sense.

Data mining and KDD are important facilitators in the unfolding evolution of the enterprise toward higher levels of decision-making maturity. Whereas the identification of tacit knowledge—or know-how—is an essentially difficult task, we can expect greater and greater increases in our ability to let data speak for themselves. Data mining and the associated data manipulation maturity involved in data mining mean that data—and the implicit knowledge that data contain—can be more readily deployed to drive the enterprise to greater market success and higher levels of decision-making effectiveness. The topic of intellectual capital development is taken up further in Chapter 7. You can also read more about it in *Intellectual Capital* (Thomas Stewart).

3

Data Mining Tools and Techniques

*Statistical thinking will one day be as necessary for efficient
citizenship as the ability to read and write.*

—H. G. Wells

If any organization is poised to introduce statistical thinking to citizens at large, proposed as necessary by the notable H. G. Wells, then surely it is Microsoft, a company that is dedicated to the concept of a computer on every desktop—in the home or office. Since SQL Server 2000 incorporates statistical thinking and statistical use scenarios, it is an important step in the direction of making statistical thinking broadly available—extending this availability to database administrators and SQL Server 2000 end users.

In spite of this potential scenario, statistically based computing has been—and to date remains—on the periphery of main line desktop computing applications. Even spreadsheets, the most prevalent form of numerically based computing applications, are rarely used for "number crunching" statistical applications and are most often used as extensive numerical calculators. From this perspective, a data mining workstation on every desktop may be an elusive dream—nevertheless, it is a dream that Microsoft has dared to have. Let's look at the facilities that Microsoft has put in place in support of this dream.

3.1　Microsoft's entry into data mining

With the advent of SQL Server 7, introduced in the fall of 1998, Microsoft took a bold step into the maturing area of decision support and business intelligence (BI). Until this time BI existed as a paradox—a technique that belonged in the arsenal of any business analyst, yet curiously absent as a major functional component of the databases they used. SQL Server 7, with OLAP services, changed this: It provided a widely accessible, functional, and flexible approach to BI OLAP and multidimensional cube data query and data manipulation. This initiative brought these capabilities out of a multifaceted field of proprietary product vendors into a more universally accessible and broadly shared computing environment.

The release of SQL Server 2000, introduced in the fall of 2000, was a similarly bold move on the part of Microsoft. As shown in this text, data unity is an essential complement to the kind of dimensional analysis that is found in OLAP. But it has been more difficult to grasp, and this is reflected in the market size of data mining relative to OLAP. Microsoft's approach to extend earlier OLAP services capabilities to incorporate data mining algorithms resulted in SQL Server 2000's integrated OLAP/data mining environment, called Analysis Services.

3.2　The Microsoft data mining perspective

The Data Mining and Exploration group at Microsoft, which developed the data mining algorithms in SQL Server 2000, describes the goal of data mining as finding "structure within data." As defined by the group, structures are revealed through patterns. Patterns are relationships or correlations (correlations) in data. So, the structure that is revealed through patterns should provide insight into the relationships that characterize the components of the structures. In terms of the vocabulary introduced in Chapter 2, this structure can be viewed as a model of the phenomenon that is being revealed through relationships in data.

Generally, patterns are developed through the operation of one or more statistical algorithms (the statistical patterns are necessary to find the correlations). So the Data Mining and Exploration group's approach is to develop capabilities that can lead to structural descriptions of the data set, based on patterns that are surfaced through statistical operations. The approach is designed to automate as much of the analysis task as possible and to eliminate the need for statistical reasoning in the construction of the analysis tools. After all, in the Microsoft model, shouldn't an examination of a database to find likely prospects for a new product simply be a different kind of query? Traditionally, of course, a query has been constructed to retrieve particular fields of information from a database and to summarize the fields in a particular fashion. A data mining query is a bit different—in the same way that a data mining model is different from a traditional database table. In a data mining query, we specify the question that we want to examine—say, gross sales or propensity to respond to a targeted marketing offer—and the job of the data mining query processor is to return to the query station the results of the query in the form of a structural model that responds to the question.

The Microsoft approach to data mining is based on a number of principles, as follows:

- Ensuring that data mining approaches scale with increases in data (sometimes referred to as megadata)

- Automating pattern search

- Developing understandable models

- Developing "interesting" models

Microsoft employed three broad strategies in the development of the Analysis Services of SQL Server 2000 to achieve the following principles:

1.   As much as possible data marts should be self-service so that anyone can use them without relying on a skilled systems resource to translate end-user requirements into database query instructions. This strategy has been implemented primarily through the development of end-user task wizards to take you through the various steps involved in developing and consuming data mining models.

2.   The query delivery mechanism—whether it is OLAP based or data mining based—should be delivered to the user through the same interface. This strategy was implemented as follows:

    - OLE DB, developed to support multidimensional cubes necessary for OLAP, was extended to support data mining models. This means that the same infrastructure supports both OLAP and data mining.

    - After initial development, the data mining implementation was passed on to be managed and delivered by the OLAP implementation group at Microsoft. This means that both

OLAP and data mining products have been developed by the same implementation team, with the same approach and tool set.

3.   There should be a universal data access mechanism to allow sharing of data and data mining results through heterogeneous environments with multiple applications. This strategy is encapsulated in the same OLE DB for data mining mechanism developed to support this principle. Thus, heterogeneous data access, a shared mining and multidimensional query storage medium and a common interface for OLAP queries and data mining queries, is reflected in the OLE DB for data mining approach.

The Data Mining and Exploration group has identified several important end-user needs in the development of this approach, as follows:

■ Users do not make a distinction between planned reports, ad hoc reports, multidimensional reports, and data mining results. Basically, an end user wants information and does not want to be concerned with the underlying technology that is necessary to deliver the information.

■ Users want to interact with the results through a unified query mechanism. They want to question the data and the results and work with different views of the data in order to develop a better understanding of the problem and a better understanding of how the data illuminate the problem.

■ The speed of interaction between the user and the results of the query is very important. It is important to make progress to eliminate the barrier between the user and the next query in order to contribute to a better understanding of the data.

At a basic level, the Data Mining and Exploration group has achieved its goals with this implementation of SQL 2000. Here's why:

■ The group has made great progress in the self-service approach. The incorporation of wizards in all major phases of the data mining task is a significant step in the direction of self-service. By aligning OLAP and data mining information products within a generalized Microsoft Office framework, and by creating common query languages and access protocols across this framework, the group has created an environment where skills developed in the use of one Office product are readily transferable to the use and mastery of another product. Thus, for example, skills in Excel can later be brought to bear in the navigation of an OLAP cube.

- Prior to SQL Server 2000 production and release, the data mining algorithms developed by Microsoft's Data Mining and Exploration group were delivered to the SQL Server OLAP services group (Plato group) for implementation. The main thrust of this initiative was to ensure that data mining products were delivered through the same framework as OLAP products. This relationship with the Plato group led to the development of the data mining code name, Socrates. The advantage of this development direction is clear: The end user can access OLAP services and data mining services through the same interface (this is a relatively rare achievement in decision support and business intelligence circles, where OLAP style reports and data mining reports are generally separate business entities or, at the very least, separate—and architecturally distinct—product lines within the same organization).

- In the process of moving from SQL Server 7 to SQL Server 2000, Microsoft upgraded the OLE DB specification, originally developed as an Application Programming Interface (API) to enable third parties to support OLAP services with commercial software offerings, to an OLE DB for data mining API (with a similar goal of providing standard API support for third-party Information System Vendors' [ISVs] data mining capabilities).

- The OLE DB for DM (data mining) specification makes data mining accessible through a single established API: OLE DB. The specification was developed with the help and contributions of a team of leading professionals in the business intelligence field, as well as with the help and contributions of a large number of ISVs in the business intelligence field. Microsoft's OLE DB for DM specification introduces a common interface for data mining that will give developers the opportunity to easily—and affordably—embed highly scalable data mining capabilities into their existing applications. Microsoft's objective is to provide the industry standard for data mining so that algorithms from practically any data mining ISV can be easily plugged into a consumer application.

While the wizard-driven interface is the primary access mechanism to the data mining query engine in SQL 2000, the central object of the implementation of data mining in SQL Server 2000 is the data mining model. A Data Mining Model (DMM) is a Decision Support Object (DSO), which is built by applying data mining algorithms to relational or cube data and which is stored as part of an object hierarchy in the Analysis Services directory. The model is created and stored in summary form with dimensions, patterns, and relationships, so it will persist regardless of the disposition of the data on which it is based. Both the DMM and OLAP cubes can be accessed through the same Universal Data Access (UDA) mechanism. This addition of data mining capability in Microsoft SQL 2000 represents a major new functional extension to SQL Server's capabilities in the 2000 release.

This chapter shows how Microsoft's strategy plays to the broadened focus of data mining, the Web, and the desktop. It discusses the Microsoft strategy and organization, the new features that have been introduced into SQL 2000 (Analysis Services), and how OLE DB for data mining will create new data mining opportunities by opening the Microsoft technology and architecture to third-party developers.

3.3 Data mining and exploration (DMX) projects

During the development of Analysis Services, the DMX group worked with a number of data mining issues from scaling data mining algorithms to large collections of data; to data summary and reduction; and analysis algorithms, which can be used on large data sets. The DMX areas of emphasis included classification, clustering, sequential data modeling, detecting frequent events, and fast data reduction techniques. The group collaborated with the database research group to address implementing data mining algorithms in a server environment and to look at the implications and requirements that data mining imposes on the database engine. As indicated previously, the DMX group also worked hand in glove with other Microsoft product groups, including Commerce Server, SQL Server, and, most especially, the Plato group (BI OLAP Services).

Commerce Server is a product that is integrated with the Internet Information Server (IIS) and SQL Server and helps developers build Web sites that accept financial transactions and payments, display product catalogs, and so forth. The DMX group developed the predictor component (used in cross-sell, for example) in the 3.0 version of Commerce Server and is developing other data mining capabilities for subsequent product releases.

The DMX group is also looking at scalable algorithms for extracting frequent sequences and episodes from large databases storing sequential data. The main challenge is to develop scaling mechanisms to work with high-dimensional data—that is, data with thousands or tens of thousands of variables. It is also developing methods to integrate database back-end products and SQL databases in general.

3.4 OLE DB for data mining architecture

The OLE DB for data mining (DM) specification is an extension of the OLE DB for OLAP services specification introduced in the earlier version of SQL Server 7. The main goal of this specification is to introduce support for data mining algorithms and data mining queries through the same facilitating mechanism.

OLE DB for DM was constructed as an extension of the earlier specification introduced to support OLAP algorithms and OLAP queries. OLE DB for DM extends and builds upon the earlier specification so that no new OLE DB interfaces are added. Rather, the specification defines a simple query language, very similar to the familiar SQL syntax, and defines specialized schema row sets, which consumer applications can use to communicate with data mining providers.

OLE DB for DM is designed to support most popular data mining algorithms. Using OLE DB for DM, data mining applications can tap into any tabular data source through an OLE DB provider, and data mining analysis can now be performed directly against a relational database.

A high level view of the OLE DB for DM architecture is shown in Figure 3.1. As with the earlier OLE DB for OLAP specification, both clients and servers are supported, as is SQL Server and other OLE DB data sources (illustrated in the lower part of the diagram). As shown in the top of the diagram, OLAP applications, user applications, and system services, such as Commerce Server and a variety of third-party tools and applications, can plug into the OLE DB for DM facility. Access can be via wizards or programmatically as an OLE DB command object. This is particularly useful for third-party applications (which may provide or consume data mining functions through OLE DB for DM).

To bridge the gap between traditional data mining techniques and modern relational database management systems (RDBMS), OLE DB for DM defines important new concepts and features, including the following:

- *Data mining model.* The data mining model is like a relational table, except that it contains special columns that you can use to derive the patterns and relationships that characterize the kinds of discoveries

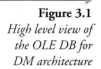

Figure 3.1
High level view of
the OLE DB for
DM architecture

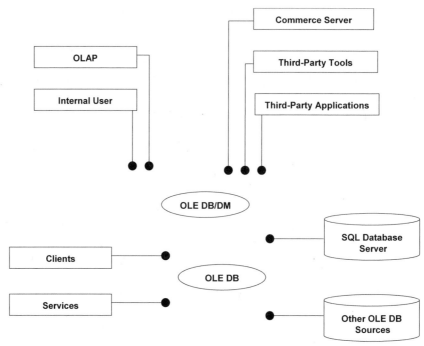

that data mining reveals, such as what offers drive sales or the characteristics of people who respond to a targeted marketing offer. You can
also use these columns to make predictions; the data mining model
serves as the core functionality that both creates a prediction model
and generates predictions. Unlike a standard relational table, which
stores raw data, the data mining model stores the patterns discovered
by your data mining algorithm. To create data mining models, you
use a CREATE statement that is very similar to the SQL CREATE
TABLE statement. You populate a data mining model by using the
INSERT INTO statement, just as you would populate a table. The
client application issues a SELECT statement to make predictions
through the data mining model. A prediction is like a query in that it
shows the important fields in a given outcome, such as sales or probability of response. After the data mining model identifies the important fields, it can use the same pattern to classify new data in which
the outcome is unknown. The process of identifying the important
fields that form a prediction's pattern is called *training*. The trained
pattern, or structure, is what you save in the data mining model.

OLE DB for Data Mining is an extension of OLE DB that lets
data mining client applications use data mining services from a broad

variety of providers. OLE DB for Data Mining treats data mining models as a special type of table. When you insert the data into the table, a data mining algorithm processes the data and the data mining model query processor saves the resulting data mining model instead of the data itself. You can then browse the saved data mining model, refine it, or use it to make predictions.

- *OLE DB for Data Mining schema rowsets.* These special-purpose schema rowsets let consumer applications find crucial information, such as available mining services, mining models, mining columns, and model contents. SQL Server 2000 Analysis Services' Analysis Manager and third-party data mining providers populate schema rowsets during the model creation stage, during which the data is examined for patterns. This process, called learning or training, refers to the examination of data to discern new patterns or, alternatively, the fact that the data mining model is trained to recognize patterns in the new data source.

- *Prediction join operation.* To facilitate deployment, this operation, which is similar to the join operation in SQL syntax, is mapped to a join query between a data mining model (which contains the trained pattern from the original data) and the designated new input data. This mapping lets you easily generate a prediction result tailored to the business requirements of the analysis.

- *Predictive Model Markup Language (PMML).* The OLE DB for Data Mining specification incorporates the PMML standards of the Data Mining Group (DMG), a data mining consortium (http://www.oasis-open.org/cover/pmml.html). This specification gives developers an open interface to more effectively integrate data mining tools and capabilities into line-of-business and e-commerce applications.

3.4.1   How the Data Mining Process Looks

Data to be mined is a collection of tables. In an example I discuss later, you have a data object that contains a customer table that relates to a promotions table—both of which relate to a conference attendance table. This is a typical data mining analysis scenario in which you use customer response to past promotions to train a data mining model to determine the characteristics of customers who are most likely to respond to new promotions. Through data mining, you first use the training process to identify historical patterns of behavior, then use these patterns to predict future behavior.

Data mining accomplishes this prediction through a new data mining operator, the prediction join, which you can implement through Data Transformation Services (DTS). DTS provides a simple query tool that lets you build a prediction package, which contains the trained data mining model and which points to an untrained data source that you want predicted outcome from. For example, if you had trained a data source to look for a pattern that predicts likely customer response to a conference invitation, you could use DTS to apply this predicted pattern to a new data source to see how many customers in the new data will likely respond. DTS's ready-made mechanism of deploying data mining patterns provides a valuable synergy among data mining, BI, and data warehousing in the Microsoft environment.

The collection of data that make up a single entity (such as a customer) is a *case*. The set of all associated cases (customers, promotions, conferences) is the *case set*. OLE DB for Data Mining uses nested tables—tables stored within other tables—as defined by the Data Shaping Service, which is part of Microsoft Data Access Components (MDAC). For example, you can store product purchases within the customer case. The OLE DB for Data Mining specification uses the SHAPE statement to perform this nesting.

A significant feature of SQL Server 2000's data mining functionality is ease of deployment. With DTS, you can easily apply the results of previously trained models against new data sources. The strategy is to make data mining products similar to classic data processing products so that you can manipulate, examine, extract data from, and deploy data mining models in the same way as you would any table in a typical database. This approach recognizes that data mining, as organizations usually practice it, requires the data mining analyst to work outside the standard relational database. When you mine outside the database, you create a new database, which leads to redundancy, leaves room for error, takes time, and defeats the purpose of the database. So, a major objective of SQL Server 2000 is to embed the data mining capability directly in the database so that a mining model is as much a database object as a data table is. If this approach is widely adopted in the industry, it will eliminate significant duplication of effort in the creation of data warehouses that are built especially for data mining projects. This approach will also eliminate the time needed to produce specialized data mining tables and the potential threats to data quality and data integrity that the creation of a separate data mining database implies. Finally, directly embedding data mining capability will eliminate the time lag that the creation of a specialized data table inevitably entails. As the demand for data mining products and enhancements increases, this time factor may prove to be the element that finally leads to the universal adoption of data mining functionality as an intrinsic component of a core database management system (DBMS).

3.4.2   Standards

Not all generally accepted standards turn out to be the best. Often it is a marketing victory rather than a technological victory when a standard gets adopted (the SONY betamax versus JVC standard in videotape technology is a case in point). It is not clear at this point whether the OLE DB for DM standard will be broadly subscribed to, but, if it is, it will mean that data mining models available in various vendors' products will be available as products to consume, refine, or extend in any other vendor's product that subscribes to the standard.[1] One of the things that is particularly exciting about the Microsoft standard is that the standard accommodates not only data mining views of the data but OLAP views as well. So Microsoft has accomplished a seamlessness between two different styles of working with data that has been overlooked in the industry in general.

3.4.3   OLE DB for data mining concept of operations

As shown in Figure 3.2, the use of OLE DB for DM starts with the development of a mining model from a given data set. As can be seen in the second panel of the figure, the data mining method is to pass the training data table through the DM engine to produce the mining model. The model is said to be "trained" to recognize patterns, or structures, in data. The third panel shows the process of applying the mining model to the real-world data. This prediction operation involves passing a new set of unmined data through it. This process employs the mining model and the new (unmined) data. These new data are then passed through the data mining engine to produce the predicted outcome.

3.4.4   Implementation

The implementation scenario for OLE DB for DM is shown in Figure 3.3.

A major accomplishment of OLE DB for DM is to address the utilization of the data mining interface and the management of the user interface. The solution adopted in SQL Server 2000 provides for mining extensions

---

1.   At the close of 2000 only one vendor, Megaputer (http://megaputer.com), had announced full support for OLE DB for DM.

Figure 3.2
The OLE DB for
DM process

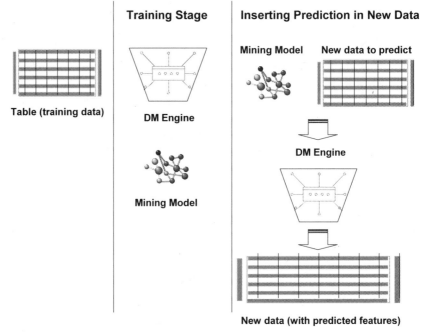

to this interface process that are supported by a number of data mining wizards, which guide the user through the data mining activity.

At a system level the DSO—data set object—model representation has been extended to support the addition of the data mining model object type.

Server components have been built to provide a built-in capability to exercise both OLAP and data mining capabilities. This is a core defining feature of the new Analysis Server. On the client side the implementation provides client OLAP and data mining engine capabilities to exploit the server delivery vehicle. The client provides complete access to both OLAP and data mining models through the OLE DB for DM specification.

Finally, with the issuance of the OLE DB for DM specification, Microsoft has provided a facility—on both the server and client sides—to provide the capability for OLE and OLE DB for DM–compliant third-party capabilities as plug ins. This provides an extensible capability for the implementation of data mining functionality in environments that conform to the OLE DB for DM specification. Currently, a number of third-party tool and application vendors provide this kind of extensibility, notably the members of the Microsoft Data Warehousing Alliance.

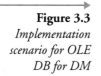

Figure 3.3
Implementation scenario for OLE DB for DM

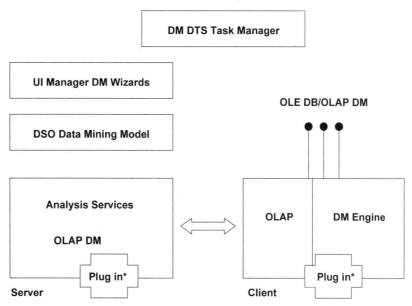

*OLE/OLE DB/DM Compliant

3.5   The Microsoft data warehousing framework and alliance

The Microsoft data warehousing framework has been designed to unify business intelligence needs and solution matching in one fast, flexible, and low-cost foundation. The stated goals are as follows:

- Deliver superior quality business intelligence and analytical applications.

- Empower organizations to turn insights into action and to close the loop between the two as quickly as possible.

- Maximize the architectural advantages of the Windows DNA 2000 platform.

The framework consists of operational, management, and analysis and planning components. A large variety of third-party applications and tools are available in the following areas:

- Extraction, transformation, and loading tools

- Analytical applications

- Query, reporting, and analysis tools
- Data mining providers

Currently, the data mining providers that are members of the Data Warehousing Alliance include the following:

- Angoss Software (KnowledgeStudio)—for further information see http://www.angoss.com
- DBMiner Technology Inc. (DBMiner)—for further information see http://www.dbminer.com
- Megaputer Intelligence (PolyAnalyst)—for further information see http://www.megaputer.com

Both Angoss Software and Megaputer Intelligence have announced SDK and component support for the OLE DB for DM standard. A large number of OLAP vendors in the Data Warehousing Alliance—for example, Knosys Inc.—have also announced support for OLE DB for DM.

For more information about the Data Warehousing Alliance and business intelligence information see http://www.microsoft.com/industry/bi.

3.6   Data mining tasks supported by SQL Server 2000 Analysis Services

Data mining can be applied to a number of different tasks. As we saw in Chapter 2, these could be broken down into three areas: outcome (predictive) models, cluster models, and affinity models. The Microsoft view uses this same breakdown of techniques (although slightly different names are used to describe them). In the area of affinity models, Microsoft has defined a type of analysis that is directed toward finding dependency relationships (dependency relationships are stronger than associations, since associations are correlated, whereas a dependency relationship is both correlated and dependent so that one effect is a precondition to another). The Microsoft world of data mining techniques appears as follows:

- Outcome models or predictive modeling, called "classification" by Microsoft
- Cluster models or segmentation
- Affinity models, including:
  - Association, sequence, and deviation analyses
  - Dependency modeling

SQL Server 2000 Analysis Services provide direct support for the first two tasks (classification and clustering). Two basic data mining algorithms are provided by Analysis Services to support classification and clustering: decision trees and cluster analysis.

Exclusive Ore (http://www.xore.com) has built both a standalone and ActiveX-based data mining package to derive association and sequence patterns from databases: Xaffinity. It is implemented in SQL—so it is highly scalable—and has an Access-based frontend—so it benefits from a standard look and feel.

3.6.1 Outcome or classification models

Outcome modeling uses a set of input variables to predict or classify the value of a target, or response, variable (this is the outcome). The target variable may be categorical (having discrete values such as reply/did not reply) or continuous values (such as dollar amount purchased). When the target is categorical, predictive modeling is referred to as a classification task—that is, which combinations of the input variables can be used to reliably classify the target. When the target variable is continuous, then the model is typically described as a regression model, since regression is the most common type of analysis that attempts to predict values of a continuous target variable based on the combined values of the input variables. Microsoft refers to this type of modeling as "classification."

3.6.2 Decision trees

Decision trees are a common and robust technique to carry out predictive modeling tasks with an outcome. Decision trees are very easy to work with; produce a highly readable, graphic display; and work well with both continuous and categorical data. With a continuous outcome, they are commonly called "regression trees." With a categorical outcome, they are commonly called "classification trees." Table 3.1 shows how data might be arranged to measure the response to a request to attend an Information Technology conference. Although this is a small data set, it would be difficult, through visual inspection alone, to determine which of the attributes (columns) in the data set, if any, were predictive of the likelihood to reply to the request to attend. Imagine, for example, trying to determine what influences probability of response in a response database of over 10,000 records: Is it type of job (title)? Gender? Number of employees or size of sales? Of course, if it is difficult to see the two-variable predictive relationships, it is impossible to see the combinations of predictive relationships that produce a strong pre-

Table 3.1   *Sample Enrollment Data Showing Response to an Offer to Attend a High-Technology Conference and Workshop*

Custnum	Title	Gender	EmploySize	SalesSize	Replied
1	CHIEF SCIENTIST	F	Small	$1M+	No reply
2	DEVELOPER	M	Small	$1M+	No reply
3	IT PROGRAMMER	M	Small	$1M+	No reply
4	IT PROGRAMMER	M	Small	$1M+	No reply
5	IT PROGRAMMER	M	Small	$1M+	No reply
6	PRODUCT MANAGER	M	Small	< $1M	No reply
7	PRODUCT MANAGER	M	Small	$1M+	No reply
8	PRODUCT MANAGER	M	Small	$1M+	No reply
9	PRODUCT MANAGER	M	Small	$1M+	Reply
10	PRODUCT MANAGER	F	Large	< $1M	Reply
11	PRODUCT MANAGER	F	Large	< $1M	Reply
12	PRODUCT MANAGER	F	Large	< $1M	Reply
13	PRODUCT MANAGER	F	Small	< $1M	No reply
14	PRODUCT MANAGER	M	Large	$1M+	No reply
15	PRODUCT MANAGER	M	Small	$1M+	No reply

dictive classification of the likelihood of replying or not. (We will answer these and other questions in the example that we construct in Chapter 5.)

Figure 3.4, based on a decision tree, reveals the predictive structure of the data: From this we can see that employee size (EmploySize) is the strongest predictor of attendance. The overall attendance rate (number who requested to attend) is 40 percent. We can see that 75 percent of employees from large companies attended, whereas only about one-quarter (actually, 27 percent) of the employees from small companies attended. So, employees from large companies are three times as likely to attend the conference. We can see that this effect of small companies reverses when sales income is considered: In the two cases where sales income for small companies was less than $1 million, attendance is 100 percent. (This indicates that, in this sample, all employees from companies with less than $1 million in annual revenues chose to attend the conference.) We are showing these results as an example: You would never base results on such a small number of records (unless you had completed substantial testing with other data sets to verify that this pattern repeats reliably in the target consumer population). If there were 10 times as much data as is shown in the example—so that all the numbers were multiplied by 10—then you might be inclined to have more confidence in the statistical reproducibility of the results.

How does a decision tree work?

As seen in Figure 3.4, a decision tree works by taking the overall data set, which is presented as the origin or root node of a decision tree at the top of the figure, and finding ways of partitioning the records or cases that occur in the root node in order to form branches. The branches are identified in the form of an upside-down decision tree. The nodes that are identified at the ends of the branches are usually called "leaves" (to extend the decision tree metaphor).

Determining the branches (splits) on the decision tree

SQL Server 2000 uses a gain ratio calculation to determine the splitting sequence for branches in a decision tree. The choice of the Gain Ratio statistic as the splitting criterion results from the fact that the Gain Ratio is a well-known, well researched and commonly-used assessment measure in academic circles. There are many splitting statistics that could be used—all have good points and bad points. The Gain Ratio is a good place to start. In

Figure 3.4
A decision tree

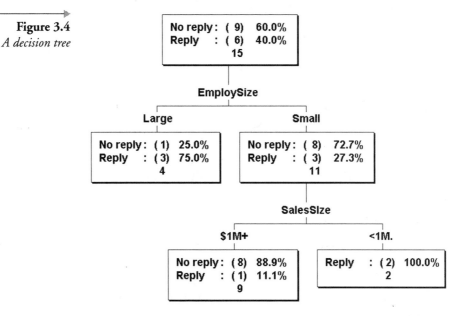

Table 3.1, Gender, Employee Size, and Sales Size would be used as potential inputs, or splitting attributes. Inputs such as Title, with a large number of potential categories, are not typically supported by entry-level data mining algorithms (although virtually all the third-party products that provide decision tree functionality in the marketplace support multiple attribute values such as those found in Title in this example). Fields such as Title are difficult to support, because the code entries in Title combine in many different ways to form branches. For example, when using the information contained in Table 3.1, there are four titles: Chief Scientist, Developer, IT Programmer, and Product Manager. There are 2^{n-1} ways that these codes can combine to form branches on a decision tree, so, in this case, there are eight different combinations to examine with a statistical algorithm. This is not a computationally intensive task, but it is with the main data set from which this example was taken (in the main data set there are 1,100 distinct codes for Title—i.e., more than 10^{300} combinations to explore in forming the branches of the decision tree). In practice, products that do sort through fields such as Title to find combinations of values from which to form branches typically use heuristics to find the branches. One common heuristic is to simply look for binary partitions. This is the approach behind various binary decision tree products, notably Salford Systems' CART product. Other heuristics include adaptations of Kass's CHAID algorithms. These adaptations are discussed in Biggs, de Ville, and Suen, 1991.

Not all fields in the data set are as difficult to examine as fields such as Title. Other fields, such as Employee Size and Sales Size, combine in numerical order—that is, Small–Medium–Large involves only looking at Small–Medium versus Large or Small versus Medium–Large branches (Small–Large versus Medium branches break the numerical order, so they are not valid branch combinations).

The way in which gain ratio is calculated is illustrated in Table 3.2. In this table we can see that, overall, there were nine no's and six yes's. If you had to guess what the outcome of the 15 cases were and you had no other information, then your best strategy would be to guess "no." Using this strategy would yield six mistakes (the number of yes's in the node of the tree that represents the overall number of cases). In the case of Sales, Gender, and Employee, assume that you are given a little more information—that is, the distributions of responses (yes) versus no responses (no) within each of these categories. Using this guessing strategy and taking advantage of this extra information would yield a total number of mistakes of one for Sales, three for Gender, and four for Employee. So, in this case, it would make most sense to partition the root node of the tree according to Sales, since

Table 3.2   *Gain Ratio Calculations for Various Potential Branch Partitions*

	Overall		Sales			Gender			Employee	
	Yes	No		Yes	No		Yes	No		Yes	No
	6	9	<$1M	5	0	Female	4	1	Large	3	1
			$1M+	1	9	Male	2	8	Small	3	8
Mistakes	6			1	0		2	1		3	1

this will result in the fewest number of errors. Notice that any partition results in fewer errors than the errors that result in the root node where no additional information is available. This illustrates a general principle in statistics: The more information you have about an area the greater the knowledge you have about the area.

This general idea of choosing splits that minimize errors has been extended to the calculation of the information value, or entropy. The gain ratio is the ratio of the reduction in entropy over the entropy of the parent split (in this case, the parent split is the topmost node of the decision tree—that is, the node with 15 cases in it). This calculation is used in growing the decision tree in Analysis Server. So, using the calculations presented here, we can see that the gains ratio for Sales is (6-1/6); the gains ratio for Gender is (6-3/6); and the gains ratio for Employee Size is (6-4/6)—that is, 5.8, 5.5, and 5.3, respectively. So, the split that is chosen is the one that maximizes gains ratio; in this case, this is Sales Size.

The decision tree algorithm in Analysis Server always works with binary splits. For multiple values each attribute is first assigned to a unique branch, and then, in steps, two branches are merged until only two branches exist. Cases with missing values are excluded from the split search on that input and also from the numerator of the gain ratio. Missing values are considered as an additional branch in the tree.

In a real-life target marketing task there would be far more attributes for each potential conference attendee and the numbers of potential attendees would be very large. When the scale of the problem increases, it is certainly difficult to manually assess predictive characteristics so automatic techniques, as shown here, are necessary. This difficulty of assessing the predictive power of multiple attributes is true, to a lesser extent, even with sophisticated OLAP tools. The role of data mining and decision trees is to provide this ability to assess the combined predictive power of multiple attributes. Decision trees scale well with many attributes having many values and many records in the data. Because of this, they turn out to be extremely useful for a wide range of predictive modeling and classification tasks.

The background of decision trees

There have been numerous types of approaches used in multidimensional knowledge discovery. Outcome methods try to use the information contained in many fields in the data store to explain variations in the outcome field—that is, the field that contains the question (profit, defects, interest rate, and so on). One of the earliest methods used multiple regression, a standard statistical technique, which uncovers the pattern of dependencies between multiple predictor fields and the outcome.

Other methods include decision trees, which show the combined dependencies between multiple inputs and the outcome as a number of decision branches that show how the value of the outcome changes with different values in the inputs. Decision tree methods of knowledge discovery were developed in order to compensate for some of the problems that were encountered using multiple regression as a data mining tool. Decision tree methods are fashioned after a mental problem-solving capacity, used by humans, called "induction." In an inductive approach we proceed incrementally, by steps, first finding a solution and then looking for a solution within this solution and so on. The decision tree method first finds a branch, or partition, to explain variability in the root node and then looks for a new branch within the branches that are discovered in the root node and so on. This is the incremental inductive approach. This process of induction is the direct precursor of the decision tree implementation used in Microsoft's SQL Server 2000 implementation.

Problems with past decision tree approaches

Decision tree techniques were developed by statisticians who wanted to overcome the limitations of the statistical technique of multiple, linear regression. There are many problems with linear regression: As the name implies, the basic statistical model assumes that relationships are linear. So, the relationship between age and height is treated as a linear one: For every increment in years of age there is a corresponding increment in height. This relationship is constant, linear, and additive. That is, the increment from year to year is constant, and it increases additively from year to year in linear fashion. We know now that this relationship is not constant: During the teenage years, for example, it is common for people to go through growth spurts where the rate of growth is several times the rate before or after the teenage years. We also know that this is not additive, nor is it linear: In most cases, with sufficient aging, people lose height as their bones, ligaments, and cartilage shrink and compress after years of use.

The basic regression statistical model also requires that data elements be quantitative rather than qualitative. So, regression has difficulty handling marital status (e.g., Mr., Mrs., Miss) in a modeling situation. Regression also has difficulty in detecting spurious relationships in a data store. A spurious relationship is produced when an association between two fields can be shown to be the result of some other predetermining factor. For example, the relationship between seasonal sales and gross margin may be a spurious one if we can show that the relationship is actually a result of a predisposing relationship between discount rate and gross margin (discount rates may be higher in the summer and this may be what is causing the variation in the gross margin, not the season).

Morgan and Sonquist (1963) were applied statisticians at the University of Michigan who were interested in developing a statistical analysis technique that would allow them to deal with applied social and economic problems in a better way than was possible using existing standard statistical regression techniques. They developed a technique that was modeled after the way humans went about solving problems (see Belson and Hunt, Marin and Stone in the references). They proposed an automatic interaction detector, which they called AID. The interaction detector referred to the ability to introduce qualitative fields, such as marital status, into a regression analysis in order to check for the presence of spurious relationships and nonlinear relationships. They suggested a mechanical, or automatic, system, which would mimic the steps that an experienced data analyst might go through to determine the strong interaction effects in data.

In the terminology of Morgan and Sonquist a spurious relationship is an interaction; the true relationship is obscured by an interaction between the outcome and another data field. The automatic interaction detector technique involves an exhaustive examination of all possible relationships between predictor fields and the outcome field to determine the strongest, or best, prediction. When this is found, the data are partitioned into two separate groups determined by the selected predictor field. This is the beginning of the construction of the decision tree. The process is repeated, inductively, for the descendant groups formed by the selection of the strongest predictor. The result was a series of partitions, or branches, in the data, where each partition produced a new data set, which was, in turn, split up. The final result was a series of branches resembling a decision tree.

The Morgan and Sonquist procedure was implemented as a computer program, called AID (for automatic interaction detector) at the University of Michigan in the early 1970s. When it was introduced, AID was enthusiastically received by many researchers, statisticians, and data analysts. The advantage of decision trees, over both regression and neural networks, is that the models they provide are easier to interpret than the mathematically intense regression and neural network models. Because of the way a decision tree is built, the analyst has more control over the construction of the model and can assemble a more valid and reliable final model. The beauty decision trees and the original AID program is that they addressed this problem of hidden dependencies and spurious relationships.

But there were some problems with AID noted by observers at the time. The best example of these problems was documented by Einhorn (1972). Essentially, Einhorn showed that, if anything, AID was too aggressive at identifying relationships and dependencies in data. AID had no mechanism to discriminate meaningful relationships from meaningless relationships; often AID fell into the trap of selecting relationships that were a result of random fluctuations in the data set. In short, AID frequently produced decision trees that were the result of chance effects in the data rather than a true reflection of the theory of operation of the question under examination. This is the problem of overfitting.

The concept of induction was also the inspiration behind another precursor to the decision tree approach used in SQL Server 2000: a top-down induction of decision tree approach, called ID3, developed by Ross Quinlan at the University of Sydney, Australia (in Michie, 1979). A series of improvements to ID3 culminated in the development of the C4.5 method of tree induction, which is the direct precursor to the algorithm used in SQL Server 2000. The C4.5 algorithm, together with its most recent successor, C5, resolves a number of problems and provides for methods to deal with both qualitative and quantitative attributes, missing values, and overfitting.

Solutions to early data mining problems

In the mid-1970s, a method of addressing the shortcomings of AID was published by a statistician named Kass (1976, 1980). The approach he employed depends on applying the lessons of statistical hypothesis testing to the decision trees produced by AID. This is one of the origins of modern decision tree methods employed in SQL Server 2000.

Kass reasoned that branches identified by AID could be tested using standard statistical tests to determine whether they were a chance effect of fluctuations in the data. Statistical tests are used in this capacity all the time (to determine, for example, whether increases in the height of wheat grown with a particular fertilizer are a result of the fertilizer or just a result of random fluctuations in the data used to measure the height of the wheat). So Kass found a way to apply modern statistics to determine the statistical strength of each of the branches on the decision tree. When the branch was too weak statistically, it would not be identified as a branch in the decision tree.

In the early 1980s, a validation approach emerged to remedy the problems with AID (see Breiman, Friedman, Olshen, and Stone). In a validation approach the data being analyzed are split up into a training (or learning) data set and test (or validation) data set. When a branch is identified in the training data set, the algorithm checks to see if the same branch is present in the test data set. If it is, then the branch is considered to be a valid and repeatable finding. If it is not, then this is considered a case of overfitting. This approach complements the statistical approach of Kass, since, while statistical approaches are based on statistical theory, validation approaches are based on an examination of the actual properties of data. Validation looks closely at data that are used to build the decision tree. If too many fluctuations are observed, then, as with the statistical approach employed by Kass, the branch is rated poorly and is not presented in the final decision tree display. The results of this validation approach are published in Breiman et al. (see references).

3.6.3   Segmentation (clustering)

Segmentation is the process of grouping or clustering cases together based on their shared similarities to a set of attributes. Decision trees also find segments, but the segments are always defined with respect to a particular outcome variable. So, the values or codes on one branch of the decision tree can be seen to form a cluster, where the cases in that cluster—here a leaf on the decision tree—have a shared similarity in terms of the attribute of the branch that forms the decision tree. The branch that identifies the shared similarity of the cases in the leaf—or cluster—has been formed with respect to a particular outcome (e.g., respond or did not respond). If there is no outcome variable, or if you want to see how observations group together in terms of their shared values in multiple outcome variables, then clustering is the technique of choice.

The goal of cluster analysis is to identify groups of cases that are as similar as possible with respect to a number of variables in the data set yet are as different as possible with respect to these variables when compared with any other cluster in the grouping. Records that have similar purchasing or spending patterns, for example, form easily identified segments for targeting different products. In terms of personalized interaction, different clusters can provide strong cues to suggest different treatments.

Clustering is very often used to define market segments. A number of techniques have evolved over time to carry out clustering tasks. One of the oldest clustering techniques is K-means clustering. In K-means clustering the user assigns a number of means that will serve as bins, or clusters, to hold the observations in the data set. Observations are then allocated to each of the bins, or clusters, depending on their shared similarity. Another technique is expectation maximization (EM). EM differs from K-means in that each observation has a propensity to be in any one bin, or cluster, based on a probability weight. In this way, observations actually belong to multiple clusters, except that the probability of being in each of the clusters rises or falls depending on how strong the weight is.

Microsoft has experimented with both of these approaches and also with the idea of taking many different starting points in the computation of the bins, or clusters, so that the identification of cluster results is more consistent (the traditional approach is to simply identify the initial K-means based on random assignment). The current Analysis Server in SQL Server 2000 employs a tried-and-true, randomly assigned K-means nearest neighbor clustering approach.

If we examine a targeted marketing application, which looks at the attributes of various people in terms of their propensity to respond to different conference events, we might observe that we have quite a bit of knowledge about the different characteristics of potential conference participants. For example, in addition to their Job Title, Company Location, and Gender, we may know the Number of Employees, Annual Sales Revenue, and Length of Time as a customer.

In traditional reporting and query frameworks it would be normal to develop an appreciation of the relationships between Length of Time as a customer (Tenure) and Size of Firm and Annual Sales by exploring a number of two-dimensional (cross-tabulation) relationships. In the language of multidimensional cubes we would query the Tenure measure by Size of Firm and Annual Sales dimensions. We might be inclined to collapse the dimension ranges for Size of Firm into less than 50, 50 to 100, 100+ to

500, 500+ to 1,000, and 1,000+ categories. We might come up with a similar set of ranges for Annual Sales. One of the advantages of data mining—and the clustering algorithm approach discussed here—is that the algorithms will discover the natural groupings and relationships among the fields of data. So, in this case, instead of relying on an arbitrary grouping of the dimensional attributes, we can let the clustering algorithms find the most natural and appropriate groupings for us.

Multidimensional data records can be viewed as points in a multidimensional space. In our conference attendance example, the records of the schema (Tenure, Size of Firm) could be viewed as points in a two-dimensional space, with the dimensions of Tenure and Size of Firm. Figure 3.5 shows example data conforming to the example schema. Figure 3.5(a) shows the representation of these data as points in a two-dimensional space.

By examining the distribution of points, shown in Figure 3.5(b), we can see that there appear to be two natural segments, conforming to those customers with less than two years of tenure on the one hand and those with more than two on the other hand. So, visually, we have found two natural groupings.

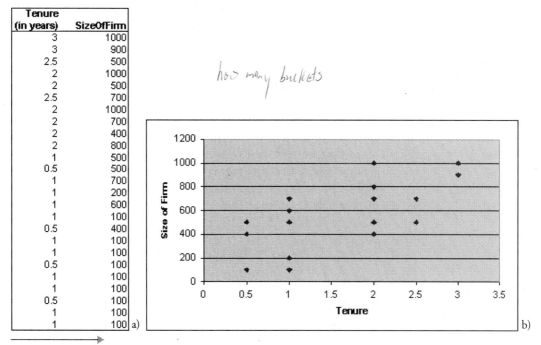

Tenure (in years)	SizeOfFirm
3	1000
3	900
2.5	500
2	1000
2	500
2.5	700
2	1000
2	700
2	400
2	800
1	500
0.5	500
1	700
1	200
1	600
1	100
0.5	400
1	100
1	100
0.5	100
1	100
1	100
0.5	100
1	100
1	100

a)

b)

Figure 3.5   *Clustering example; a) data, b) distribution*

Knowledge of these two natural groupings can be very useful. For example, in the general data set, the average Size of Firm is about 450. The numbers range from 100 to 1,000. So there is a lot of variability and uncertainty about this average. One of the major functions of statistics is to use increased information in the data set to increase our knowledge about the data and decrease the mistakes, or variability, we observe in the data. Knowing that an observation belongs in cluster 1 increases our precision and decreases our uncertainty measurably. In cluster 1, for example, we know that the average Size of Firm is now about 225, and the range of values for Size of Firm is 100 to 700. So we have gone from a range of 900 (1,000 − 100) to a range of 600 (700 − 100). So, the variability in our statements about this segment has decreased, and we can make more precise numerical descriptions about the segment. We can see that cluster analysis allows us to more precisely describe the observations, or cases, in our data by grouping them together in natural groupings.

In this example we simply clustered in two dimensions. We could do the clustering visually. With three or more dimensions it is no longer possible to visualize the clustering. Fortunately, the K-means clustering approach employed by Microsoft works mathematically in multiple dimensions, so it is possible to accomplish the same kind of results—in even more convincing fashion—by forming groups with respect to many similarities.

K-means clusters are found in multiple dimensions by computing a similarity metric for each of the dimensions to be included in the clustering and calculating the summed differences—or distances—between all the metrics for the dimensions from the mean—or average—for each of the bins that will be used to form the clusters. In the Microsoft implementation, ten bins are used initially, but the user can choose whatever number seems reasonable. A reasonable number may be a number that is interpretable (if there are too many clusters, it may be difficult to determine how they differ), or, preferably, the user may have some idea about how many clusters characterize the customer base derived from experience (e.g., customer bases may have newcomers, long-timers, and volatile segments). In the final analysis, the user determines the number of bins that are best suited to solving the business problem. This means that business judgement is used in combination with numerical algorithms to come up with the ideal solution.

The K-means algorithm first assigns the K-means to the number of bins based on the random heuristics developed by Microsoft. The various observations are then assigned to the bins based on the summed differences between their characteristics and the mean score for the bin. The true aver-

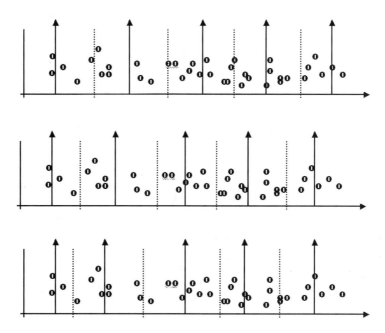

Figure 3.6
*Multiple iterations
to find best
K-means clusters*

age of the bin can now only be determined by recomputing the average based on the records assigned to the bin and on the summed distance measurements. This process is illustrated in Figure 3.6.

Once this new mean is calculated, then cases are reassigned to bins, once again based on the summed distance measurements of their characteristics versus the just recomputed mean. As you can see, this process is iterative. Typically, however, the algorithm converges upon relatively stable bin borders to define the clusters after one or two recalculations of the K-means.

3.6.4   Associations and market basket analysis using distinct count

Microsoft has provided a capability to carry out market basket analysis since SQL Server 7. Market basket analysis is the process of finding associations between two fields in a database—for example, how many customers who clicked on the Java conference information link also clicked on the e-commerce conference information link. The DISTINCT COUNT operation enables queries whereby only distinct occurrences of a given product purchase, or link-click, by a customer are recorded. Therefore, if a customer clicked on the Java conference link several times during a session, only one occurrence would be recorded.

DISTINCT COUNT can also be used in market basked analysis to log the distinct number of times that a user clicks on links in a given session (or puts two products for purchase in the shopping basket).

3.7 Other elements of the Microsoft data mining strategy

3.7.1 The Microsoft repository

The Microsoft repository is a place to store information about data, data flows, and data transformations that characterize the life-cycle process of capturing data at operational touch points throughout the enterprise and organizing these data for decision making and knowledge extraction. So, the repository is the host for information delivery, business intelligence, and knowledge discovery. Repositories are a critical tool in providing support for data warehousing, knowledge discovery, knowledge management, and enterprise application integration.

Extensible Markup Language (XML) is a standard that has been developed to support the capture and distribution of metadata in the repository. As XML has grown in this capacity, it has evolved into a programming language in its own right (metadata do not have to be simply passive data that describe characteristics; metadata can also be active data that describe how to execute a process). Noteworthy characteristics of the Microsoft repository include the following:

- *The XML interchange.* This is a facility that enables the capture, distribution, and interchange of XML—internally and with external applications.

- *The repository engine.* This includes the functionality that captures, stores, and manages metadata through various stages of the metadata life cycle.

- *Information models.* Information models capture system behavior in terms of object types or entities and their relationships. The information model provides a comprehensive road map of the relations and processes in system operation and includes information about the system requirements, design, and concept of operations. Microsoft created the Open Information Model (OIM) as an open specification to describe information models and deeded the model to an independent industry standards body, the Metadata Coalition. Information models are described in the now standard Unified Modeling Language (UML).

The role of metadata in system development, deployment, and maintenance has grown steadily as the complexity of systems has grown at the geometric rate predicted by Moore's Law. The first prominent occurrence of metadata in systems was embodied in the data dictionaries that accompanied all but the earliest versions of database management systems. The first data dictionaries described the elements of the database, their meaning, storage mechanisms, and so on.

As data warehousing gained popularity, the role of metadata expanded to include more generalized data descriptions. Bill Inmon, frequently referred to as the "father" of data warehousing, indicates that metadata are information about warehouse data, including information on the quality of the data, and information on how to get data in and out of the warehouse.

Information about warehouse data includes the following:

- System information

- Process information

- Source and target databases

- Data transformations

- Data cleansing operations

- Data access

- Data marts

- OLAP tools

As we move beyond data warehousing into end-to-end business intelligence and knowledge discovery systems, the role of metadata has expanded to describe each feature and function of this entire end-to-end process. One recent effort to begin to document this process is the Predictive Model Markup Language (PMML) standard. More information about this is at the standard's site: http://ww.oasis-open.org/cover/pmml.html.

3.7.2   Site server

Microsoft Site Server, commerce edition, is a server designed to support electronic business operations over the Internet. Site Server is a turn-key solution to enable businesses to engage customers and transact business on line. Site Server generates both standard and custom reports to describe and analyze site activity and provides core data mining algorithms to facilitate e-commerce interactions.

Site Server provides cross-sell functionality. This functionality uses data mining features to analyze previous shopper trends to generate a score, which can be used to make customer purchase recommendations. Site Server provides a promotion wizard, which provides real-time, remote Web access to the server administrator, to deploy various marketing campaigns, including cross-sell promotions and product and price promotions.

Site Server also includes the following capabilities:

- *Buy Now.* This is an on-line marketing solution, which lets you embed product information and order forms in most on-line contexts—such as on-line banner ads—to stimulate relevant offers and spontaneous purchases by on-line buyers.

- *Personalization and membership.* This functionality provides support for user and user profile management of high-volume sites. Secure access to any area of the site is provided to support subscription or members only applications. Personalization supports targeted promotions and one-to-one marketing by enabling the delivery of custom content based on the site visitor's personal profile.

- *Direct Mailer.* This is an easy-to-use tool for creating a personalized direct e-mail marketing campaign based on Web visitor profiles and preferences.

- *Ad Server.* This manages ad schedules, customers, and campaigns through a centralized, Web-based management tool. Target advertising to site visitors is available based on interest, time of day or week, and content. In addition to providing a potential source of revenue, ads can be integrated directly into Commerce Server for direct selling or lead generation.

- *Commerce Server Software Developer's Kit (SDK).* This SDK provides a set of open application programming interfaces (APIs) to enable application extensibility across the order processing and commerce interchange processes.

- *Dynamic catalog generation.* This creates custom Web catalog pages on the fly using Active Server pages. It allows site managers to directly address the needs, qualifications, and interests of the on-line buyers.

- *Site Server analysis.* The Site Server analysis tools let you create custom reports for in-depth analysis of site usage data. Templates to facilitate the creation of industry standard advertising reports to meet site advertiser requirements are provided. The analytics allow site managers to classify and integrate other information with Web site usage data to get a more complete and meaningful profile of site visitors and their behavior. Enterprise management capabilities enable the central administration of complex, multihosted, or distributed server environments. Site Server supports 28 Web server log file formats on Windows NT, UNIX, and Macintosh operating systems, including those from Microsoft, Netscape, Apache, and O'Reilly.

- *Commerce order manager.* This provides direct access to real-time sales data on your site. Analyze sales by product or by customer to provide insight into current sales trends or manage customer service. Allow customers to view their order history on line.

3.7.3   Business Internet Analytics

Business Internet Analytics (BIA) is the Microsoft framework for analyzing Web-site traffic. The framework can be used by IT and site managers to track Web traffic and can be used in closed-loop campaign management programs to track and compare Web hits according to various customer segment offers. The framework is based on data warehousing, data transformation, OLAP, and data mining components consisting of the following:

- Front-office tools (Excel and Office 200)

- Back-office products (SQL Server and Commerce Server 2000)

- Interface protocols (ODBC and OLE DB)

The architecture and relationship of the BIA components are illustrated in Figure 3.7.

On the left side of Figure 3.7 are the data inputs to BIA, as follows:

- Web log files—BIA works with files in the World Wide Web Consortium (W3C) extended log format.

- Commerce Server 2000 data elements contain information about users, products, purchases, and marketing campaign results.

- Third-party data contain banner ad tracking from such providers as DoubleClick and third-party demographics such as InfoBase and Abilitech data provided by Acxiom.

Data transformation and data loading are carried out through Data Transformation Services (DTSs).

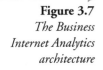

Figure 3.7
*The Business
Internet Analytics
architecture*

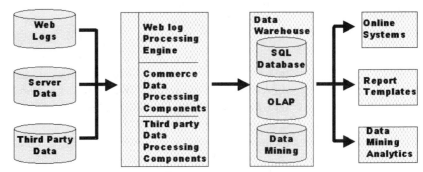

The data warehouse and analytics extend the analytics offered by Commerce Server 2000 by including a number of extensible OLAP and data mining reports with associated prebuilt task work flows.

The BIA Web log processing engine provides a number of preprocessing steps to make better sense of Web-site visits. These preprocessing steps include the following:

- Parsing of the Web log in order to infer metrics. For example, operators are available to strip out graphics and merge multiple requests to form one single Web page and roll up detail into one page view (this is sometimes referred to as "sessionizing" the data).

- BIA Web processing merges hits from multiple logs and puts records in chronological order.

This processing results in a single view of user activity across multiple page traces and multiple servers on a site. This is a very important function, since it collects information from multiple sessions on multiple servers to produce a coherent session and user view for analysis.

The next step of the BIA process passes data through a cleansing stage to strip out Web crawler traces and hits against specific files types and directories, as well as hits from certain IP addresses.

BIA deduces a user visit by stripping out page views with long lapses to ensure that the referring page came from the same site. This is an important heuristic to use in order to identify a consistent view of the user. BIA also accommodates the use of cookies to identify users. Cookies are site identifiers, which are left on the user machine to provide user identification information from visit to visit.

The preprocessed information is then loaded into a SQL Server–based data warehouse along with summarized information, such as the number of hits by date, by hours, and by users. Microsoft worked on scalability by experimenting with its own Microsoft.com and MSN sites. This resulted in a highly robust and scalable solution. (The Microsoft site generates nearly 2 billion hits and over 200 GB of clickstream data per day. The Microsoft implementation loads clickstream data daily from over 500 Web servers around the world. These data are loaded into SQL Server OLAP services, and the resulting multidimensional information is available for content developers and operations and site managers, typically within ten hours.)

BIA includes a number of built-in reports, such as daily bandwidth, usage summary, and distinct users. OLAP services are employed to view Web behavior along various dimensions. Multiple interfaces to the resulting reports, including Excel, Web, and third-party tools, are possible. Data mining reports of customers who are candidates for cross-sell and up-sell are produced, as is product propensity scoring by customer.

A number of third-party system integrators and Information System Vendors (ISVs) have incorporated BIA in their offerings, including Arthur Andersen, Cambridge Technology Partners, Compaq Professional Services, MarchFirst (www.marchFirst.com), Price Waterhouse Coopers, and STEP Technology. ISVs that have incorporated BIA include Harmony Software and Knosys Inc.

4

Managing the Data Mining Project

You can't manage what you can't measure.

—Tom DeMarco

Pulling data together into an analysis environment—called here a *mining mart*—is an essential precondition to providing data in the right form and providing the right measurements in order to produce a timely and useful analysis. Mining mart assembly is the most difficult part of a data mining project: Not only is it time-consuming, but, if it is not done right, it can result in the production of faulty measurements, which no data mining algorithm, no matter how sophisticated, can correct.

It is important to understand the difference between a data warehouse, data mart, and mining mart. The data warehouse tends to be a strategic, central data store and clearing house for analytical data in the enterprise. Typically, a data mart tends to be constructed on a tactical basis to provide specialized data elements in specialized forms to address specialized tasks. Data marts are often synonymous with OLAP cubes in that they are driven from a common fact table with various associated dimensions that support the navigation of dimensional hierarchies. The mining mart has historically consisted of a single table, which combines the necessary data elements in the appropriate form to support a data mining project. In SQL Server 2000 the mining mart and the data mart are combined in a single construct as a Decision Support Object (DSO). Microsoft data access components provide for access through the dimensional cube or through access to a single table contained in a relational database.

Table 4.1   *Time Devoted to Various Data Mining Tasks (Pyle, 1999)*

	Time	Importance
Business understanding	20%	80%
Exploring the problem	10%	15%
Exploring the solution	9%	14%
Implementation specification	1%	51%
Data preparation and mining	80%	20%
Data preparation	60%	15%
Data surveying	15%	3%
Modeling	5%	2%

There can be a lot of complexity in preparing data for analysis. Most experienced data miners will tell you that 60 percent to 80 percent of the work of a data mining project is consumed by data preparation tasks, such as transforming fields of information to ensure a proper analysis; creating or deriving an appropriate target—or outcome—to model; reforming the structure of the data; and, in many cases, deriving an adequate method of sampling the data to ensure a good analysis.

Data preparation is such an onerous task that entire books have been written about just this step alone. Dorian Pyle, in his treatment of the subject (Pyle, 1999) estimates that data preparation typically consumes 90 percent of the effort in a data mining project. He outlines the various steps in terms of time and importance, as shown in Table 4.1.

4.1   The mining mart

In its simplest form, the mining mart is a single table. This table is often referred to as a "denormalized, flat file."

Denormalization refers to the process of creating a table where there is one (and only one) record per unit of analysis and where there is a field—or attribute—for every measurement point that is associated with the unit of analysis. This structure (which is optimal for analysis) destroys the usual normalized table structure (which is optimal for database reporting and maintenance).

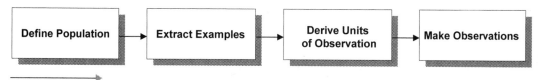

Figure 4.1   *Building the analysis data set—process flow diagram*

The single table data representation has evolved for a variety of reasons—primarily due to the fact that traditional approaches to data analysis have always relied on the construction of a single table containing the results. Since most scientific, statistical, and pattern-matching algorithms that have been developed for data mining evolved from precursors to the scientific or statistical analysis of scientific data, it is not surprising that, even to this day, the most common mining mart data representation is a single table view to the data. Microsoft's approach to SQL 2000 Analysis Services is beginning to change this so that, in addition to providing support for single table analysis, SQL 2000 also provides support for the analysis of multidimensional cubes that are typically constructed to support OLAP style queries and reports.

In preparing data for mining we are almost always trying to produce a representation of the data that conforms to a typical analysis scenario, as shown in Figure 4.1.

What kinds of observations do we typically want to make? If we have people, for example, then person will be our unit of observation, and the observation will contain such attributes as height, weight, gender, and age. For these attributes we typically describe averages and sometimes the range of values (low value, high value for each attribute). Often, we will try to describe relationships (such as how height varies with age).

4.2   Unit of analysis

In describing a typical analytical task, we quickly see that one of the first decisions that has to be made is to determine the unit of analysis. In the previous example, we are collecting measurements about people, so the individual is the unit of analysis. The typical structure of the mining mart is shown in Figure 4.2.

If we were looking at people's purchases, a wireless phone or a hand-held computer, then the product that was purchased would typically be the unit of analysis, and, typically, this would require reformatting the data in a dif-

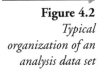

Figure 4.2
*Typical
organization of an
analysis data set*

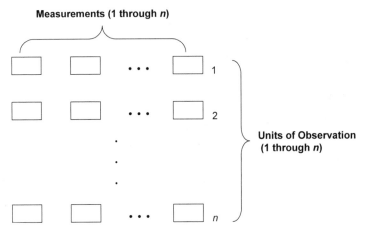

ferent manner. The data table would typically be organized as shown in Figure 4.3.

If this information comes from an employee enrollment form, for example, then there will be very little data preparation involved in producing the analytical view of the data. In the simplest case there is a 1:1 transformation of the customer measurements (fields, columns) to the analytical view. This simple case is illustrated in Figure 4.4.

In the Microsoft environment, in order to make the analytical view accessible to the data mining algorithm, it is necessary to perform the following steps:

1.   Identify the data source (e.g., ODBC).

2.   Establish a connection to the data source in Analysis Services.

3.   Define the mining model.

There are many themes and variations, however, and these tend to introduce complications. What are some of these themes and variations?

Figure 4.3
*Field layout of a
typical analysis
data set*

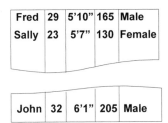

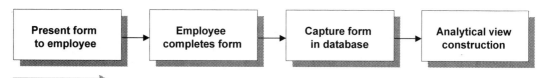

Figure 4.4 *Simple 1:1 transformation flow of raw data to the analytical view*

4.3   Defining the level of aggregation

In cases where the unit of analysis is the customer, it is normal to assume that each record in the analysis will stand for one customer in the domain of the study. Even in this situation, however, there are cases where we may want to either aggregate or disaggregate the records in some manner to form new units of analysis. For example, a vendor of wireless devices and services may be interested in promoting customer loyalty through the introduction of aggressive cross-sell, volume discounts, or free service trials. If the customer file is extracted from the billing system, then it may be tempting to think that the analysis file is substantially ready and that we have one record for each customer situation. But this view ignores three important situations, which should be considered in such a study:

1.   Is the customer accurately reflected by the billing record? Perhaps one customer has multiple products or services, in which case there may be duplicate customer records in the data set.

2.   Do we need to draw distinctions between residential customers and business customers? It is possible for the same customer to be in the data set twice—once as a business customer, with a business product, and another time as a residential customer—potentially with the same product.

3.   Is the appropriate unit of observation the customer or, potentially, the household? There may be multicustomer households, and each customer in the household may have different, but complementary, products and services. Any analysis that does not take the household view into account is liable to end up with a fragmented view of customer product and services utilization.

In short, rather than have customers as units of observation in this study, it might well be appropriate to have a consuming unit—whether a business on one hand or a residential household on the other—as the unit of analysis. Here the alternatives represent an aggregation of potentially multiple customers.

4.4   **Defining metadata**

It is not usually sufficient to publish data as an analytical view without defining the attributes of the data in a format readable by both people and machines. Data, in their native form, may not be readily comprehensible—even to the analyst who produced the data in the first place.

So in any data publication task it is important to define data values and meanings. For example:

Customer (residential customer identification)

Name (last name, first name of customer)

Age (today's date, DOB; where DOB is date of birth)

Gender (allowable values: male, female, unknown)

Height (in feet and inches)

Weight (in pounds)

Purchases (in dollars and cents)

This type of information will provide the analyst with the hidden knowledge—metaknowledge—necessary to further manipulate the data and to be able to interpret the results.

It is now common to encode this type of metadata information in XML format so that, in addition to being readable by people, the information can be read by machines as well.

```
<customer>
   <attributes>
      <name> Customer's name; eg. Dennis Guy</name>
      <age> Age calculated as Today's date - DOB </age>
      <gender> Gender … value values
         <male> 'Male' </male>
         <female> 'Female' </female>
         <unknown> 'unknown' </unknown>
      </gender>
      <weight> Weight in pounds </weight>
      <purchases> Purchases in dollars and cents </
purchases>
   </attributes>
</customer>
```

4.5   Calculations

Typical calculations when the individual is the unit of analysis include the calculation of age—as shown previously—or durations (e.g., length of time as a customer) or aggregations (e.g., number of purchases over the last period).

It is also typical to check data for extreme values and to transform, or eliminate, extreme values that are found. Extreme values can have a biasing effect on the identification of the form of a relationship, so this is why it is normal to process them in some way. The effect of extreme values is illustrated in Figure 4.5.

As shown in Figure 4.5, one or more extreme values can significantly change the apparent form of a relationship, and this can lead to false or misleading results. This is particularly true in cases where the extreme values are entered in error, typically due to a data-entry error (entering a 7 instead of a 2, for example, when transcribing).

Figure 4.5
Example effect of extreme values on shaping the form of the relationship

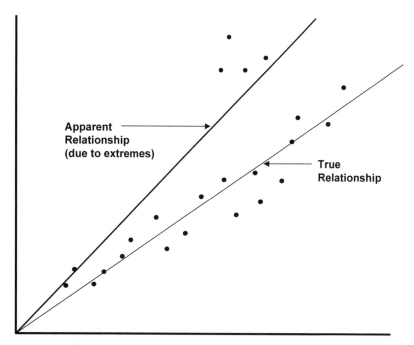

4.5.1   How extreme is extreme?

In most cases it is pretty simple to see an extreme value simply by reporting the results in the form of a scatter plot or histogram. The scatter plot shown in Figure 4.5 makes it pretty clear where the extreme values are since they deviate visually from the mass of points on the diagram.

There are theoretical methods to determine whether extreme values are plausible in a distribution of numbers. This can be determined by looking at a normal distribution (often called the *Bell curve* and sometimes referred to as *Gaussian*, named after the mathematician Gauss who identified the distribution).

From this distribution, illustrated in Figure 4.6, we know that the vast majority of values will lie in the vicinity of the average (or *mean* as it is called by statisticians). It is possible to tell how many extreme values there should be by referring to the theoretical properties of the normal distribution (as originally worked out by Gauss). According to Gauss, 67 percent of the observations should fall within ±1 standard deviation (s.d.) of the mean—or average—value. Statisticians have many words to describe average and use the specific term *mean* to describe the average that is computed for a number, such as height, which has a continuous range of values (as opposed to gender, which has a discrete number of values).

Most people know how to compute the mean. Knowledge of how to compute the standard deviation is much less common. The standard deviation is based on the calculation of the mean. The mean is calculated as the sum of individual measurements divided by the number of observations:

Sum $(ht_1 + ht_2 + \ldots + ht_n)/n \ldots$

here *ht* is all the height observations from 1 to *n* in the data set.

The standard deviation is the sum of the squared deviations of each individual observation from the mean (computed by subtracting the observation value from the mean value and then multiplying the result by itself). This sum is then divided by the number of observations, and the square root of the entire result is taken. The multiplication—or squaring—is carried out to eliminate negative results.

Typical transformations of extreme values may use the standard deviation as a point of departure. For example, according to the theoretical properties of the normal distribution, it is known that ±1 standard deviation contains over 68 percent of the observations, ±2 standard deviations contain over 94 percent of the observations, and ±3 standard deviations contain over 99 percent of the data. So, if there are a lot of extreme values in the data, it may be

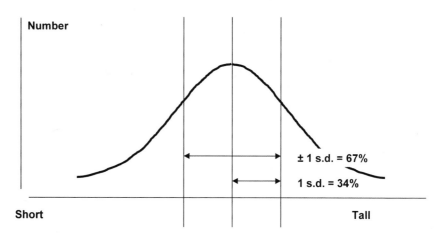

Figure 4.6
Example of the normal, bell-shaped (or Gaussian) distribution

reasonable to reset any observation that is over three standard deviations to an average value or a missing value.

Another strategy may be to apply logistic transformations to the data. Logistic transformations are usually carried out to compress extreme values into a more normal range. This is because the logistic transformation pushes extreme values closer to the average than less extreme values, as illustrated in Figure 4.7. Here we can see that the characteristic S shape of the logistic function captures more and more of the extremely low and high val-

Figure 4.7
Using the logistic transformation to squeeze extremely low and high values toward the center of the S shape

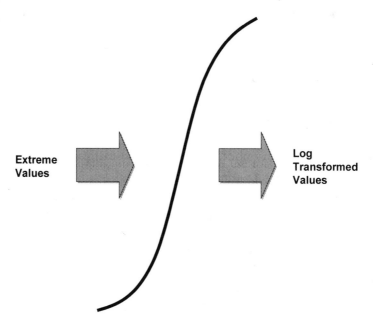

ues in a range of values that is closer to the elongated center of the transformation.

A general purpose "softmax" procedure for computing this function is presented in Pyle, 1999.

4.6   Standardized values

Some data mining algorithms—for example, cluster analysis—are based on the calculation of distance measurements to determine the strength of a relationship between the various fields of values being used in the analysis. As can be seen in Figure 4.8, the distance between height and weight is relatively short as compared with the distance between either of these measurements and the amount of dollars spent. This indicates that the relationship between height and weight is much stronger than the relationship between either of these measurements and amount of dollars spent.

These distances are used as measurements in the calculation of relationships to detect patterns in data mining algorithms such as cluster analysis. In order to compute these distances so that they can be consistently used and applied across all the components in the analysis, it is important that the components and relationships all be measured on the same scale. This

Figure 4.8
Relationship between various measurements when measured on a common scale

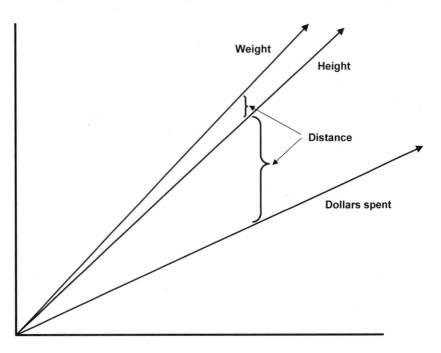

way, differences in the strength of a relationship are clearly a function of the distance between the components—as opposed to a function of the fact that the components have been measured on different scales (e.g., height in feet, weight in pounds, and amount in dollars). If different scales are used, then there can be no valid comparisons of the relative distances between the components. For this reason, it is usual to reduce all measurements to a common scale. Typically, the common scale that is used is normalized or standardized scores.

Standardized scores use the standard deviation of the score in the calculation, as follows:

Standard score = Original measurement/standard deviation
                  of the original measurement

Standardized scores always produce a measurement that has a mean of zero and a standard deviation of one. Obviously, standardized scores can only be computed for continuously valued fields.

4.7   Transformations for discrete values

In cases where the field of information contains discrete values—for example, gender—it is typical to create multiple scores, each with a value of 0 or 1 in a process that is typically referred to as 1 of N coding. This means that discrete values are expressed at a level of measurement similar to the standardized scores that have been derived for the continuously valued fields of information. So, discrete fields of information and continuous fields of information can be combined in the same analysis.

In the case of gender, the 1 of N values would be male … 1 or 0; female … 1 or 0; and unknown … 1 or 0. If the observation is male, then the male 1 of N indicator is set to 1 and the other two indicators are set to 0.

4.8   Aggregates

The tables we have been looking at contain summary measurements of the object (in this case person) we expect to observe. It is sometimes necessary to examine detail records associated with the object in order to create summary measurements. For example, in a sales application it may be necessary to derive a measurement of purchase activity from the last year in order to derive a number of purchases field. This requires us to aggregate values in multiple records to create a roll-up value in the summary record. Figure 4.9 illustrates this process of taking the values contained in multiple detail

Figure 4.9
*Rolling up the
values contained in
detail records to
create a summary
record*

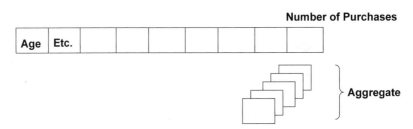

records in order to create a summary, or aggregate, so that there is one summary record for multiple detail records. A typical summary is the total cash spent by a customer across multiple transactions in a retail setting. In Web commerce applications, it is usually necessary to create a summary that reflects one session per user, regardless of the number of detail records that record page hits.

Many summary values are possible when aggregating records, as shown in Table 4.2.

In marketing applications, the creation of these kinds of summary measurements enables you to derive date of purchase (time since last purchase), frequency (how many purchases per period), and monetary value (average or sum) indicators for the analysis. These are strong and universal indicators of purchasing behavior in many marketing applications.

4.8.1   Calculated fields

As discussed previously, in the derivation of Age (from date of birth), it is normal to have calculated values in data preparation tasks. The calculation of Age involved the use of subtraction (Age = Today's Date – Date of Birth).

Table 4.2   *Typical Kinds of Aggregate Summary Measurements Possible with Detail Record Roll-Ups*

Sum	Sum of all values in the detail records
Average	Average of all values in the detail records
Minimum	Smallest value in the detail records
Maximum	Largest value in the detail records
Number	Number of detail records
First	First date when dates are present on the detail record
Last	Last date when dates are present

Calculation typically requires such standard arithmetic operators as addition (+), subtraction (−), multiplication (*), division (/), and, sometimes, logarithms, exponentiation (antilogs), power operations (square), and square roots.

We saw the logarithmic operation earlier (in transformations) as well as the square root (in manipulation of squared deviations in the calculation of standard deviation). Division was used in the derivation of frequency in the aggregation of the purchase detail records.

4.8.2   Composites

Composites are values that are created from separate variables, or measurements, and are typically formed to serve as proxies for some other useful measurement or concept to be included in the analysis. For example, while customer lifetime value is frequently absent from an analysis, it may be possible to form a proxy for this value through the creation of a composite. As indicated, the measurements of date of purchase, frequency, and monetary value have been demonstrated to consistently predict and describe customer persistency and value in various market studies. It may be useful to form a composite value that combines these three values to serve as a proxy for lifetime value. This strategy has the additional virtue of combining many separate measurements into one global measurement, which serves to simplify the analysis.

In forming the composite it is important to determine what weight and level of measurement will be used to capture the contribution of the individual components. In forming a date of purchase, frequency, and monetary value composite it is easiest to assume that the individual components contribute in equal measure to the formation of the composite value. Since these three values are measured in different terms, it is useful to reduce them all to a standard unit of measurement by creating standard scores for each of them.

In producing the composite score the component values may be simply added or multiplied together. Many different types of composites can be constructed and many different types of composite construction techniques can be used—some of them can be quite elaborate and sophisticated. For example, clustering algorithms may be used to cluster observations together with regard to common measurements. Once the cluster is created, the cluster can be used as a composite representation of the component scores used to produce the cluster. This is one of the many uses for the clustering facilities provided in SQL 2000.

4.8.3 Sequences

Sequences are often useful predictors or descriptors of behavior. Many data mining applications are built around sequences of product purchases, for example. Sequences of events can frequently be used to predict the likelihood of customer defection (diminishing product purchase or use over time), and, in financial applications (e.g., the analysis of stock prices) sequences can often be used to predict a given outcome.

In predicting anything that is time dependent—for example, a stock price or a temperature—it is normal to have a data set that is organized as shown in Table 4.3.

To deal with this as a typical analytical data set, it is necessary to reform the data so that each observation reflects a cross-section—in essence flipping the multiple time dependencies from rows to columns. (See Figure 4.10.)

In arranging the time-oriented observations across the columns, a number of summary measurements can be derived: t_1 high (high value at time 1—e.g., highest hourly stock price), t_1 low (low value at time 1—e.g., lowest hourly stock price), t_2 high, t_2 low, high–low difference t_1, high–low difference t_2. Frequencies can also be computed: high followed by low by time period, low followed by low by time period, and so on.

Once the data set is reformatted in this manner, the time-derived measurements (sequences, differences, and so on) become predictors or descriptors as in any other analysis, and the outcome measurement (e.g., return on investment) can then be modeled as a function of any one of the predictors that have been captured as summary measurements in the columns of the analysis table.

Table 4.3 *Organization of Time-Oriented Data Sets*

Outcome	Time
O_1	T_1
O_2	T_2
...	...
O_n	T_n

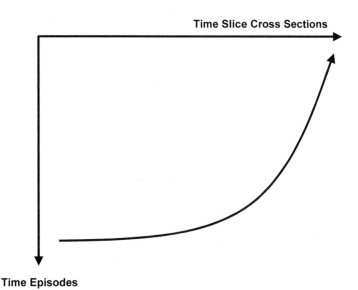

Figure 4.10
Including time in the analysis by taking episodic time observations and creating one cross-sectional time slice record

Time Slice Cross Sections

Time Episodes

4.8.4   Normalization and denormalization

It is usual for operational and relational databases to be stored in normalized form. This storage method is useful in the construction of high-performance operational databases but is difficult, if not impossible, to analyze. For example, a banking database is likely to contain a field with account type in one column and, possibly, transaction amount and date in other columns, as shown in Table 4.4.

In order to format these data for analysis, it is necessary to denormalize them, as shown in Table 4.5.

Table 4.4   *Normalized Account Transaction Table*

Account	Date	Transaction Amount
Checking	Jul-22-99	$123.00
Savings	Jan-5-00	$1,004.25
Money Mart	Aug-12-99	$2,500.00
Checking	May-5-00	$43.57
CD	Jan-22-00	$1,000.00

Table 4.5 *Denormalized Table with Transactional (Detail) Records Summarized (Aggregated, Rolled Up) to One Record per Customer*

Total Checking Transactions	Total Savings Transactions	Total Money Mart Transactions	Total CD Transactions
$ pppp.pp	$ qqqq.qq	$ rrrr.rr	$ ssss.ss

In Table 4.5, the individual transactions for each customer are summed and placed in a separate column to facilitate analysis. This summarization is often called *detail record roll up* or *data aggregation*. All the transactional records for a given individual are summarized (often the total or average, or both, is calculated), and this summary is placed in the columns of one summary record created for one individual.

4.8.5 Trends

There are some simple but effective ways to calculate trends in detail records. Trend information can be useful for predicting prices or activity changes as a precursor to defection or product loss (churn). For example:

(Period 4 – Period 3)/(Period 2 – Period 1)

The periods in question can be days, weeks, months, or quarters.

Another useful trend indicator is a measurement of the variability in a sequence of records. This can be calculated by using the standard deviation. Other trends include the calculation of the spread—that is, the difference between the high and low in any period.

4.8.6 Sampling

If you have too many records (cases or observations) to analyze easily, it is quite reasonable to sample from the main data set in order to get a more manageable (but still representative) subset of records to work with. So, if you have 500,000 records, for example, it is possible (and reasonable) to take a 1 percent sample, which would produce 5,000 records (a 10 percent sample would produce 50,000 records).

The concept of sampling has been used for a very long time, as statisticians and mathematicians sought to determine the properties and characteristics of various phenomena. They came to the understanding that, since all incidents of any given phenomenon under consideration could not be examined, it was a practical necessity to instead look at the idea of creating samples of observations so as to have a reasonable chance of determining the characteristics of the phenomenon, as reflected in the sample.

Once the concept of sampling was developed, a further concept—that of determining a method so as to ensure that the sample results would reflect the properties of the population from which the sample was derived—was established. In essence, the goal of sampling is to pick a subpopulation of the phenomenon in such a manner that any results in the subpopulation can be generalized to the parent population. In order to avoid the introduction of biases in the sample, the concept of random sampling was developed. The idea of a random sample is to ensure that each member of the parent population has an equal chance of being selected for the sample. Samples are selected randomly so as to minimize the chance of introducing biases in the selection of the sample.

By the turn of the twentieth century, random sampling techniques had developed to the point where they became essential instruments in a variety of areas, notably in agricultural studies.

The situation that led to a highly developed science of sampling is illustrated in Figure 4.11, which depicts four fields of grain grown under different conditions. In order for agricultural researchers to test new varieties of grain or different types of fertilizer or crop rotations, it was common to plant crops under different circumstances and then to sample the results in order to compare the success or failure of the circumstances.

Figure 4.11
Origins of sampling— assessing various treatments in agricultural plots

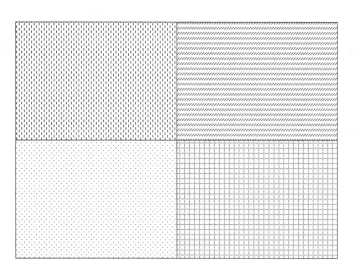

To see whether grains tended to grow taller, for example, the researcher resorted to a random sampling technique whereby every nth wheat plant was harvested and measured in order to determine the average height of the wheat grown under the circumstance to be tested.

4.8.7   How good are the results?

The degree of confidence you can have in the results depends on the size of the sample you use. Large samples tend to be more reliable than small samples.

Table 4.6 tells you how big your sample has to be to produce results at a given level of confidence. As you can see, sample sizes of between 5,000 and 15,000 provide an extremely high degree of confidence and a high degree of precision (as indicated by the tolerated error). Bear in mind that in using these guidelines you are making the normal (and normally correct) assumption that the data are normally distributed (the normal distribution is the typical bell-shaped curve shown in Figure 4.6). In the example of height, the normal curve would show that most people are of average height while fewer and fewer people are exceptionally short and fewer and fewer are exceptionally tall).

4.8.8   Confidence limits

Confidence limits refers to the overall probability that the database you are working with is an anomaly—that is, a chance or freak occurrence, which does not accurately reflect the real world as captured by the database from which you are sampling. As you can see, the larger the sample database, the less likely it is that you will have anomalous results. The 95 samples in 100 is the 95 percent confidence level. Here you can be confident that you

Table 4.6   *Simple Random Sample Errors Assuming Normal Distributions*

Tolerated Error	95 Samples in 100	99 Samples in 100
1%	9,604	16,587
2%	2,401	4,147
3%	1,067	1,843
4%	600	1,037
5%	384	663

would produce misleading results only five times out of 100. At a 99 percent confidence level (99 samples in 100) there is only one chance in 100 that you would expect to get misleading results. As you require more confidence you will want to create larger samples.

The tolerated error refers to the amount of potential imprecision you are prepared to tolerate around the identification of the values that form the partitions on the decision tree. With a 1 percent tolerated error (the highest level), the branches of the decision tree will reflect real differences between values within +1 percent or –1 percent. This means that income differences that have been identified as separate branches for region, education level, or gender will be accurate by +1 percent or –1 percent. At the 5 percent tolerance level, your results are only good by +5 percent to –5 percent. This will be fine if there are big differences between the various groupings of codes that form the partitions of the decision tree (and if the standard deviation is small). If there are small differences between the codes that form the branches of the decision tree, and if a difference of +5 percent or –5 percent could influence whether a category gets grouped with one branch or another, then 5 percent will not be a very satisfactory tolerance level.

In practice, this means that a sample size of 5,000 to 15,000 is more than adequate in most situations. Sample sizes greater than this, in the range of 50,000 cases or more, are almost certain to produce results that are as good as working with the entire database.

4.9   Enrichments

The process behind enrichments is illustrated in Figure 4.12. Here we see that multiple sources of outside data may be added to the basic set of information that is known (typically) about a customer. A customer's location may be used as a locator, for example, to establish the social and economic characteristics of the neighborhood where the customer lives. Customer life style data, provided by external data source providers, may also be appended to the customer record.

Enrichments provide the possibility of constructing a richer analytical model. This, in turn, can lead to superior explanation, description, and better predictive models.

Typically enrichment data is appended to the data warehouse, data mart or mining mart by matching the enrichment data against a customer identifier, a household identifier, or a neighborhood identifier. Neighborhood data can be propagated to household or customer level records and, of

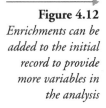

Figure 4.12
Enrichments can be added to the initial record to provide more variables in the analysis

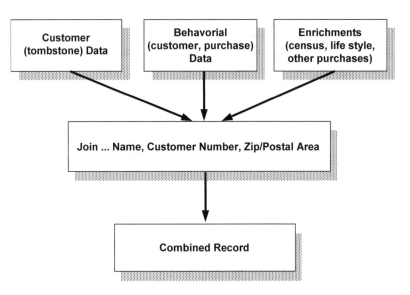

course, customer level data and household data can be aggregated up to the neighborhood level. Typically, the neighborhood level match field is zip or postal code.

There are many sources of enrichment data. Popular vendors include Acxiom (www.acxiom.com), Experian (www.experian.com) and Equifax (www.equifax.com).

4.10   Example process (target marketing)

Target marketing is one of the most prevalent application areas for data mining. Target marketing includes direct mail offers to selected customers or selected locations or events. Other forms of target marketing includes outbound telemarketing calls, door drops, magazine, letter or periodical inserts and, in the case of in-bound service enquiries, matching messages to caller characteristics. The process described in Figure 4.13 applies to a wide range of targeted marketing situations. In the case study developed in following chapters we are using a situation where new and existing customer lists have been gathered and an offer has been sent out in the mail. These steps correspond to the Identify Main File, Draw Sample, Prepare test materials, Target test population and Gather responses boxes shown in Figure 4.13. Typically, a marketing organization will use a subset of their main marketing file, potentially adding some new enrichments in the form of new prospect data (perhaps a purchased mailing list) and will typically test the response to an offer with this subset. A number of themes and variations

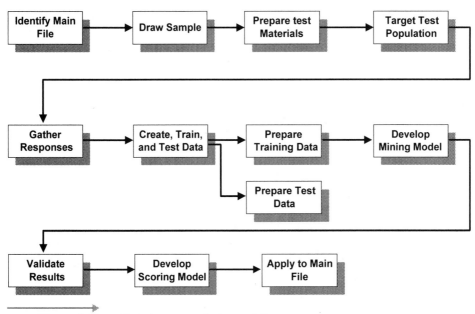

Figure 4.13   *Typical target marketing modeling process*

may be tried: for example, different prices, incentives or coupons may be included in the offer in order to test which type of offer is most compelling. When the responses are returned the sub set data is updated with a respond–did not respond indicator.

Once the response indicator is appended to the test data set the scene is set for the beginning of the data mining analysis. The data is split into training and test data partitions so that any models that are developed during the training (or learning) phase of the analysis can be tested or validated on a fresh data set. Unlike classical statistics, which uses the theoretical properties of data and data distributions to test the validity of results, data mining relies on the empirical properties of data—usually in the form of a test data set—to confirm the validity of the data mining results. Data mining algorithms explore countless potential patterns of relationships when they are run against the training data set so are prone to "over-fitting" the data (over-fitting is a situation where the pattern that is extracted from the data is specific, or unique to that particular data set, and will not generalize well to novel data sets). Verifying data mining results with respect to a test or validation data set is an effective way to guard against over-fitting.

Data mining and the associated search for promising patterns is the only way to sort through the various fields of information that could combine to describe the propensity of a prospect to respond to a given offer. Responses can be affected by many factors, including personal background, personal life style and preferences, length of time as a customer, other products or services purchased from the same vendor, type of offer and even the time of day or day of week that the offer was made. Sorting through all these potential drivers of response rate is a job for data mining algorithms—one which they are well-adapted to accomplish. In the end the data mining step will produce one or more predictive models that will show which factors, in which combinations, come together to drive probability of response.

As shown in the diagram presented in Figure 4.13, once the data mining model has been developed it is passed on to a validation step that checks the veracity of the model with respect to the test or validation data (as described above). Once the model is validated then the target marketer is ready to apply the model to the target population (designated as the "Main File" in the diagram in Figure 4.13). In order to apply the data mining model (or models) to the target population typically a scoring model (or models) is produced. As indicated above, the data mining model shows which factors combine as a pattern or model to show what is driving response rate. Typically, this pattern can be expressed as an equation or as a set of decision rules. The equation or decision rules are deposited on a scoring file and this scoring file is used to assign a probability of response to the records in the target population. When the attributes of the record in the target population contain values that suggest a high combined score for probability of response then these attributes, when matched against the scoring algorithm, will tend to produce a high probability of response. In this fashion, a score is assigned to every record in the target population data set.

Typically, the scores that are assigned on the records of the target population range from 0 to 1. A value of .5 on the record would indicate that the target has an equal probability of responding. A value of .9 indicates a 90% probability of responding and a value of .25 means that the target prospect has a 25% chance of responding. Once the scores are applied to the main file the target marketer has to make the choice of which members on the file to contact. Typically, this means selecting a cut off probability of response to contact. The decision of the cut off probability usually boils down to a dollars and cents decision: if the expected value from a respondent is in the range of, say, $500 and if it costs $50 to target the responder, then, in general, I would make money with the targeting if I target everyone with an expected probability of response that is greater than 10%.

This explains a bit about the business and process of target marketing. Obviously, the profitability or loss of a campaign depends upon many factors. Clearly, the accuracy of the estimated probability of response is a critical component of the business success of the target marketing strategy. This explains the interest in the efficacy and reliability (and, from a cost point of view, the ease of use) of data mining algorithms in the targeted marketing area. While the example above assumed that a test data set was selected it is also possible to use the results of previous targeting campaigns as proxies for a test set and, in this fashion, collect history of targetings and propensities to respond over time (thus increasing the value of the in-house marketing file).

4.11 The data mart

The database contains a table for customer data, a table for promotions, and a table for conference attendances, shown in Figure 4.14. The database is partially normalized; since the customer table contains company information a separate company table would need to be identified to produce a database in normal form. A normalized database facilitates database updates and database integrity (if the company changes address, for example, it is only necessary to change the entry once in the company table). As we will see later, however, when mining data as a relational table it is very useful to have important information about a customer collected in one table. Other aspects of this database, including SQL statements to produce a data mining mart, are described in Chapter 5. Here it is shown how to process the

Figure 4.14
Data model for the targeted marketing case study

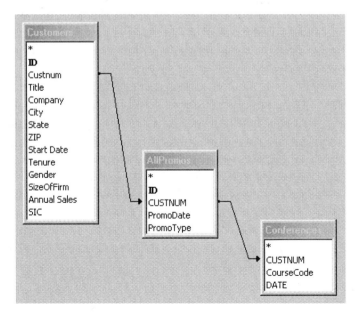

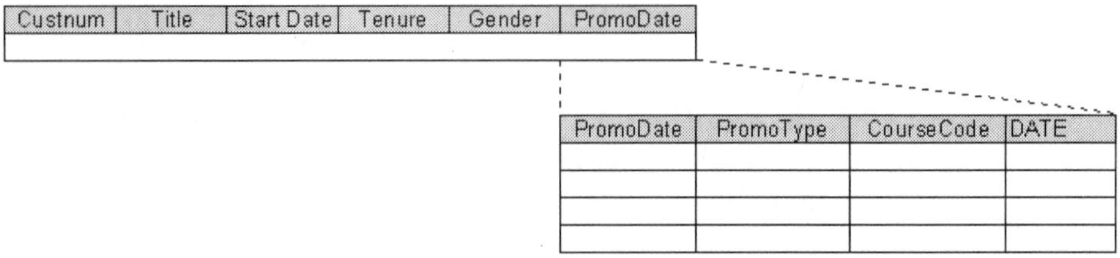

Custnum	Title	Start Date	Tenure	Gender	PromoDate

PromoDate	PromoType	CourseCode	DATE

Figure 4.15   *Example of the hierarchical nature of a Microsoft data mining analysis case*

data tables to produce both star schemas, for multidimensional viewing, as well as relational tables for mining.

The way this information is stored assigns a record for each field of data in a table. So for each customer record there may be one or more promotions with one or more conference attendances in response to the promotions. The collection of related records constitutes a case. For all customers, the collection of customer cases is called the case set. Different case sets can be constructed from the same physical data. How the case set is assembled determines how the mining is done. The focus of the analysis could be the customer, the promotions or the conference attendances. We could even do the analysis at the company. If the focus is the customer then such attributes as Gender and tenure could be used to predict the behavior of future customers.

In our example, we can see that the main unit of analysis—called the case—is the customer and that the promotional detail is contained, in a nested, hierarchical fashion, within the customer. This is illustrated in Figure 4.15.

In situations where information is nested in a hierarchical fashion as shown in Figure 4.19 it is necessary to be careful when specifying the case level key in the data mining analysis since this will be used to determine the case base, or unit of analysis. Considerations on defining the unit of analysis and examples on identifying the key to define the case base are taken up in Chapter 5.

5

Modeling Data

Information is the enemy of intelligence.

—Donald Hall

In the recent past there has been a growing recognition that we are suffering from what has sometimes been called a "data deluge." In Chapter 2 we outlined a data maturity hierarchy, which suggested that we turn data into intellectual capital through successive, and successively sophisticated, refinements. Data are turned into information through grouping, summarizing, and OLAP techniques such as dimensioning. But too much information can contribute to the overwhelming effect of data deluge. Further, information, which, as we can see, is data organized for decision making, can be further refined. By processing information through the lens of numerical and statistical search algorithms, data mining provides a facility to turn information into knowledge. Data can be organized along many dimensions of potential analysis. But to find the subset of dimensions that are most important in driving the outcome or phenomenon under investigation requires the kind of automated search algorithms that are incorporated in SQL Server 2000. This chapter provides detailed examples of how to use the Analysis Server data mining functionality to carry out typical outcome or predictive modeling (classification) and clustering (segmentation) tasks.

The chapter begins with a review of how to go about setting up an OLAP cube to perform preliminary data scanning and analysis as a first step to data mining. It shows how both the data mining model and the OLAP cube model are different representations of the same data source and how

Analysis Manager stores both sets of models in the same folder. A simple set of wizards is available to create and examine both OLAP and data mining models. A very common data mining scenario is built to illustrate the analysis: target marketing.

As indicated in Chapter 1, potentially the most common data mining scenario is to sort through multiple dimensions containing multiple drivers in the data and combinations of drivers in order to determine the specific set of data drivers that is determining an outcome. These drivers can be data elements (such as a gender field) or even operational measures of a concept (such as earnings–expenses to provide an index of purchasing power). The most common outcome is a probability of purchase or probability of response to an offer. This is a typical target marketing scenario.

The target marketing example that has been selected for discussion in this chapter is taken from a marketing scenario discussed in the previous chapters. The organization under investigation offers educational workshops and conferences in a variety of emerging technology areas and contacts its potential customers in several ways, including sending targeted offers to prospect lists drawn from both new and previous customer inquiries. Our example enterprise wants to determine the characteristics of people who have responded to previous offers, according to the event that was offered, in order to construct more effective prospect lists for future event offerings. This is the kind of problem that data mining is ideally suited to solve.

5.1   The database

The database captures the important data that are necessary to run the conference delivery business that serves as our example case study. The basic organization of the database is shown in Figure 5.1.

5.2   Problem scenario

The problem scenario builds on the data mart assembly description discussed in Chapter 4. As shown there, the enterprise—which we shall call Conference Corp.—provides industry-leading exposure to new trends and technologies in the area of information technology through conferences, workshops, and seminars. It promotes through targeted offers—primarily through the delivery of personalized offers and the delivery of associated conference brochures. The exclusive, "by invitation only" nature of the

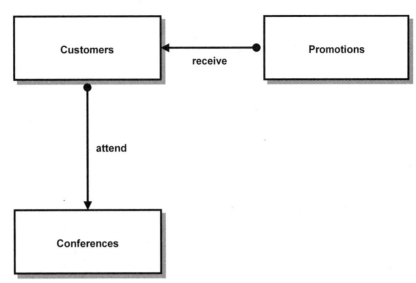

Figure 5.1
*Information model
for the "New
Trends in
Information
Technology"
conference and
workshop enterprise*

events requires the development of high-quality promotional materials, which are normally sent through surface mail. Such quality places a premium on targeting, since the materials are expensive to produce. The enterprise consistently strives for high response and attendance rates through continual analysis of the effectiveness of its promotional campaigns.

The database is organized around the customer base and carries tables relating to the promotions that have been sent to customers and the attendances that were registered.

As we can see, the information model shown in Figure 5.1 provides the core data tables needed to accomplish the target marketing task: Customers receive many promotions for many events. Once they receive the promotion, they may ignore it or may register and attend the event being promoted. Our job is to look at promotional "hits and misses": What characteristics of customers who have been contacted predispose them to attend the promoted event? Once we know these characteristics, then we will be in a good position to better target subsequent promotions for our events. This will lower our promotional costs and will enable us to provide better service to our customers by providing them with information that is more appropriate to their interests. This produces a personalization effect, which is central to building customer loyalty over time. Thus, the benefit of this targeted approach includes the promotional savings that accrue through targeting a customer grouping that is more likely to respond to an offer, as

Figure 5.2
Data tables used to support targeted marketing application information model

Customers
Custnum
Title
Company
City
State
ZIP
Start Date
Tenure
Gender
EmploySixe
SalesSize
SIC

Promotions
CUSTNUM
PromoDate
PromoType

Conferences
CUSTNUM
CourseCode
DATE

well as the benefit of providing targeted, personalized messages to customers and prospects.

The contents of the data tables used to populate the information model are shown in Figure 5.2. All databases in these exercises are available at http://www.vitessimo.com/.

5.3   Setting up analysis services

The first task is to publish your data source in the Windows NT or 2000 environment by establishing a data source name (DSN). The Data Sources (ODBC) settings are accessed in NT through Start → Settings → Control Panel, and in Windows 2000 the appropriate access path is Start → Settings → AdministrativeTools.

Figure 5.3
The first step in defining a data source name— defining source data driver

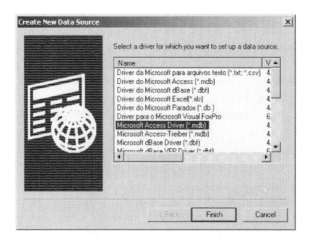

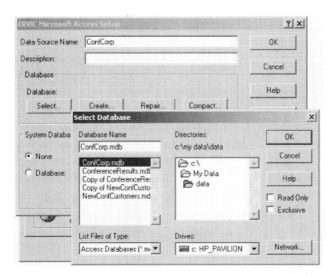

Figure 5.4
Designating the database to be used as the data source name

Open the Data Sources (ODBC) by double-clicking and then select the System DSN tab. Click Add to display the Create New Data Source window, as shown in Figure 5.3.

In the Create New Data Source window, select Microsoft Access Driver (*.mdb). Now click Finish. This will present the ODBC Microsoft Access Setup dialog, displayed in Figure 5.4. Under Data Source Name, enter ConfCorp (or whatever name you choose). In the Database section click Select.

In the Select Database dialog box, browse to the ConfCorp.mdb database and Click OK.

Click OK in the ODBC Microsoft Access Setup dialog box.

Click OK in the ODBC Data Source Administrator dialog box.

To start Analysis Manager, from the Start button on the desktop select Programs → Microsoft SQL Server → Analysis Services → Analysis Manager. Once Analysis Manager opens, then, in the tree view, expand the Analysis Services selection. Click on the name of your server. This establishes a connection with the analysis server, producing the display shown in Figure 5.5.

5.3.1   Setting up the data source

Right-click on your server's name and click New Database. Once you have defined the new database you can associate a data source to it by right-clicking the Data Sources folder and selecting New Data Source. In the Data

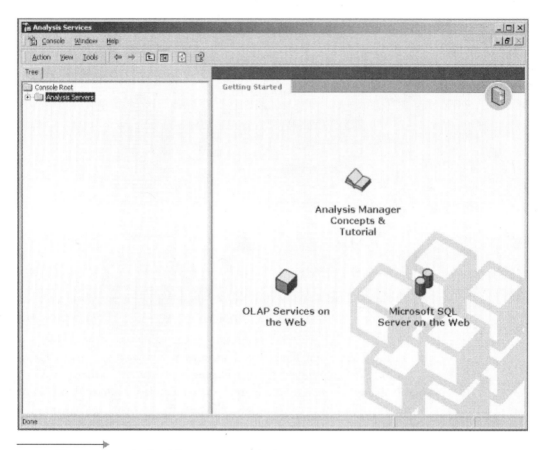

Figure 5.5   *Analysis Manager opening display*

Link Properties dialog box select the Provider tab and then click Microsoft OLE DB Provider for ODBC Drivers. This will allow you to associate the data source with the DSN definition that you established through the Microsoft Data Sources (ODBC) settings earlier. Select the Connection tab. In the database dialog box, shown in Figure 5.6, enter the DSN that you have identified—here called ConfCorp—and then click OK.

In the tree view expand the server and then expand the ConfCorp database that you have created. As shown in Figure 5.7, the database contains the following five nodes:

1.   Data sources

2.   Cubes

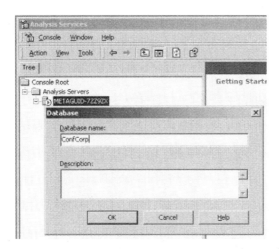

3.   Shared dimensions

4.   Mining models

5.   Database roles

As shown in Figure 5.8, you can use the Test Connection button to ensure that the connection was established (if so, you will receive a confirmatory diagnostic). At this point you can exit by selecting OK. Exit the Data Link Properties dialog by selecting OK.

Figure 5.8
*Testing the
database
connection*

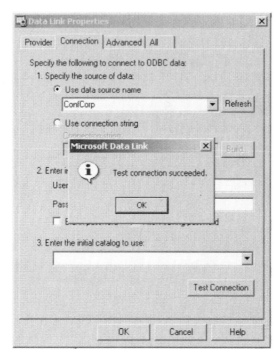

5.4   Defining the OLAP cube

Now that you have set up the data source you can define the OLAP cube. Start by expanding the ConfCorp database and then selecting the Cubes tree item. Right-click, then as shown in Figure 5.9, select New Cube and Wizard.

In the Welcome step of the Cube Wizard, select Next. In the Select a fact table from a data source step, expand the ConfCorp data source, and then click FactTable. You can view the data in the FactTable by clicking Browse data, as shown in Figure 5.10.

To define the measurements for the cube, under fact table numeric columns, double-click LTVind (Life Time Value indicator).

To build dimensions, in the Welcome to the Dimension Wizard step, click Next. This will produce the display shown in Figure 5.11. In the *Choose how you want to create the dimension* setup, select *Star Schema: A single dimension table*. Now select Next.

In the *Select the dimension table* step, click Customer and then click Next.

Figure 5.9
Building a new cube from the Database Definition in Analysis Manager

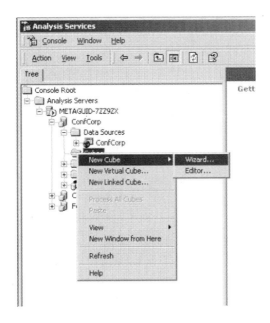

In the *Select the dimension type*, click Next. As shown in Figure 5.12, to define the levels for the dimension, under *Available columns*, double-click the State, City, and Company columns. Click Next.

Figure 5.10
Browsing the cube fact table data

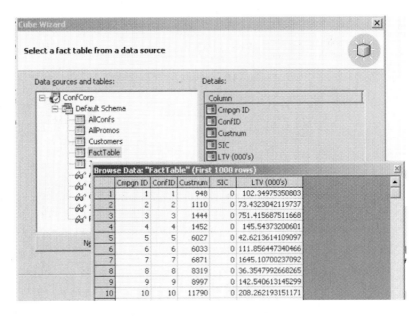

Figure 5.11
Setting up the cube—defining the source schema

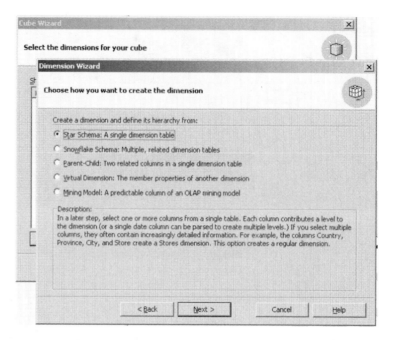

Figure 5.12
Definition of the cube dimensions and levels

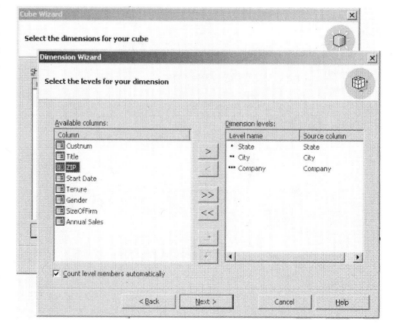

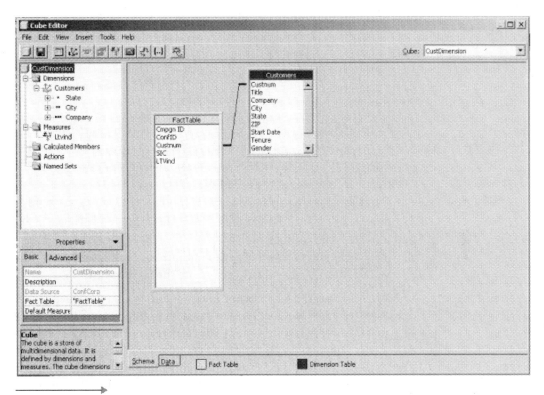

Figure 5.13   *Example of a cube with fact table and one dimension*

In the *Specify the Member Key Column* step, click Next. Also click *Next for the Select Advanced options* step. In the last step of the wizard, type Customer in the Dimension name box, and keep the *Share this dimension with other cubes* box selected. Click Finish.

This will produce a display of the OLAP cube that you have built, illustrated in Figure 5.13.

You can either save the cube for processing later or process the cube immediately (to process immediately select the close box).

If you select the close box you will get a window, shown in Figure 5.14, that asks you whether you want to save the cube. Select Yes to save the cube and to enter cube processing to set up the dimensions for the analysis.

This will set up the cube for processing. Processing is necessary to look ahead for the potential reporting dimensions of the cube so as to make the

Figure 5.14
Saving the cube for processing

dimensional results available for query in a responsive manner (since there are potentially a large number of queries, the processing is done ahead of time to ensure that the queries are processed and stored in the database to enable quick responses to a user request).

You will be asked what type of data store you want to create: Molap, Rolap, or Holap. These dimensional storage options are explained in the Microsoft Press publication *Data Warehousing with SQL Server 7.0*. Essentially, these techniques allow the user to optimize query responsiveness with disk space savings. The data store options are shown in Figure 5.15.

Once you select the data storage method you will be presented with a storage optimization window, as illustrated in Figure 5.16. This window will give you an opportunity to tune the relative contributions of preprocessed queries and associated storage against potential query responsiveness. To start, simply select the defaults (including the default "Performance gain" of 50 percent). Select Start to launch the storage–query responsiveness process, as shown in Figure 5.16.

Figure 5.15
Defining the cube storage types

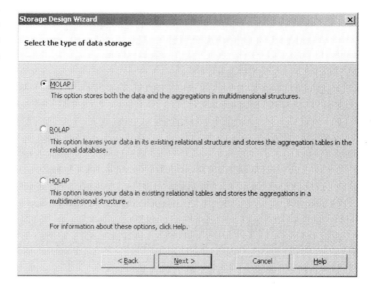

Figure 5.16
*Setting up the
cube query
responsiveness
process*

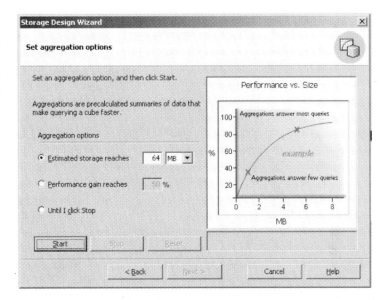

Figure 5.16
*Setting up the
cube query
responsiveness
process*

This will produce the actual query responsiveness distribution, as shown in Figure 5.17.

Once Analysis Services has finished processing, the cube that you have defined, it will produce a display indicating that the processing has been successful. You can examine the processing results window, shown in Figure 5.18, to see the various processing steps (the window displays the SQL that it used to produce the dimensional cube reports).

Figure 5.17
*Actual predicted
query
responsiveness
display*

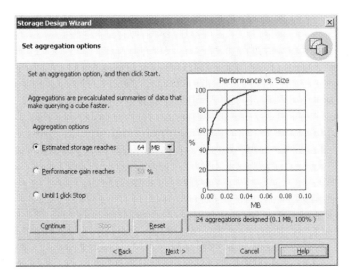

Figure 5.18
*Cube processing
results window*

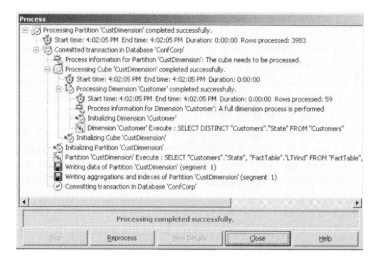

Once the cube has finished processing, you can view the results. As shown in Figure 5.19, to view the cube processing results select the cube in the Analysis Services server tree, select Cube, right-click, and Browse.

This will produce a browsable table as shown in Figure 5.20.

If you like, you can open up the various categories and drill down to state-level aggregations to get a better view of the results. An example of drill down is shown in Figure 5.21.

Figure 5.19
*Cube processing
results*

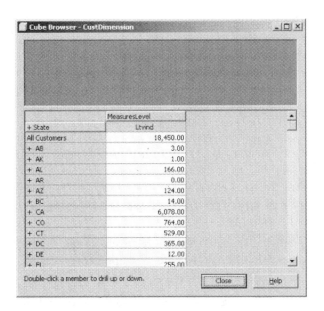

Figure 5.20
Results of cube browsing operation

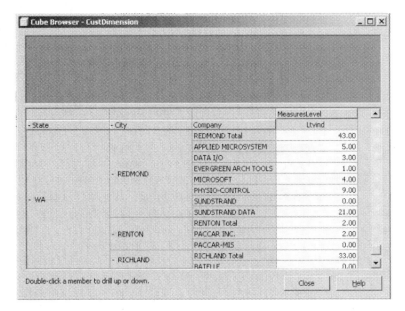

Figure 5.21
Cube drill down

Figure 5.22
*Adding dimensions
to the cube*

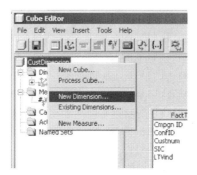

5.5   Adding to the dimensional representation

So far what we have shown is relatively simple. Let's add a few more dimensions to the display to be in a position to produce a more comprehensive view of our promotion and conference programs.

To do this, we need to go back to the server tree display in Analysis Services and, once the cube is selected, right-click to produce the New Dimension selection in the cube definition, as shown in Figure 5.22.

Once this is done, it provides the ability to add as many new dimensions as are necessary to complete the preliminary picture of the conference program that we need to support our descriptive analysis of the conference promotional results. Figure 5.23 shows the display that allows us to add the Promotional dimension to the analysis.

Figure 5.23
*Adding a
dimension
(promotion) to the
cube*

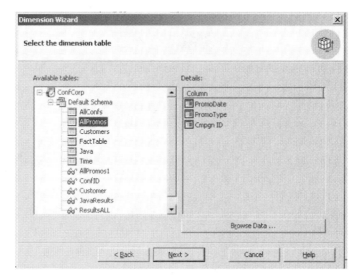

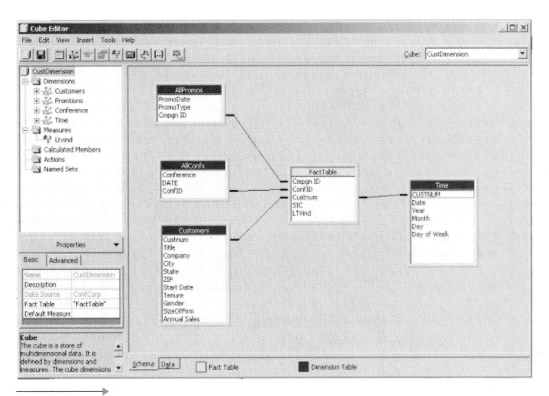

Figure 5.24 *Completed star schema representation for the conference results*

This allows us to add enough dimensions to provide a comprehensive overview of the promotional program results, which includes the relevant dimensions of promotions, corresponding conferences attendances, and the associated time (or seasonality) results. The star schema that supports this reporting framework is shown in Figure 5.24.

This allows you to produce multidimensional reports, as shown in Figure 5.25.

Here we see that, overall, the e-commerce conference is attracting the most attendances from people with a relatively higher lifetime value index. But we can also see that there are many other possible views of the conference program. To see the effect of other dimensions all you have to do is pick up a dimension with the mouse by left-clicking on the dimension and moving it into the Measurement level column of the OLAP display. Figure 5.26 shows the kinds of multidimensional displays that are possible using this drag-and-drop, cross-dimensional view operation.

Figure 5.25
*Top-level cube for
the conference
attendance results*

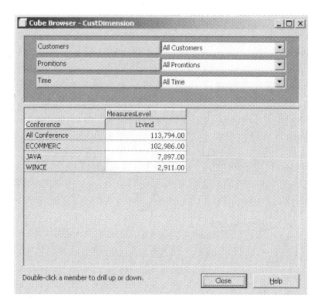

Here we can see, for example, the growth of the e-Commerce program—in terms of Life Time Value indicators—from 1998 to 1999. We
can also see that the Java program and the Windows CE operating system
programs were introduced in 1999.

Figure 5.26
*Dragging and
dropping various
dimensions*

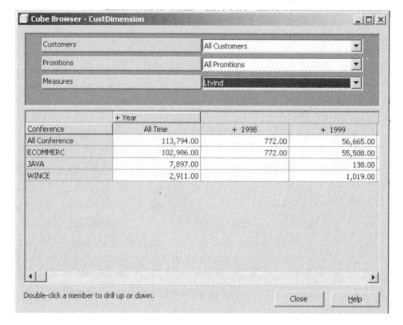

While this kind of presentation is informative and necessary to meet that standard reporting needs of the enterprise, it is not well adapted to finding the critical dimensions and dimensional values, that drive a particular business decision. For example, from this kind of display, it is hard to see what the most important drivers of a decision to attend a particular conference are. Data mining is well adapted to address this kind of investigative question. And, of course, that is why Microsoft followed up the implementation of OLAP cube reporting in Microsoft SQL Server 7 with the implementation of data mining in SQL Server 2000. The data mining capabilities provided in SQL Server 2000 are described in the following sections.

5.6   Building the analysis view for data mining

5.6.1   Analysis problem

We need to determine the characteristics of customers and prospects who are most likely to respond to our promotional offer. This means that we have to assemble an analysis data set containing responses and nonresponses to our offer. Further, we have to assemble a data set that has enough distinguishing information in it to enable us to distinguish the propensity to respond on the basis of key discriminating characteristics.

Our business experience suggests that the propensity to respond is a function of customer characteristics, such as type of job and employer characteristics, such as size of firm and annual sales. Response rates also vary according to other customer characteristics, such as length of time as a customer, whether the customer has attended previous events, and so on. Finally, in the past, business managers have observed that the propensity to respond is related to the offer type, discount, and coupon policies, as well as how many promotions have been sent to the targeted prospect.

It is very difficult to sort through all these potential predictors of customer response in order to find the unique combination of attributes that will best describe the profile of the customer who is most likely to respond without some sort of automated pattern search algorithm. As shown below, data mining decision trees are particularly suited to carrying out this kind of automated pattern search.

Once the analysis has been completed below we will see that the best predictor of response—length of time as a customer—while seemingly useful, reveals a problem: since short term customers are most likely to respond

Figure 5.27
*Analytical model
for the response
analysis*

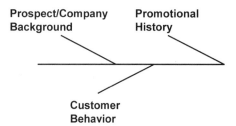

to campaigns this means that customer loyalty in the installed customer base is low. However, data mining can be useful in exploring and cultivating the most loyal customers in order to increase their life time value. The most loyal customers turn out to be males who either come from very small firms or very large firms. Whereas the long term response rate to campaigns is very low at 1 percent it turns out that males in this small or large firm category respond at a rate of 8 percent. So Conference Corp can increase response rate and stimulate customer loyalty by targeting more of this market segment in the future.

Among females the keys to increasing response rate are also revealed by the data mining model: Females in mid-size firms (neither small nor large as in the case of males) with moderate income are the best targets. Here the response rate increases to approximately 15 percent.

The analytical model for this approach is illustrated, in the form of an Ishikawa diagram, in Figure 5.27.

5.6.2 Unit of analysis

As we can see from Figure 5.27, there are four potential units of analysis, as follows:

1.   The company (1,955 records or cases in the data set)

2.   The individual customer (3,984 records or cases in the data set)

3.   The response (there are 9,934 responses in the data set: 8,075 for the e-commerce conference [55 percent]; 1,467 for the Java conference [10 percent], and 392 for the Windows CE conference [3 percent] for an overall response rate of about 68 percent)

4.   The promotion (14,589 incidents or cases in the data set)

It might be tempting to see the customer as the unit of analysis; however, if we think about it, the unit of analysis has to be the promotion itself.

We want to look at each and every promotion and examine whether the promotion produced a response or not.

So, promotion is the unit of analysis and response is the outcome that we want to examine and explain. In our case, the "explanation" will be through the construction of a predictive model, which uses the characteristics on the analysis record to discriminate between responders and nonresponders.

5.7 Setting up the data mining analysis

In order to develop a model of the effectiveness of promotions and the associated customer attributes that predict promotional response, the data need to be expressed in the appropriate format. Attendance is viewed as a function of customer and promotional characteristics.

Attendance (outcome/target) ← Customer Characteristics + Promotional Activities

The data representation that supports this type of analysis is shown in Figure 5.28.

Figure 5.28
Construction of the analysis record— the customer case

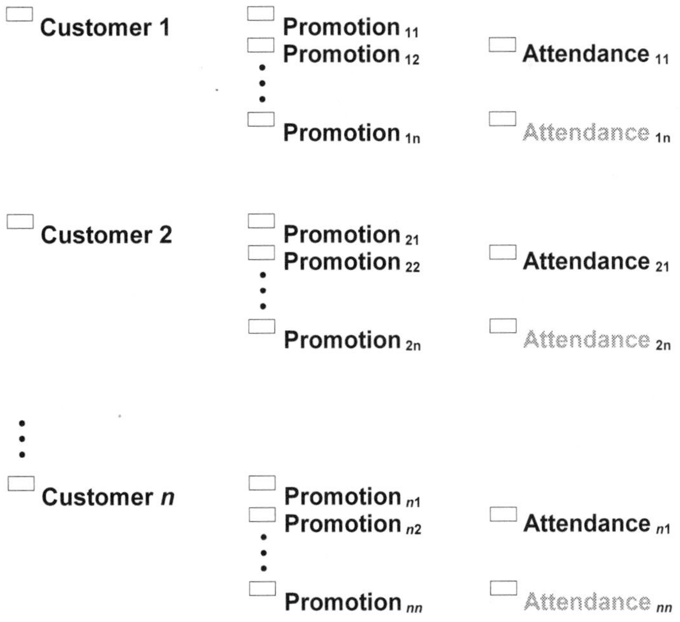

Customer 1   Promotion $_{11}$
              Promotion $_{12}$ Attendance $_{11}$
              ⋮
              Promotion $_{1n}$ Attendance $_{1n}$

Customer 2   Promotion $_{21}$
              Promotion $_{22}$ Attendance $_{21}$
              ⋮
              Promotion $_{2n}$ Attendance $_{2n}$

⋮

Customer n Promotion $_{n1}$
              Promotion $_{n2}$ Attendance $_{n1}$
              ⋮
              Promotion $_{nn}$ Attendance $_{nn}$

As can be seen, the unit of analysis is the promotion. This means that copies of the "host" customer record for each promotion will be propagated through the analysis file (the result of executing a right join in the query that forms the Customer–Promotion link). There may be one or more conference attendances that can result from the promotional records on file, so these attendances need to be added to the analysis view. This is accomplished by a left join between the Promotions and Attendances tables (this join precedes the former join).

5.7.1 Query construction

Three tables need to be joined to produce the analysis view, as shown in the following SQL join expression:

```
SELECT Customers.*, AllPromos.*,
[Conferences].[CourseCode], [Conferences].[DATE]

FROM Customers RIGHT JOIN (AllPromos LEFT JOIN
Conferences ON
([AllPromos].[CUSTNUM]=[Conferences].[CUSTNUM]) AND
([AllPromos].[PromoDate]=[Conferences].[DATE])) ON
[Customers].[Custnum]=[AllPromos].[CUSTNUM];
```

Note: Since the example database is in Microsoft Access we can use non-ANSI compliant SQL for this query. The Transact-SQL query, in particular the OUTER join, would be different.

The first join—a left outer join—includes all records from the promotional AllPromos table and only those records in the Conference table where the promotional date and the conference date are equal (this latter business rule is how we establish that a given conference attendance resulted from a particular promotion). This results in a join between the promotional and conference attendance tables that allows us to see which promotions resulted in a conference attendance (attendance types include e-Commerce, Java, and Windows CE).

The next join—a right outer join—delivers all the promotional and conference attendances and attaches the associated customer and company fields to the record. This duplicates customer and company information for each promotion and conference attendance, so that these potential discriminators are available for the analysis of response/no response. As indicated, there are 14,589 promotional offers, which resulted in 9,934 attendances.

5.8   Predictive modeling (classification) tasks

The relational database shown in Figure 5.1 has been defined as a Microsoft Access database. So, the first task to accomplish in bringing the data into the analysis is to establish the database as an ODBC data source.

As with the dimensional example, begin by setting up the system data source (DSN) to establish a connection between Analysis Manager and the conference response data in the ODBC data source administrator, as shown in Figure 5.29.

In Windows 2000, go to Settings, Control Panel, and then Administrative Tools. Double-click on Data Sources (ODBC).

As illustrated in Figure 5.30, on the System DSN tab, click Add. Select Microsoft Access Driver and then click Finish.

This will bring you to the Data Link Properties sheet, shown in Figure 5.31. Select the Connection tab, set the check box *Use data source name*, and fill in the Access database name (in this case, Conference).

This will present the Select Database dialog box. Use the Select button to browse to the Conference.mdb database. Click OK.

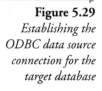

Figure 5.29
Establishing the ODBC data source connection for the target database

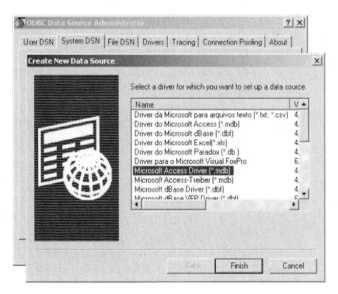

Figure 5.30
Data Link
Properties

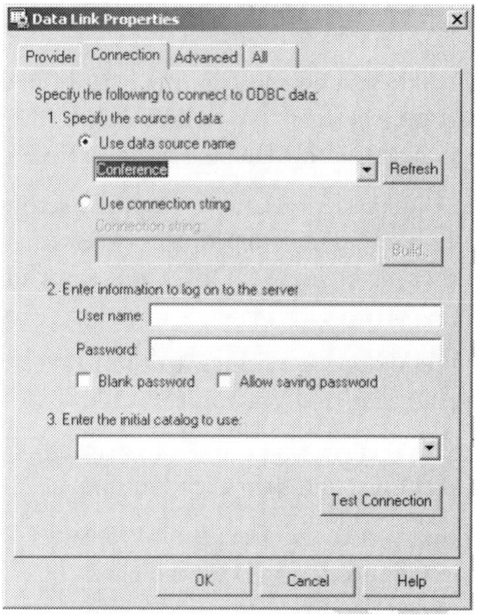

Now back out of the ODBC source data selection sequence: In the ODBC Microsoft Access Setup dialog box, click OK. In the ODBC Data Source Administrator dialog box, click OK.

Figure 5.31
Access Database
Setup dialog box

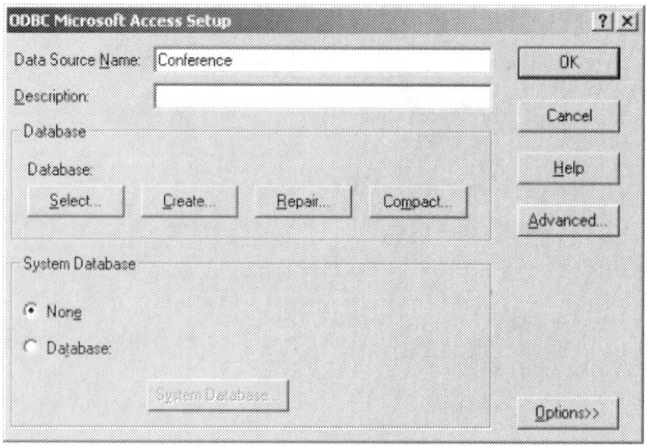

5.9   Creating the mining model

Now we want to create a mining model using Microsoft Decision Tree to develop a predictive model, which will tell us who is likely to respond to the promotional offer. Here we define a mining model in the analytical data mart.

Begin by starting up Analysis Manager. As shown in Figure 5.32, go to the start menu, select Microsoft SQL Server, then Analysis Services, and, finally, Analysis Manager.

Once you have started up Analysis Manager go to the tree view and expand Analysis Services. Click on the name of your server to establish a connection with the Analysis Server. To set up a new database, right-click on your server name and then click New Database. In the Database dialog box enter Conference in the Database name box and then click OK.

As shown in Figure 5.33, the new conference database created by this operation contains the following five nodes:

1.   Data sources

2.   Cubes

3.   Shared dimensions

4.   Mining models

5.   Database roles

So far we can see that the operations in creating a data mining view of the data are the same as creating a dimensional view of the data.

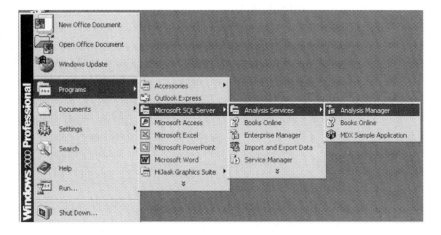

Figure 5.32
*Analysis Manager
startup sequence*

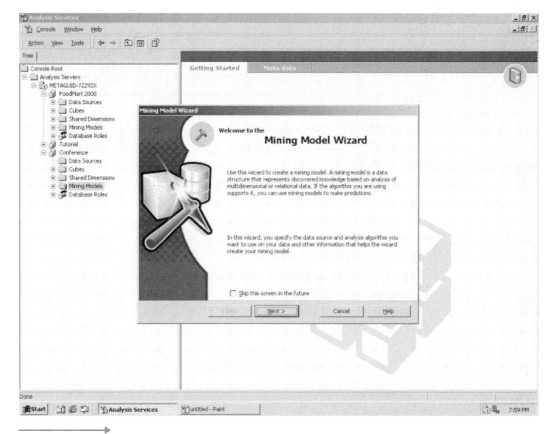

Figure 5.33   *The Data Mining wizard created from the Mining Models folder in Analysis Services*

Figure 5.33 shows the opening dialog for the Data Mining wizard. We start by selecting the table that contains the results (attendance at conference). Begin by starting up Analysis Services (if it is not already started). Then open Conference Results and go to Mining Models. Right-click and select New Mining Model. To invoke the wizard, right-click on the Mining Models folder, and then select New Mining Model from the shortcut menu.

Once the Mining Model wizard has been displayed, click Next in the select source type window, select Relational Data, and then select Next.

In the select case window, shown in Figure 5.34, select the Conference table from the available tables. Click Next.

Once you select the Conference database, the associated tables and views will become available. Select the JavaResults view, shown in Figure 5.35.

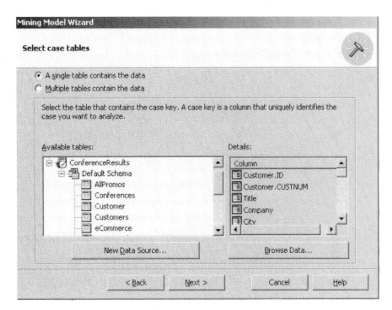

Figure 5.34
*Mining Model
wizard relational
table selection view*

The wizard will now step you forward to select the data mining technique. We want to use decision trees, so in the select data mining technique window select Microsoft decision trees as the technique. Click Next.

Figure 5.35
*Selecting a
database table view
for analysis*

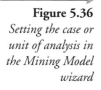

Figure 5.36
*Setting the case or
unit of analysis in
the Mining Model
wizard*

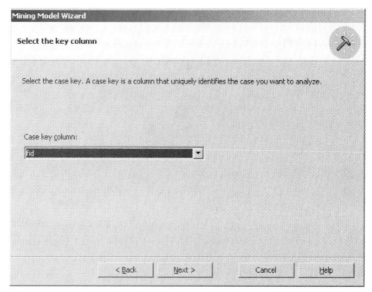

Next, we need to identify the case base or unit of analysis for the modeling task. When we created this view, we formed an ID field to indicate that the unit of analysis would be the result of the promotional table join. Use this ID to establish the case, or unit, of analysis.

As shown in Figure 5.36, in the Select key column step of the wizard, select ID for the Case key column. Click Next.

As a final step to setting up the analysis task, we need to select the outcome or target of the analysis. The view has highlighted the field Outcome for this purpose. In the wizard, select the field Outcome in the Predictable Columns dialog, as shown in Figure 5.37. The wizard also presents the inputs, or predictors, you can select in the model as well. As shown in Figure 5.37, select Tenure, Gender, Size of Firm, and PromoDate as inputs. This provides us with indicators of all the dimensions of analysis that we have established for this model: Personal/company characteristics, customer behavior characteristics, and promotion characteristics.

As shown in Figure 5.38, save the model as PromoResults.

If you select the *Save and process now* check box, the model will begin to work with the training data in order to find a good predictive model based on a decision tree. The model execution is shown in Figure 5.39.

The model execution view will indicate that it has found the best model by posting a Finish message to the window. Select Done to view the results.

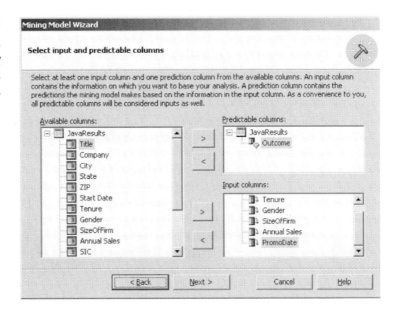

Figure 5.37
Setting up the model target and inputs for the decision tree

As shown in Figure 5.40, there are three main areas in the decision tree display: the main display, which provides a detailed view of the tree; a content navigator, which shows a high-level, summarized view of the tree (with the area shown in the detailed view outlined); and an attributes results browser, which provides a statistical summary of the current highlighted node.

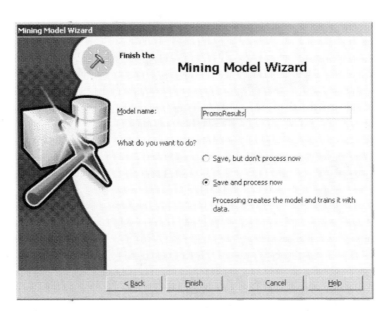

Figure 5.38
Saving the data mining model specification

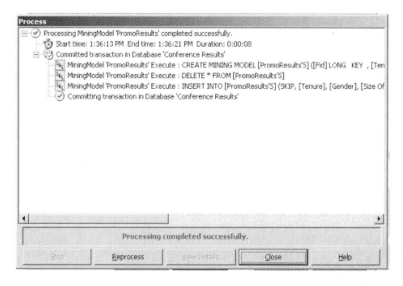

Figure 5.39
*Model execution
diagnostics—
training a decision
tree*

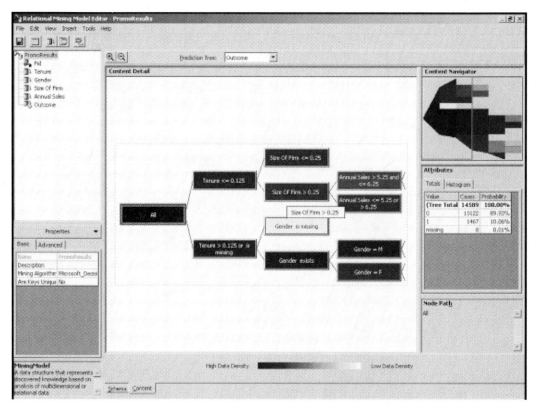

Figure 5.40   *Typical decision tree display*

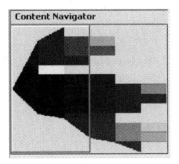

Figure 5.41
Content navigator

5.10   The tree navigator

Expanded views of the content navigator and attributes results browser are shown in Figures 5.41 and 5.42, respectively. The content navigator allows you to browse through the entire tree (which, in some cases, can be very large) in order to identify the area of the tree that you want to view in more detail. The nodes of the tree are presented as boxes. The various colors in the boxes point to the density of the outcome (a greater proportion of responses is shown with a denser color).

The attributes results browser, shown in Figure 5.42, allows you to highlight any given node of the tree in order to produce a statistical summary of the results in the node. As shown in Figure 5.42, there are 14,589 cases in the analysis data set. The response, attendance at a Java conference, accounts for 10 percent of the cases in the analysis.

The attributes window indicates that of the 14,589 cases selected for this analysis a total of 1,467, or approximately 10 percent, replied to the promo-

Figure 5.42
Attributes results browser—root node statistics

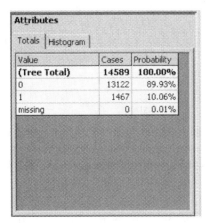

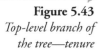

Figure 5.43
Top-level branch of
the tree—tenure

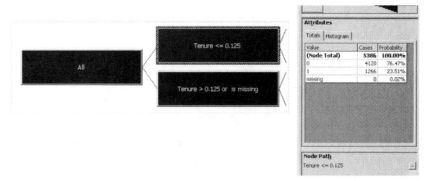

tional offer with a conference attendance. The conference organizer wants to use the decision tree method to gain an appreciation of how this attendance varies according to key customer characteristics. The organizer is also interested in developing a decision rule to help distinguish low-probability attendees from high-probability attendees. These decision rules can be used to increase the probability of success in future conference offerings.

At the highest level of the decision tree, we can see that the most important distinguishing characteristic that separates likely response to a conference offer is tenure; that is, length of time as a customer. In the attribute table, shown in the lower right-hand pane in Figure 5.43, we see that if tenure is less than or equal to 0.125, then the probability of response climbs from the average of about 10 percent to 23.51 percent. Since tenure is expressed in years, this means that the highest probability of a response to a promotion comes from customers who have been recruited very recently (365 × .125 = 45.25 days), probably for the specific offer of this campaign.

The attributes results for the lower node (tenure > 0.125), displayed in Figure 5.44, show the results for the higher-tenure members of the database: those who have been on the database for over 45 days. Among high tenure customers, the probability of response has dropped to about 2 percent. We are beginning to run out of data with this low-response group: Only 201 cases are available in this group—a very low number. As the number of cases in a group begins to drop, the statistical accuracy of results tends to become more and more suspect.

Let's see how far the Microsoft algorithm grows the results. This will provide more information about the characteristics of longer-term customers who are most likely to return for more events after the initial conference they attended has come and gone. This part of the tree browser, displayed in Figure 5.44, shows us that if tenure is high and the customer is female, then the probability of response drops even further to about 1 percent (there are

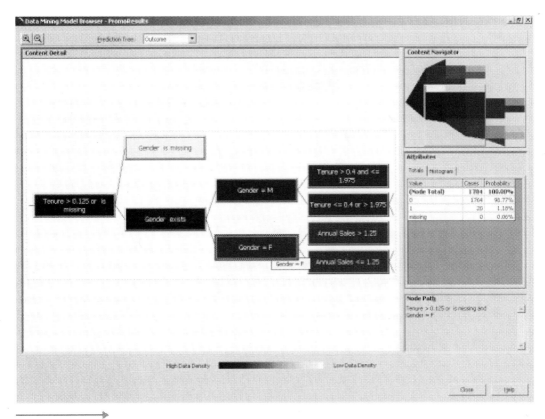

Figure 5.44   *Results for higher-tenure members of the target population*

20 females in the database, which yield an average attendance rate of 1.18 percent). Notice also that there is one low-density data node for cases where the Gender field was missing. It turns out that in this node the attendance rate is zero (this probability indicates that poor data quality reflects poor customer loyalty).

Among the 7408 males at this level of the tree, displayed in Figure 5.45, we can see that the attendance rate is 2.46 percent—roughly 2.5 times more likely to attend a promoted event than females.

Figure 5.45   *Higher tenure male attendance rates*

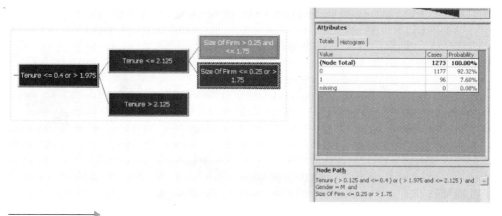

Figure 5.46   *Increased response among males with high tenure*

Figure 5.46 shows that males who have an relatively long tenure (≥ 1.125 years) and who come from relatively small firms (≤ 0.25) or, at the other extreme, from relatively large firms (> 1.75) are most likely to attend: 7.6 percent. This places this group at about the same level as the overall attendance rate of 10 percent and indicates that these people can be targeted as a means of increasing loyalty and lifetime value.

As shown in Figure 5.47, females who come from firms with relatively low annual sales and who come from a midrange size of firm (> 1.75 and ≤ 3.25) are also good targets. This group had an attendance rate of 14.85 percent. Notice that there are only 14 "positive" occurrences of attendance

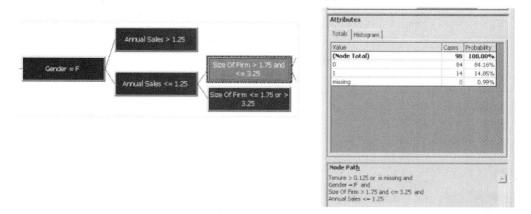

Figure 5.47   *Example of response by selected female attributes*

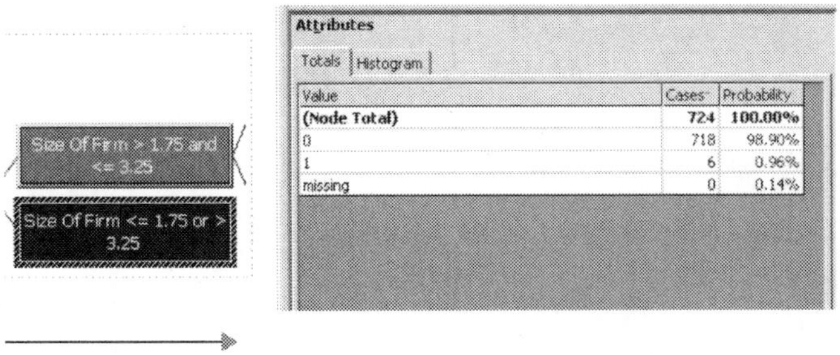

Figure 5.48   *A small number of "positive" cases*

in this node. This is a relatively small number to base results on, even though these results are statistically valid.

There are no attendances in the Annual Sales > 1.25 node and in the Size of Firm ≤ 1.75 or > 3.25 node, shown in Figure 5.48. We see that there are only 6 of 724 "positive" cases (less than 1 percent). Six cases is a very small number to base marketing results on and, while it may be possible to demonstrate that the results are statistically valid from a theoretical point of view, it is definitely recommended to verify these results with respect to a holdout sample or validation database to see whether these results could be expected to generalize to a new marketing target population.

5.11 Clustering (creating segments) with cluster analysis

Cluster analysis allows us to segment the target population reflected in our database on the basis of shared similarities among a number of attributes. So, unlike decision trees, it is not necessary to specify a particular outcome to be used to determine various classes, discriminators, and predictors. Rather, we just need to specify which fields we want the data mining clustering algorithm to use when assessing the similarity or dissimilarity of the cases being considered for assignment to the various clusters.

To begin the data mining modeling task it is necessary to specify the source data. As with the decision tree, developed in the previous section, we will point the Data Mining wizard at the Conferences.mdb data source and pick up the customer table as the analysis target. As shown in Figure 5.49, in this case we will be clustering on customers and will use their shared similarities according to various characteristics or attributes to determine to which cluster they belong.

Figure 5.49
Identifying the source table to serve as the clustering target

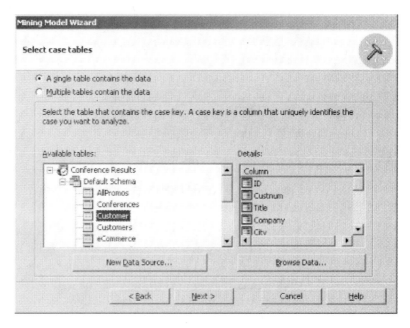

Figure 5.50
Selecting the cluster data mining method

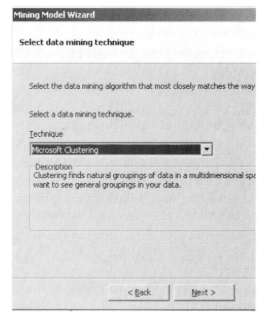

Figure 5.51
Selecting the case key to define the unit of analysis

Once the target data table has been identified, the Modeling wizard will request us to specify the data mining technique. As shown in Figure 5.50, select clustering as the data mining method.

As in all data mining models, we are asked to indicate the level of analysis. This is contained in the case key selected for the analysis. As shown in Figure 5.51, at this point we want the level of analysis to be the customer level, so we specify the customer as the key field.

The Analysis wizard then asks us to specify the fields that will be used to form the clusters. These are the fields that will be used to collectively gauge the similarities and dissimilarities between the cases to form the customer clusters. We select the fields shown in Figure 5.52.

Once the fields have been selected, we can continue to run the cluster model. After processing, we get the results presented in Figure 5.53.

Figure 5.52
Selecting the fields to use in calculating similarity measures to define the clusters

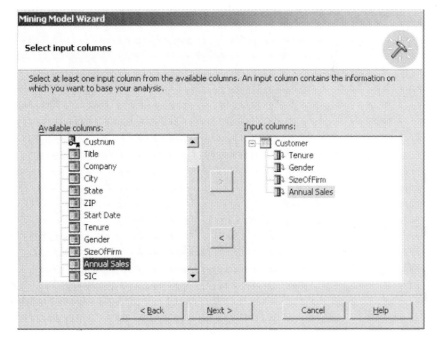

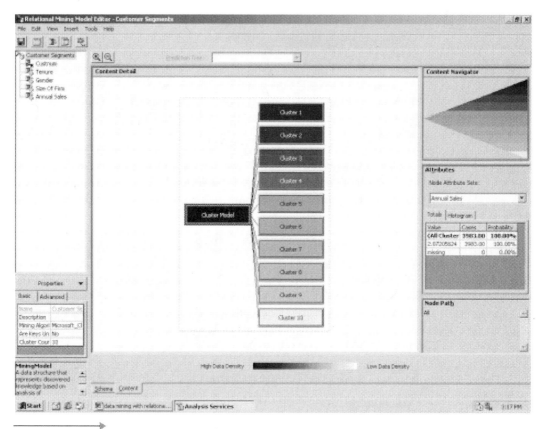

Figure 5.53   *Default display produced by the cluster analysis modeling procedure*

In Figure 5.53 we see that by default, the cluster procedure has identified ten clusters. The content detail and content navigator areas use color to represent the density of the number of observations.

We can browse the attribute results to look at the characteristics of the various clusters. Although we can be confident that the algorithm has forced the clusters into ten homogenous but optimally distinct groups, if we want to understand the characteristics of the groups then it may be preferable to tune the clustering engine to produce a fewer number of clusters. Three clusters accomplish this. There are many different quantitative tests to determine the appropriate number of clusters in an analysis. In many cases, as illustrated here, the choice is made on the basis of business knowledge and hunches on how many distinct customer groupings actually exist. Having determined that three clusters are appropriate, we can select the

Figure 5.54
*Using the
properties dialog to
change the number
of clusters*

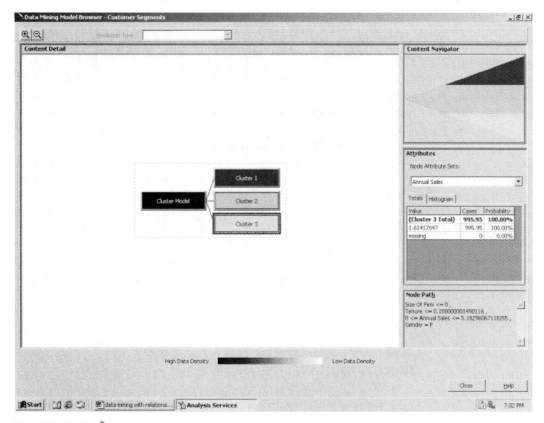

Figure 5.55 *Identification of three clusters resulting from changes to the number of cluster properties*

properties dialog and change the number of clusters from ten to three. This is shown in Figure 5.54.

This will instruct Analysis Server to recalculate the cluster attributes and members by trying to identify three clusters rather than the default ten clusters. To complete this recalculation you need to go back to the data mining model, reprocess the model, and then browse the model to see the new results. The new results are displayed in Figure 5.55.

As shown in Figure 5.55, the attributes pane shows which decision rules can be used to characterize the cluster membership. Each decision rule will result in classifying a case into a unique cluster. The cluster that is found will depend upon how the preconditions of the cluster decision rule match up to the specific attributes of the case being classified.

Here are the decision rules for classifying cases (or records) into the three clusters. Note that the fields used as preconditions of the decision rule are the same fields we indicated should be used to calculate similarity in the Mining Model wizard.

Cluster 1. Size Of Firm = 0 ,
Annual Sales = 0 ,
$0.100000001490116 \leq$ Tenure ≤ 1.31569222413047 ,
Gender = M

Cluster 2. $6.65469534945513 \leq$ Size Of Firm ≤ 9 ,
$1.06155892122041 \leq$ Annual Sales ≤ 9 ,
$0.100000001490116 \leq$ Tenure ≤ 3.00482080240072 ,
Gender = F

Cluster 3. Size Of Firm ≤ 0 ,
Tenure ≤ 0.100000001490116 ,
$0 \leq$ Annual Sales ≤ 5.18296067118255 ,
Gender = F

5.11.1   Customer segments as revealed by cluster analysis

These decision rules provide a statistical summary of the cases in the data set once they have been classified in the various clusters. Here we can see that Cluster 1 characterizes customers from generally small, general low sales volume firms. Cluster 1 members also have generally short tenure. Cluster 3 is primarily a female cluster and has the very short tenure members while Cluster 2 draws on customers from the larger, high sales volume firms.

This tends to suggest that we have Small, low sales volume customers who tend to be males. Among female customers they are either longer term customers from generally larger, higher sales companies or very short term customers from small, medium sales companies.

We can see here that Cluster techniques and Decision Tree techniques produce different kinds of results: the decision tree was produced purely with respect to probability of response. The Clusters, on the other hand, are produced with respect to Tenure, Gender, Size of Firm and Annual Sales. In fact, in clustering, probability of response was specifically excluded.

5.11.2   Opening (refreshing) mining models

As indicated in Chapter 3, mining models are stored as Decision Support Objects in the database. The models contain all the information necessary to recreate themselves, but they need to be refreshed in order to respond to new data or new settings. To retrieve a previously grown mining model, go to Analysis Services and select the mining model you want to look at. For example, as shown in Figure 5.56, open the Analysis Server file tree and highlight the previously produced mining model entitled "PromoResults."

Go to the Action menu or right-click the mouse and execute Refresh. This will bring the mining results back. Once the model is refreshed, go to the Action menu and select Browse to look at the model results.

Figure 5.56
Navigating to the Analysis Services tree to retrieve a data mining model

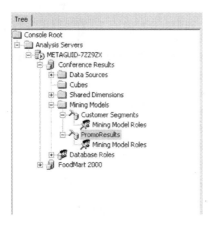

5.12   Confirming the model through validation

It is important to test the results of modeling activities to ensure that the relationships that have been uncovered will bear up over time and will hold true in a variety of circumstances. This is important in a target marketing application, for example, where considerable sums will be invested in the targeting campaign. This investment is based on the model results, so they better be right! The best way to determine whether a relationship is right or not is to see whether it holds up in a new set of data drawn from the modeled population. In essence, in a target marketing campaign, we would like to apply the results of the analysis to a new set of data, where we already know the answer (whether people will respond or not), to see how well our model performs.

This is done by creating a "test" data set (sometimes called a "hold back" sample), which is typically drawn from the database to be analyzed before the analytical model is developed. This way we can create a test data set that hasn't been used to develop the model. We can see that this test data set is independent of the training (or learning data set), so it can serve as a proxy for how a new data set would perform in a model deployment situation. Of course, since the test data set was extracted from the original database, it contains the answer; therefore, it can be used to calculate the validity of the model results. Validity consists of accuracy and reliability: How accurately do we reproduce the results in a test data set and how reliable is this finding. Reliability is best tested with numerous data sets, drawn in different sets of circumstances over time. Reliability accumulates as we continue our modeling and validation efforts over time. Accuracy can be calculated on the basis of the test data set results.

5.12.1   Validation with a qualitative question

Qualitative questions—such as respond/did not respond—result in decision trees where the components of the nodes on the branches of the tree show a frequency distribution (e.g., 20 percent respond; 80 percent do not respond). In this case the decision tree indicates that the majority of cases will not respond. To validate this predicted outcome a test or hold back sample data set is used. Each data record in the test sample is validated against the prediction that is suggested by the decision tree. If the prediction is correct, then the valid score indicator is incremented. If the prediction is incorrect, then the invalid score indicator is incremented. At the end of the validation procedure the percentage of valid scores to invalid scores is calculated. This is then displayed as the percentage accuracy of the validated decision tree model.

5.12.2   Validation with a quantitative question

In the case of a quantitative outcome, such as dollars spent, accuracy can be calculated using variance explained according to a linear regression model calculated in a standard statistical manner. In this case, some of the superior statistical properties of regression are used in calculating the accuracy of the decision tree. This is possible because a decision tree with quantitative data summarized in each of the nodes of the decision tree is actually a special type of regression model. So the statistical test of variance explained, normally used in regression modeling, can be used with decision trees.

Thus, the value of a quantitative field in any given node is computed as consisting of the values of the predictors multiplied by the value for each predictor that is derived in calculating the regression equation. In a perfect regression model this calculation will equal the observed value in the node and the prediction will be perfect. When there is less than a perfect prediction, the observed value deviates from the predicted value. The deviations from these scores, or residuals, represent the unexplained variance of the regression model.

The accuracy that you find acceptable depends upon the circumstances. One way to determine how well your model performs is to compare its performance with chance. In our example, there were about 67 percent, or two-thirds, responders and about one-third nonresponders. So, by chance alone, we expect to be able to correctly determine whether someone responds two-thirds of the time. Clearly then, we would like to have a model that provides, say, an 80 percent accuracy rate. This difference in accuracy—the difference between the model accuracy rate of 80 percent and the accuracy rate given by chance (67 percent)—represents the gain from using the model. In this case the gain is about 13 percent. In general, this 13 percent gain means that we will have lowered targeting costs and increased profitability from a given targeting initiative.

5.13   Summary

Enterprise data can be harnessed—profitably and constructively—in a number of ways to support decision making in a wide variety of problem areas. The "trick" is to deploy the best pattern-searching tools available to look through the enterprise data store in order to find all relevant data points to support a decision and, more importantly, to determine how these data points interact with one another to affect the question under examination.

This is where decision tree products show their value as an enterprise data and knowledge discovery tool. Decision trees search through all relevant data patterns—and combinations of patterns—and present the best combinations to the user in support of decision making. The decision tree algorithm quickly rejects apparent (spurious) relationships and presents those combinations of patterns that—together—produce the effect under examination. It is both multidimensional, in an advanced numerical processing manner, and easy to use in its ability to support various user models of the question under examination.

In summary, the SQL 2000 decision tree presents critical benefits in support of the enterprise knowledge discovery mission, as follows:

- It is easy to use and supports the user's view of the problem domain.

- It works well with real-world enterprise data stores, including data that are simple, such as "male" and "female," and data that are complex, such as rate of investment.

- It is sensitive to all relevant relationships, including complex, multiple relationships, yet quickly rejects weak relationships or relationships that are spurious (i.e., relationships that are more apparent than real).

- It effectively summarizes data by forming groups of data values that belong together in clusters, or branches, on the decision tree display.

- It employs advanced statistical hypothesis testing procedures and validation procedures to ensure that the results are accurate and reproducible (in a simple manner, behind the scenes, so that users do not need a degree in statistics to use these procedures).

- The resulting display can be quickly and easily translated into decision rules, predictive rules, and even knowledge-based rules for deployment throughout the enterprise.

In a similar manner, the SQL 2000 clustering procedure provides critical benefits when a particular field or outcome does not form the focus of the study. This is frequently the case when, for example, you are interested in placing customers into various classes or segments that will be used to describe their behavior in a variety of circumstances. As with the decision tree, the cluster procedure provides a range of benefits, including the following:

- The Data Mining wizard makes it easy to use.

- It is possible to define, ahead of time, how many clusters you feel are appropriate to describe the phenomenon (e.g., customer segments) that you are viewing.

- The attributes of the clusters can be easily examined.

- As with decision tree models, cluster models can be described and deployed in a variety of ways throughout the enterprise.

Knowledge discovery is similar to an archeological expedition—you need to sift through a lot of "dirt" in order to find the treasure buried beneath the dig. There is no shortage of dirt in enterprise operational data, but there are real treasures buried in the vaults of the enterprise data store. The SQL Server 2000 decision tree is an indispensable tool for sifting through multitudes of potential data relationships in order to find the critical patterns in data that demonstrate and explain the mission-critical principles necessary for success in the knowledge-based enterprise of the twenty-first century.

6

Deploying the Results

The customer generates nothing. No customer asked for electric lights.

—W. Edwards Deming

W. Edwards Deming, in his tireless efforts to apply statistical concepts in the pursuit of ever-more quality outputs, was instrumental in changing the way products are conceived, designed, and developed. In the Deming model, novelty emerged from the determined application of quality principles throughout the product life cycle. The Deming quality cycle is similar to the data mining closed-loop "virtuous cycle," which was outlined in Chapter 2. The application of data mining results, and the lessons to be learned from the application of these results to the product/market life cycle, begins with the deployment of the results. In the same way that tireless application of quality principles throughout the product life cycle has been shown to lead to revolutionary new ways of conceiving, designing, and delivering products, so too can the tireless deployment of data mining results to market interventions lead to similar revolutionary developments in the product and marketing life cycle.

If information is data organized for decision making, then knowledge could be termed data organized for a deployable action. As seen in the example developed in Chapter 5, data, once analyzed, yield up their secrets in the form of a decision rule, a probability to purchase, or perhaps a cluster assignment. The deployment of the decision rule, probability to purchase, or cluster assignment could be embodied in a specific, point solution to a particular problem (e.g., identify cross-sell opportunities on a Web site or at a customer call center). Another deployment could be a multistage, multi-channel delivery system (e.g., in what is normally referred to as campaign management, send offers to prospects through several channels with various frequencies and periodicities while measuring the results in order to determine not only what characteristics of prospects are most likely to lead to responses but which approach methods, frequencies, and timing provide incremental response "lift"). In assessing the potential value of a deployable result, it is common to talk about lift. Lift is a measure of the incremental value obtained by using the data mining results when compared with the results that would normally be achieved in the absence of using the knowledge derived from data mining.

In this chapter, we will show how to implement a target marketing model by scoring the customer database with a predictive query. We also show how to estimate return on investment with a lift chart.

6.1   Deployments for predictive tasks (classification)

Data Transformation Services (DTS), which are located in the Enterprise Services of SQL Server 2000, can be used to build a prediction query to score a data set using a predictive model developed in Analysis Manager. The predictive query is used to score unseen cases and is stored as a DTS package. This package can be scheduled for execution using DTS to trigger the package at any time in the future, under a variety of conditions. This is a very powerful way to create knowledge about unclassified cases, customers who have responded to a promotional offer, or customers who have visited your Web site.

Figure 6.1 illustrates the procedure that is necessary to create a prediction query. First, start up DTS Designer by going to the desktop start menu, selecting Programs, pointing to Microsoft SQL Server, and then selecting Enterprise Manager. In the console tree, expand the server that will hold the package containing the Data Mining Prediction Query task. Right-click the Data Transformation Services folder, and then click New Package.

In DTS Designer, from the Task tool palette, drag the icon for the Data Mining Prediction Query task onto the workspace. This icon appears in the DTS Package (New Package) dialog shown in Figure 6.1.

As an option, as shown in Figure 6.1, in the Data Mining Prediction Query Task dialog box, type a new name in the Name box to replace the

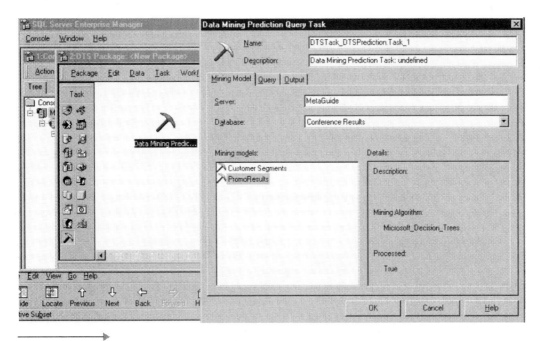

Figure 6.1   *Building a prediction query task in DTS Designer*

default name for the task. As another option, type a task description in the Description box. This description is used to identify the task in DTS Designer. In the Server box, type the name of the Analysis Server containing the data mining model to be used as the source for the prediction query. The server name—MetaGuide, used in the example in Figure 6.1—is the same as the computer name on the network.

From the Database list, select the database that contains the mining model to be queried. Here we select ConferenceResults, and this provides either the CustomerSegments data mining model (DMM) for the cluster results or PromoResults DMM for the response analysis.

If the mining model you want to use for the prediction query is not already highlighted in the Mining Models box, select a mining model from the box by clicking on its name or icon. As shown in Figure 6.1, you can view some of the properties of the mining model in the Details box.

Click the Query tab, and then, in the Data source box, either type a valid ActiveX Data Objects (ADOs) connection string to the case table containing the input and predictable columns for the query, or, to build the connection string, click the edit (...) button to launch the Data Link Properties dialog box.

Figure 6.2
DTS Prediction
Query Builder

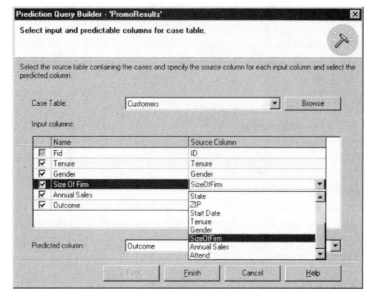

In the Prediction query box, type the syntax, or click New Query to launch Prediction Query Builder, as shown in Figure 6.2. If you choose to build the query yourself, note that the prediction query syntax must conform to the OLE DB for DM specification. For more information about the OLE DB for DM specification, see the list of links on the SQL Server Documentation Web site at http://www.microsoft.com/sql/support/docs.htm.

As shown in Figure 6.2, once the Prediction Query Builder has launched, you can build a query. The query asks you to associate the prediction with a new table.

Once the associations are made, the query builder is complete, and you can click OK to finish creating the task.

When the query is executed, it produces the query code shown in the query output box, displayed in Figure 6.3.

As can be seen by examining the code produced by the Prediction Query Builder, prediction queries are run by means of the SELECT statement. The prediction query syntax is as follows:

```
SELECT [FLATTENED] <SELECT-expressions> FROM <mining
model name>
PREDICTION JOIN <source data query> ON <join condition>
[WHERE <WHERE-expression>]
```

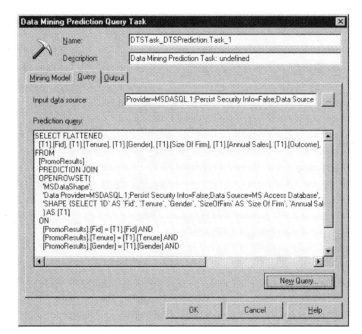

Figure 6.3
*Running the
prediction query
task with
Prediction Query
Builder*

The <mining model name> identifies the mining model that will be used to generate the predictions. After the source data have been identified, a relationship between these data and the data in the mining model must be defined. This is done using the PREDICTION JOIN clause. The <source data query> token identifies the set of new cases that will be predicted. As seen in the code, the mining model entitled PromoResults will be used to generate new values for the ID, Tenure, and Gender fields.

The query language shown in Figure 6.3, which will be stored as a DTS package, is as follows:

```
SELECT FLATTENED
  [T1].[Fid], [T1].[Tenure], [T1].[Gender], [T1].[Size Of
Firm], [T1].[Annual Sales], [T1].[Outcome],
[PromoResults].[Outcome]
FROM
  [PromoResults]
  PREDICTION JOIN
  OPENROWSET(
  'MSDataShape',
  'Data Provider=MSDASQL.1;Persist Security
Info=False;Data Source=MS Access Database',
  'SHAPE {SELECT 'ID' AS 'Fid', 'Tenure', 'Gender',
'SizeOfFirm' AS 'Size Of Firm', 'Annual Sales', 'Attend'
```

Figure 6.4
Defining the output data source for the prediction query task

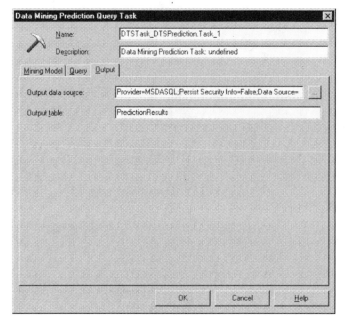

```
AS 'Outcome' FROM 'Customers' ORDER BY 'ID'}'
) AS [T1]
ON
[PromoResults].[Fid] = [T1].[Fid] AND
[PromoResults].[Tenure] = [T1].[Tenure] AND
[PromoResults].[Gender] = [T1].[Gender] AND
[PromoResults].[Size Of Firm] = [T1].[Size Of Firm] AND
[PromoResults].[Annual Sales] = [T1].[Annual Sales] AND
[PromoResults].[Outcome] = [T1].[Outcome]
```

In the Data Mining Prediction Query dialog you can select the Output tab to define an outcome data source, as shown in Figure 6.4.

As shown in Figure 6.4, the results of the prediction query task are going to be produced in a new table entitled PredictionResults. Click OK to finish creating the task. To save the task in a DTS package in DTS Designer, click Save on the package menu. Figure 6.4 shows the result of this save operation.

As shown in Figure 6.5, you can save the package in the following four ways:

1.   *As a Microsoft SQL Server table.* This allows you to store packages on any instances of SQL Server on your network. This is the option used in Figure 6.5.

Figure 6.5
Saving the query prediction package in DTS

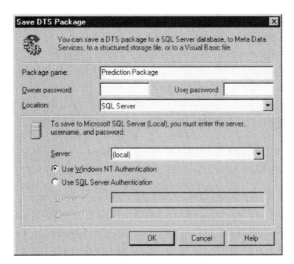

2. *SQL Server 2000 metadata services.* With this save option, you can maintain historical information about the data manipulated by the package and you can track the columns and tables used by the package as a source or destination.

3. *As a structured storage file.* With this save option, you can copy, move, and send a package across the network without having to store the file in a SQL Server database.

4. *As a Microsoft Visual BASIC file.* This option scripts out the package as Visual BASIC code; you can later open the Visual BASIC file and modify the package definition to suit your specific purposes.

Once the package is saved, as shown in Figure 6.5, it can be saved and executed according to a defined schedule or on demand from the DTS Prediction Package window. To execute, click on the prediction icon and trigger the Execute Step selection. This will create an execution display, as shown in Figure 6.6.

Once the predictive query has been run, you will be notified that the task has completed successfully. This is illustrated in Figure 6.7.

If you were to go to the data table that was classified with the predictive model (here the table has been defined as PredictionResults), you would find the results shown in Table 6.1.

In Table 6.1, we see that the PromoResults_Outcome column has been added by the predictive query engine.

Figure 6.6
DTS package
execution

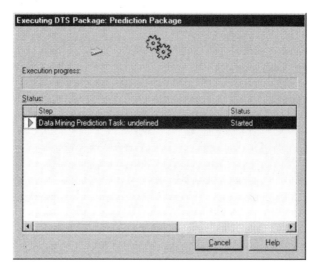

If we append the actual attendance score recorded for this data set and sort the columns by predicted attendance, the results would be as shown in Table 6.2.

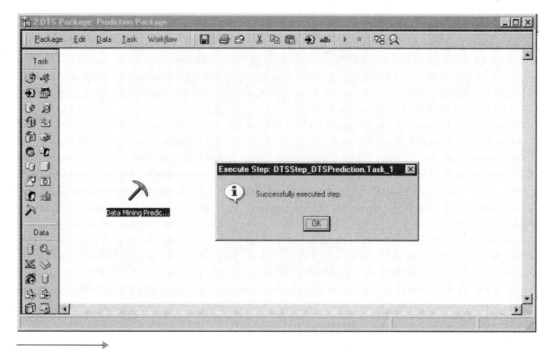

Figure 6.7   *Notification of successful package execution*

Table 6.1   *Prediction Results Table Created by the Prediction Query Task*

T1_Fid	T1_Tenure	T1_Gender	T1_Size of Firm	T1_Annual Sales	PromoResults_Outcome
1	2.1	M	0	0	0
2	2	M	0	0	0
3	4.2	M	0	0	0
4	2.2	M	0	0	0
5	3.1	M	0	0	0
6	4.1	M	0	0	0
7	2.1	M	0	0	0
8	2.1	F	0	0	0
9	3.1	M	0	0	0
10	2.1	F	0	0	0
11	3.1	M	0	0	0
12	4.2	M	0	0	0

Table 6.2   *Results of the Prediction (PromoResults_Outcome) and Actual Results*

T1_Fid	T1_Tenure	T1_Gender	T1_Size of Firm	T1_Annual Sales	PromoResults_Outcome	Actual
2523	0.1	M	9	6	1	1
2526	0.1	M	3	2	1	1
2534	0.1	M	3	0	1	1
2536	0.1	M	9	9	1	1
2545	0.1	M	0	0	1	1
2625	0.1	M	0	0	1	1
2626	0.1	M	0	0	1	1
2627	0.1	M	0	0	1	1
2628	0.1	F	0	0	1	1
2629	0.1	M	0	0	1	1
2630	0.1	M	7	4	1	1

Overall, in this data set there were 604 occurrences of an attendance and the predictive query correctly classified 286 of these. So the overall attendance rate is 14.7 percent (604 of 4,103 cases), and the predictive model correctly classified 47.4 percent of these (286 of 604 positive occurrences).

These types of results are very useful in targeted marketing efforts. Under normal circumstances it might be necessary to target over 30,000 prospects in order to get 5,000 attendees to an event where the expected response rate is 14.7 percent. With a 47.4 percent response rate this reduces the number of prospects that have to be targeted to slightly over 10,000.

6.2   Lift charts

Lift charts are almost always used when deploying data mining results for predictive modeling tasks, especially in target marketing. Lift charts are useful since they show how much better your predictive model is when compared with the situation where no modeling information is used at all. It is common to compare model results with no model (chance) results in the top 10 percent of your data, top 20 percent, and so on. Typically, the model would identify the top 10 percent that is most likely to respond. If the model is good, then it will identify a disproportionate number of responders in the top 10 percent. In this way it is not uncommon to experience model results in the top 10 percent of the data set that are two, three, and even four or more times likely to identify respondents than would be found with no modeling results.

Lift charts are used to support the goals of target marketing: to produce better results with no increase in budget and to maintain results with a budget cut (target fewer, but better chosen, prospects).

Data mining predictive models can be used to increase the overall response rate to a target marketing campaign by only targeting those prospects who, according to the data mining model developed with historic results, are most likely to respond. The lift chart in Figure 6.8 illustrates the concept.

In Figure 6.8, we show a lift chart that results when all prospects on the database are assigned a score developed by the predictive model decision tree. This score is probability of response. So every member of the database has a score that ranges from 0 (no response) to 1 (100 percent likely to respond). Then the file is sorted so that the high probabilities of response prospects are ranked at the head of the file and the low probabilities of response prospects are left to trail at the end of the file.

Figure 6.8
*Lift chart showing
cumulative
captured response*

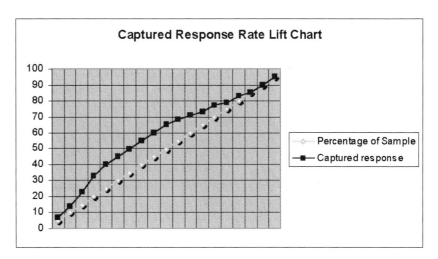

If the data mining model is working, then the data mining scoring should produce more responders in, say, the top 10 percent than the average response rate for all members in the data file. The lift chart shows how well the predictive model works. In the lift chart let us assume that the overall response rate is 10 percent. This overall response rate is reflected in the diagonal line that connects the origin of the graph to the upper right quadrant. If the data mining results did not find characteristics in the prospect database that could be used to increase knowledge about the probability to respond to a targeting campaign, then the data mining results would track the random results and the predicted response line would overlap the lower left to upper right random response line.

In most cases, the data mining results outperform the random baseline. This is illustrated in our example in Figure 6.8. We can see that the first 5 percent of the target contacts collected about 9 percent of the actual responses. The next increment on the diagonal—moving the contacts to 10 percent of the sample—collects about 12 percent of the responses and so on. By the time that 25 percent of the sample has been contacted we can see that 40 percent of the responses have been captured. This represents the cumulative lift at this point. This is a ratio of 40:25, which yields a lift of 1.6. This tells us that the data mining model will enable us to capture 1.6 times the normal expected rate of response in the first 25 percent of the targeted population.

The lift chart for the query shown in Table 6.2 is displayed in Figure 6.9.

With a good predictive model it is possible to improve the performance, relative to chance, by many multiples. This example shows the kind of lift

Figure 6.9
*Lift chart for
predictive query*

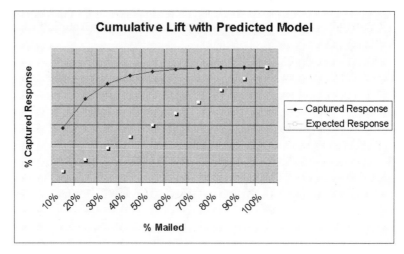

that can be expected if, instead of only capturing a response rate of about 10 percent, you capture a response rate of approximately 50 percent. The second 20 percent of the example shows that approximately two-thirds of the responses have been captured. The overall response rate was about 19 percent, which means that the first two deciles produce lift factors of 5:1 and 3:1, respectively. Using the results of the first 20 percent would mean that a targeting campaign could be launched that would produce two-thirds of the value at one-fifth of the cost of a campaign that didn't employ data mining results. This provides a dramatic illustration of the potential returns through the construction of a data mining predictive model.

Figure 6.10
*Backing up and
restoring the
database*

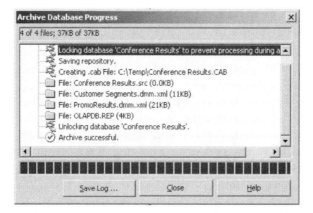

6.3 Backing up and restoring databases

To back up your database simply right-click on the database under the Analysis Servers in Analysis Manager. Select Database Archive Database. You will be prompted with a save location. When you select finish, the display illustrated in Figure 6.10 will be produced.

To restore, you reverse the procedure except that, since there is no database under Analysis Server, you select the server icon and then right-click and pick Restore Database. Navigate to the restore location, select the .CAB file, and initiate the restore.

7

The Discovery and Delivery of Knowledge for Effective Enterprise Outcomes: Knowledge Management[1]

> *Knowledge is the lifeblood of the modern enterprise.*
>
> *—Anonymous*

Knowledge for the business entity is like knowledge for the human entity—it allows the entity to grow, adapt, survive, and prosper. Given the complexities, threats, and opportunities of doing business in the new millennium, no competitive entity survives long without knowledge. If knowledge is the lifeblood of the modern enterprise, then the management of knowledge is essential to the survival and success of the enterprise. Knowledge is the ultimate, potentially the only, source of competitive advantage in a complex, ever-changing world. Perhaps this is why it is so common to hear discussions about "the knowledge economy."

> *Although the adoption of knowledge management has been relatively slow—compared to the adoption of such technologies as the web—the benefits have been nevertheless impressive: huge pay-offs have been reported by such companies as Texas Instruments ($1.5 billion over 3 years), Chevron ($2 billion annually), and BP ($30 million in the first year) (as reported by O'Dell et al., 2000, and Payne and Elliott, 1997).*

In Chapter 2 we introduced the notion of knowledge management (KM). We defined it as "the collection, organization, and utilization of various methods, processes, and procedures that are useful in turning ...

---

1.   Substantial portions of this chapter are due to the many notes provided by Lorna Palmer—notes derived from her many activities in the area of knowledge management, particularly with the American Productivity and Quality Center.

technology into business, social, and economic value." We framed the discussion of knowledge discovery in databases (KDD) as a knowledge management issue; in fact, we suggested that it was the conception of KDD as a knowledge management discipline that most appropriately distinguishes it from data mining (which, by comparison, is more focused on the technical complexities of extracting meaning from data through the application of pattern search algorithms).

We can see from this approach that knowledge management and data mining are closely related and can be seen as complementary and, indeed, as synergistic endeavors. So just as we see the unity and symmetry that exists between current notions of business intelligence and data mining, we can see a similar unity and symmetry between data mining and knowledge management. In essence, these are the three major components of an effective enterprise decision-support system in that all three are necessary for the successful extraction of decision-making information from data. Knowledge

Figure 7.1

General framework for the production of empirical and experiential knowledge in support of successful enterprise outcomes

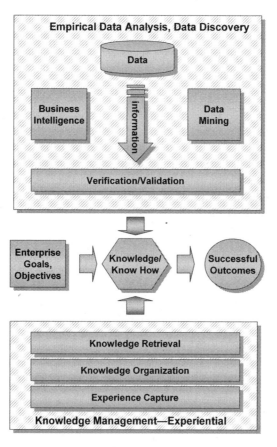

Table 7.1   *Attributes of Implicit versus Explicit Knowledge*

Implicit (Empirical) Knowledge	Tacit (Experiential) Knowledge
Formal, systematic	Insight
Objective	Judgment
Data	Know-how
Process maps	Mental models

management—in its KDD form—is essential for successful information extraction as well as for the conversion of this information into deployable actions that will work for the benefit of the enterprise.

To use a trivial example, it is impossible to know that a customer retention model could serve as a useful enterprise deployment unless it is informed by the knowledge that customers have value (and an acquisition cost) and therefore should be preserved in the interest of the business. There is a reciprocal relationship here, however. This relationship shows that while knowledge is necessary to drive the construction of the data mining model, this model, in turn, can be used to supplement and reinforce the knowledge that drives the construction of the model. Specifically, the model may show exactly which customers under what circumstances, as derived from an examination of the data, are most likely to defect and, therefore, which specific interventions are most appropriate to retain them.

A general, unified view of business intelligence, data mining, and knowledge management is shown in Figure 7.1. Here we can see that knowledge can be derived empirically from data sources or experientially through human experience. This distinction between empirically based knowledge and experientially based knowledge is often referred to as explicit versus implicit, or tacit, knowledge in knowledge management literature. Table 7.1 presents a comparison of the differences between implicit and tacit knowledge.

7.1   The role of implicit and explicit knowledge

Regardless of the source of the knowledge, in the context of the enterprise, the role of knowledge is to secure successful outcomes that are consistent with the enterprise goals and objectives. Note that there is a reciprocal relationship between empirically and experientially derived knowledge: experiential knowledge is necessary for successful empirical data analysis;

empirical data can be used to verify, validate, refine, and extend experiential notions. Clearly, the successful enterprises of the future will possess a well-orchestrated and tightly integrated knowledge management framework that will contain both empirical and experiential components. Microsoft has constructed a toolkit to enable the construction of this vision. This tool kit and the knowledge management (experiential) components of the framework that supports this vision are discussed in the pages that follow.

7.2   A primer on knowledge management

So far we have seen that knowledge management (KM) can be seen as an emerging set of strategies and approaches to capture, organize and deploy a wide range of knowledge assets so as to ensure that these assets can be used to move the enterprise to more favorable outcomes that are consistent with its goals and objectives.

Two primary paradigms for KM have emerged over the recent past:

1.   Codification: tools are very important here

2.   Noncodification: this is more of a community of practice

The difference between the two paradigms is discussed in an article in the March-April 1999 *Harvard Business Review* by Hansen, et al.:

The rise of the computer and the increasing importance of intellectual assets have compelled executives to examine the knowledge underlying their businesses and how it is used. Because KM as a conscious practice is so young, however, executives have lacked models to use as guides.

To help fill that gap, the authors recently studied KM practices at management consulting firms, health care providers, and computer manufacturers. They found two very different KM strategies in place.

In companies that sell relatively standardized products that fill common needs, knowledge is carefully codified and stored in databases, where it can be accessed and used—over and over again—by anyone in the organization. The authors call this the codification strategy. In companies that provide highly customized solutions to unique problems, knowledge is shared mainly through person-to-person contacts; the chief purpose of computers is to help people communicate. They call this the personalization strategy.

A company's choice of KM strategy is not arbitrary—it must be driven by the company's competitive strategy. Emphasizing the wrong approach or trying to pursue both can quickly undermine a business. The authors warn that KM should not be isolated in a functional department like HR or IT. They emphasize that the benefits are greatest—to both the company and its customers—when a CEO and other general managers actively choose one of the approaches as a primary strategy.

Clearly, the approach that is most amenable to a technological solution is the codification approach rather than the personalization approach.

7.2.1   Components of the knowledge management framework

The most important component of the KM framework is the underlying process itself. The first step in the management process is the discovery of knowledge. KM must then provide for the organization, planning, scheduling, and deployment of the knowledge through the enterprise. Finally, the deployment must be monitored, adjustments made where necessary and, ultimately, new knowledge must be discovered. This gives rise to the KM triangle. Knowledge discovery is at the apex of the triangle—it is the beginning and end point of KM. Once again this reiterates and reinforces the intimate link between the KM and the knowledge discovery missions.

This triangle, illustrated in Figure 7.2, is the underlying process model for all KM operations in the enterprise. It can be seen here that, while technology is a key enabler to the design, development, and implementation of a KM process, it is not the process itself. So, as with any other area of IT enablement, technology in and of itself will not produce a successful KM system.

Two other triangles are important in the description of the KM framework: enablers and knowledge stores. Enablers include culture, technology, and performance measurement to provide leadership in KM, the technol-

Figure 7.2
Components of the knowledge management process

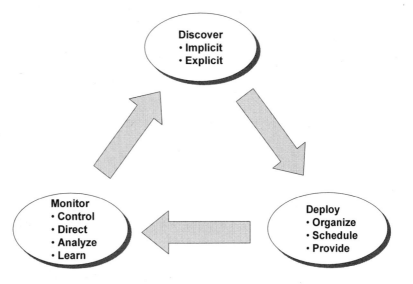

Figure 7.3
*Critical enablers of
knowledge
management*

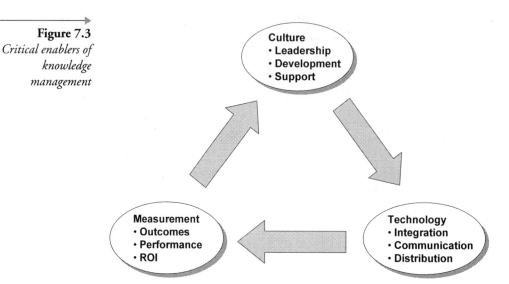

ogy necessary to carry it out, and continuous monitoring and feedback to ensure that the framework grows and evolves over time with incremental refinements and improvements. This triangle is presented in Figure 7.3.

The third component to the KM framework consists of the knowledge stores that need to be built to support the KM framework. There are many ways to organize and store knowledge. It is useful to organize knowledge in the form of people, processes, and technology. Any given enterprise out-

Figure 7.4
*Key organizational
dimensions for
knowledge stores*

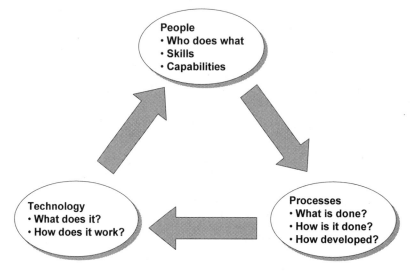

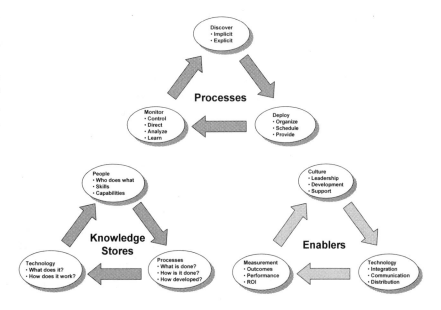

Figure 7.5
Component alignments necessary for successful knowledge management

come will critically depend on the organization and orchestration of these three capabilities so it is useful to align outcomes and the knowledge necessary to attain them along these dimensions.

Taken together, these three triangles form the core components of an effective KM framework. As shown in Figure 7.5 it is the alignment of these three sets of components that constitutes a successful architecture for the components of a KM framework.

7.2.2   Key knowledge management functionalities[2]

- Gather: Capture information from important sources in a common repository—together with its location—so it can be deployed through the group memory

- Organize: Profile the information in the repository, organize it in meaningful ways for navigating and searching, and enable pieces of information to be related to other pieces of information.

- Distribute/deliver: Harvest or acquire knowledge through an active mechanism (search interface) or a passive mechanism (push).

- Collaborate: Collaborate through messaging, workflow, discussion databases and so on.

---

2.   Adapted from Doculab's Special Report on KM Products, April 2000.

- Teach/learn: Promote distance learning.

- Analyze/refine: Analyze information in the knowledge repository (use data mining to identify relationships or patterns).

- Publish: Publish information to a broader audience, including individuals outside the organization.

- Life cycle management: Securely store, migrate, and purge information according to a set schedule.

- Mediate: Manage knowledge workers' time.

7.2.3   Delivery Architectures for Success

Many alternative architectures are possible to implement this framework. One general architecture is shown in Figure 7.6. As shown in the diagram, both implicit (empirical) knowledge and tacit (experiential) knowledge is provided for in the architecture. The data warehouse and empirical data collectors are key components to the empirical knowledge discovery, whereas communities of shared interest and technology watch agents—people who are specifically assigned this responsibility—are critical components to the knowledge network and knowledge dissemination components of the tacit (experiential) management of knowledge.

Figure 7.6
General architecture for the implementation of a knowledge management framework

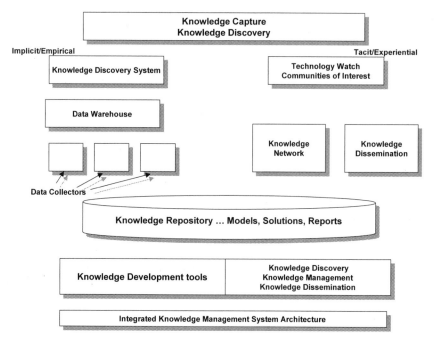

A knowledge repository (potentially multiple knowledge repositories) and knowledge development tools for the discovery and management of both implicit and tacit knowledge complete the picture of the required components as presented here.

7.2.4 Building a knowledge management system

Many approaches have been suggested for undertaking a KM project. The APQC has evolved a trademarked implementation methodology, described in the American Productivity and Quality Center's Road Map to Knowledge Management Results: Stages of Implementation™, that consists of the following stages:

Stage 1: Getting Started

- Define KM in terms people can relate to
- Identify others to join the cause
- Look for windows of opportunity
- Capitalize on the technology
- Create a compelling picture
- Know your own corporate history

Stage 2: Explore and Experiment

- Form a cross functional KM task force
- Select pilots or identify current grass roots efforts
- Find resources to support the pilots

Stage 3: Pilots and KM Initiatives

- Fund the Pilots
- Develop methodologies
- Capture lessons learned
- Land the results

Stage 4: Expand and Support

- Develop an expansion strategy
- Allocate resources

- Communicate and market the strategy

- Manage growth and control chaos

Stage 5: Institutionalize KM

- Embed KM in the business model

- Realign the organization structure and budget

- Monitor the health of KM

- Align rewards and performance evaluation

- Balance a common framework with local control

- Continue the journey

For a thorough review of the APQC process, consult the APQC road-map document by O'Dell et al., *Stages of Implementation* (see references or http://www.apqc.org). A brief review and interpretation of the various stages is provided below. This provides and opportunity to explore the content of some of the activities and considerations that may be appropriate for each of the stages.

Stage 1: Getting started

Overcome obstacles

According to the APQC there are six major obstacles to KM projects. Notice that the most prevalent obstacle is the continued existence of functional silos—and the associated myopic views—that are still prevalent in today's enterprise. It is best to recognize this at the outset and to provide for activities to build bridges and to show the benefits of cross-silo activities.

Define KM in terms people can relate to

It may prove helpful in this area to be aware of the various kinds of processes that are practiced by the enterprise and to structure the KM mission around the improvement—efficiency or profitability—of the affected processes. In this way, the KM mission is promoted in terms that are relevant to the stakeholders.

It may prove useful, from the outset, to adopt a process classification framework as a useful device for identifying the various process touch points that will be mediated by the KM project. This will enable the KM team to promote the project in terms that are relevant to the effected parts of the organization. Further, by adopting the process classification frame-

Table 7.2   *Obstacles to Knowledge Management Projects*

Obstacle	Percentage of cases
Functional silos	52%
Financial support	28%
Cynicism toward fads	12%
Internal politics	8%
Competitive pressures	4%

work at the outset, the project will be able to subsequently use it as a means of capturing and organizing information that is relevant to the various organizational touch points.

A general scheme developed by the APQC, a number of its members, and Arthur Andersen, called the Process Classification Framework is presented in Figure 7.7.

Some organizations, such as Texas Instruments (TI), a leader in the KM community, use multiple process classification frameworks. For example, TI uses a framework based on quality criteria derived from the Baldridge Award. TI also searches for excellence in each of the three areas of the disci-

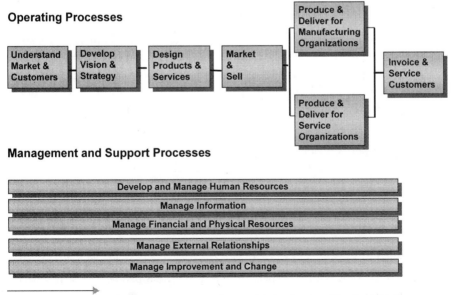

Figure 7.7   *Process classification framework (as developed by the APQC)*

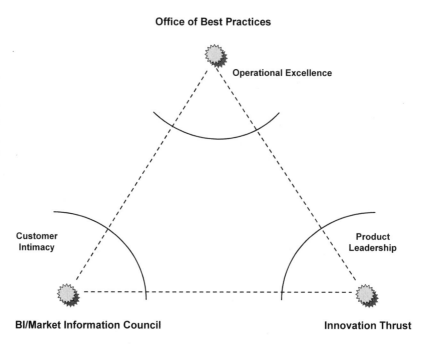

Figure 7.8
Texas Instruments knowledge management methodology oriented around Treacy and Wiersma market disciplines model

pline of market leaders developed by Treacy and Wiersma, first introduced here in Chapter 2. The TI-BEST methodology is oriented around the three areas of excellence as demonstrated in Figure 7.8.

Identify others to join the cause

Two of the most important aspects of this step are to secure executive sponsorship and to engage any task facilitators who will work throughout the project. KM may survive as a "skunkworks" project in the early days, but eventually it will be necessary to secure executive sponsorship in order to have the necessary enterprisewide implementation that is necessary to focus knowledge in the production of success. This step is vital.

Facilitators go by many names: knowledge gatekeepers, points of contact, and so on. Whatever they are called, their job is to maintain the KM system to avoid "knowledge junkyards" and to ensure that the system remains demand-driven.

It is normal to identify these facilitators on knowledge maps or knowledge yellow pages so that they can assist in the transfer of tacit knowledge through person-to-person exchanges in communities of practice or informal meeting. This is often a part-time job for these people; however, the job needs to get done so it must be budgeted and accounted for.

Look for windows of opportunity

A good point of departure is to learn from what others have done before. One of the best tools for carrying this out is to use the Arthur Andersen/ American Productivity and Quality Center (AA/APQC) external KM Assessment Tool (KMAT) to develop a snapshot of enterprise readiness for initiating KM. The tool captures readiness assessments in each of five sections that cover leadership, culture, technology, measurement, and process. The KMAT was developed with the participation of 20 organizations who formed working groups in the development of the assessment materials and scoring methods. Currently, more than 100 companies participate in the benchmark group that serves as a reference for the development of the assessment metrics.

The Leadership section contains questions on the role of knowledge in the organization, the revenue-generating possibilities in knowledge, the support of core competencies and the treatment of individuals with respect to their value in terms of the management of knowledge.

Other sections proceed in a similar fashion: Culture addresses the climate for KM along several dimensions; technological readiness and orientation towards the management of knowledge is assessed; the organization's ability to measure and improve results is assessed; and the KM processes that are currently in place are assessed. KM processes include gap analysis; intelligence-gathering; involvement of all organizational members; the presence of a formalized best practices process; and the processes in place to establish value for tacit knowledge.

More information on the KMAT and the APQC is available at http:// www.apqc.org/.

Capitalize on the technology

Technology is an important enabler. However, technology alone cannot ensure the success of KM in the enterprise. For KM processes to succeed, they must attain critical mass. This means that the systems must be able to attract users. Creators of the KM system must fill it with content and value. And the content and value needs to be available on demand. This approach requires pull technologies, in which the user specifies what is to be delivered, rather than push technologies or laissez-faire technologies (here the assumption is that if you let users know about the content they will seek it out). Pull systems promote more creativity, but they are chaotic unless there is shared understanding of what is important. Push systems may be appropriate were there is a shared agreement that a particular approach is superior to all others and that it should be adopted immediately.

Our experience with artificial intelligence has shown that the capture and execution of knowledge in software is an exceptionally difficult thing to do. So, in the context of KM, while technology can empower solutions that are based on a generally sound KM framework it cannot solve the complex requirements of a KM solution until further advances (e.g., current advances in case based reasoning) are made. For a more general viewpoint on this discussion see "The Road Ahead for Knowledge Management: An AI Perspective" by Reid G. Smith and Adam Farquhar.

Although Groupware products such as Lotus Notes and Grapevine originally formed the underpinnings of a good KM infrastructure there are now many more elements that constitute good technological practice in the KM area. Of course, the most pervasive technology is the Web and, more frequently, the Web-derived concept of the enterprise information portal (EIP). The EIP takes advantage of the ubiquity of the Web and its familiarity as a common denominator for effective retrieval and communication of information regardless of the location or status of the user (in the article noted above the wireless access to Web content in rural and otherwise inaccessible locations was cited as important support for a Web-based implementation of the KM solution). Internet and Intranet technologies have been a catalyst for the adoption of KM, especially for a pull approach because it is easier for individuals to find knowledge and peers with shared interests in a Web environment.

An extremely wide range of KM technologies are available and potentially appropriate. A comprehensive review of KM technology and solution vendors is provided in Appendix E. Microsoft KM Product Management has suggested the following evaluation criteria for selecting KM technologies:

1.   Desktop services

   ▪ Easy to use productivity suites that are integrated in all other desktop services

   ▪ Comfortable e-mail systems that support collaborative services such as shared calendars, tasks, contacts, and team-based discussions

   ▪ Web browser for browsing and presenting the documents to the user

   ▪ Simple search functionalities, like OS-integrated file search services or application-integrated search services (e.g., e-mail, discussion)

2.   Application Services

- Collaboration services with a multipurpose database for capturing the collaborative data

- Web services for providing the access layer to documented knowledge

- Indexing services for full text search of documents

3.   Operating system (OS) services

- Well-organized central storage locations like file, Web servers, and document databases

Create a compelling picture

A critical step in an enterprise's KM strategy is the identification of the value proposition that mediates the translation of its mission statement (goals and objectives) into favorable outcomes. The most powerful outcomes are achieved when the KM strategy is aligned with the enterprise value proposition.

The APQC has identified five major KM strategies:

1.   KM as a business strategy

2.   Innovation and knowledge creation

3.   Transfer of knowledge and best practices

4.   Intellectual asset management

5.   Personal responsibility for knowledge

The alignment of KM strategy with value propositions can best be illustrated by example. Perhaps the need for KM is greatest in a consulting organization where the key to business success lies in the cost-effective delivery of knowledge.

PricewaterhouseCoopers, along with the other "Big Five" consulting organizations, was faced with the need to construct and deliver a KM solution in the very early stages of the development of KM frameworks. They identified "innovation and knowledge creation" as the foundation KM strategy to support their value proposition. This proposition stated that innovation was central to business success. The competitive value of the firm was a function of the organization's innovative culture and its ability to develop unique knowledge and expertise that could differentiate it from competitors. They determined to systematically learn from their experience

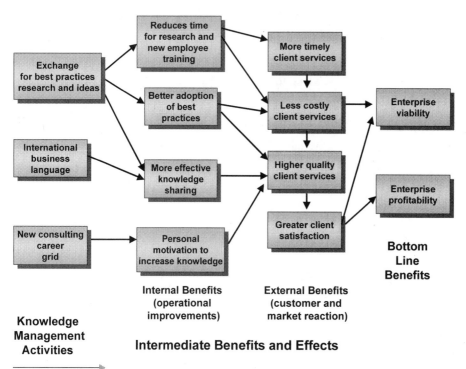

Knowledge
Management
Activities

Intermediate Benefits and Effects

Figure 7.9   *Example implementation scenario to align knowledge management strategy with value proposition*

in the field and to continuously create new knowledge in order to embed that knowledge in products and services.

The components of their KM strategy implementation, together with an illustration of the intermediate benefits and bottom line results, is presented in Figure 7.9.

Know your own corporate history

In all likelihood the enterprise will not have a culture that rewards KM. The enterprise will have to establish or amend its incentives and reward structure to promote knowledge sharing and skills transfer. This cultural change needs to be fostered with reference to what has happened in the past, why it happened and how it could be improved. The central question is "How can people be motivated and rewarded for knowledge discovery and sharing?"

Leadership must recognize excellence and best practices once the incentives are in place. This leadership and recognition will need to be reinforced continuously over a period of time until the new culture takes hold. Managers should inquire about the kind of learning that is going on, and what and how people are learning and sharing on a continuous basis.

Stage 2: Explore and experiment

Form a cross-functional KM task force

As indicated in Stage 1, one of the most prevalent obstacles to success lies in the area of functional silos and associated narrow visions and politics. A powerful way of overcoming this obstacle is through the development of a cross functional KM task force. The task force can be drawn from the communities of practice (CoP) or subject matter experts who are identified in the project.

The development and interplay between CoPs and the task force and among the CoPs themselves is central to the success of the KM initiative. The CoPs are sometimes referred to as knowledge networks, centers of excellence, knowledge ecologies, knowledge networks, and so on. Regardless of what it is called, the CoP can be considered the fundamental building block of a KM system.

The form of the CoP and its linkages should be based on pull technologies rather than push technologies. It is important to create mechanisms that enable practitioners to reach out to one another. Dixon (2000) provides a good overview of the lessons learned and organizational approaches used in the recent history of CoPs at such companies as Hewlett-Packard, Chevron, Lucent, and consulting organizations in the Big Five.

Select pilots or identify current grass roots efforts

A number of success-leaning criteria for the selection of pilots may be identified:

- The pilot issue must be important to the business
- Success in the pilot would lead to demonstrable results
- There may be an existing champion who has resources
- Pilot outcomes may be transferable to other situations
- The pilot serves as a valid test of KM principles
- The pilot will facilitate the sharing of lessons learned

Find resources to support the pilots

It will be useful to have executive sponsorship to assist in finding resources. It may be possible to borrow or sequester a resource for a given period of time, subject to some kind of midcourse review.

Stage 3: Pilots and KM initiatives

Fund the pilots

If the KM project can be framed in the context of new initiatives, then successful funding will be more likely. It may be necessary to review the return on investment of other similar KM activities to derive some measure of the likely outcome of a funding effort.

Develop methodologies

A number of important methodologies have emerged out of the experience of the APQC and others:

- CoPs
- Portals and digital dashboards
- Documents
- Yellow pages
- Templates, tools, and presentations
- CBL
- Performance support systems
- Collaborative technologies
- Workflow applications

Capture lessons learned

This is the step that closes the loop on the overall discovery, or deployment, monitor process. Moreover, as markets and enabling conditions in the enterprise change, it is a continuously advancing process. To paraphrase, KM is a journey, not a destination. Here are some of the evaluation points that could serve as the basis for the lessons-learned process:

- *KM Databases.* Observe health indicators of the knowledge base, update frequency and content usage. A skills database (e.g., a yellow pages of available skill sets) is also useful.

- *Terminology.* Keep terminology relevant and current and shared. Develop a common vocabulary and methodology.

- *Focus.* Reassess and reevaluate the focus. Establish, promote, and publicize relevant communities of practice.

- *Alignment.* Ensure that individual's goals and enterprise goals are complementary.

- *Support.* Refine support resources: coaching, tools, processes, advice, references, and training options. Reassess the KM hot line.

- *Account for cost.* People need time to learn the KM process. Account for the cost and, moving forward, attack high-cost areas to find new efficiencies.

- *Content.* Move to make every employee a producer/publisher as soon as possible. Develop and deploy common content authoring and publishing templates to facilitate the production and publication of knowledge.

- *Tacit knowledge transfer.* Tacit knowledge is hard to capture and exchange. Look to the effectiveness of communities of practice; peer assist processes; after action reviews; share fairs; lunch and learns and face-to-face meetings.

- *Common systems.* Find out which common systems work and which ones don't. Examples include common operating systems, and both front office and back office productivity tools to enable easy internal exchange.

Land the results

Measurement provides the empirical validation component of the monitoring step of the overall implementation process and provides a valid, objectively verifiable means of driving the results home. Measurement will help you determine how much you have accomplished over what period of time.

Studies conducted by APQC indicate that, on average, it takes more than two years to implement a best practice. Measurement is important to establish perspective over a longer period of time and to ensure that the momentum carries forward regardless of slips and slides in the implementation plan along the way.

Typical measurements include:

- Measures of the recency, frequency and duration of system use (e.g., use of the knowledge base; number or searches and queries per session)

- Satisfaction metrics (can be collected though customer satisfaction surveys)

- Corroborative measures in terms of customer outcomes, satisfaction, and service records

- Involvement metrics and self assessments

- Cycle time to process implementation completion

The CoPs that have been established during the project are the lever for KM follow-on and expansion. Pilot participants become the core team and advocates for future projects.

Stage 4: Expand and support

Develop an expansion strategy

The cross-functional make-up of the initial KM activity will be able to point to many areas of pain in the various constituent business process areas. It is useful to identify the various pains and to try to understand how building from the existing KM products will produce outcomes that are favorable to pain reduction and revenue generation.

Allocate resources

A number of important lessons relate to the allocation of resources:

- Budgets need to be substantial and must involve a significant reallocation of time and money or the identification of new money.

- Studies conducted by the APQC indicates that 60% of the APQC KM partners spend in excess of $1 million on KM initiatives.

- Resources to successfully support KM initiatives must also be developed and budgeted.

- An active central, cross-functional task force can help alleviate confusions and missteps

Communicate and market the strategy

There are a variety of ways to promote the results:

- Conduct awareness sessions

- Roll out special communications

- Populate Web pages and the KM portal

- Encourage favorable executive behavior

Manage growth and control chaos

An effective way to manage is through a KM coordination team. This team is most likely a cross-functional team and handles such tasks as the following:

- Coordination

- Gets leverage from lessons learned

- Provides strategic direction

- Creates a matrix, not a direct reporting, relationship

Stage 5: Institutionalize KM

Embed KM in the business model

By now there are a number of examples of where KM results have been successfully embedded in the business model of the host enterprise:

- Chevron was able to permanently reduce costs

- World Bank uses incremental knowledge to work toward reducing poverty

- Xerox has a share of the knowledge through documents ethic and has the results to show how to do it

- Siemens has built an approach that enables it to support all its knowledge-intensive businesses

Realign the organization structure and budget

Going forward, it will be necessary for the enterprise to provide for KM leadership and core group of KM enabled resources such as:

- KM professional services consisting of library and information specialists, document management specialists, communications specialists, and trainers

- Associated information technology and infrastructure including applications development, training, an IT help desk, Web standards documents, and Web support

The KM core function will be accountable for:

- Strategy development
- Templates and methodologies
- Identifying and addressing deployment issues
- Identifying IT needs
- Resources
- KM communication and promotion

Monitor the health of KM

A number of assessment services can be identified, quite possibly as a follow-on to the initial KMAT, if this was included in the KM plan:

- CoP assessments
- KM maturity/capability assessments
- Employee surveys
- Focus groups

Align rewards and performance evaluation

There are many benefits to reward or performance alignment since it can contribute to an understanding of the value of knowledge sharing. This, in turn, will reinforce the commitment to contribute to sharing and will ultimately contribute to the creation of a rewarding environment.

Some measures to consider going into the project:

- Activity and access
- Participation
- Perceived usefulness
- Success stories

Some post-project evaluation measures to consider:

- Business results: quality, cost, and cycle time
- Measures such as those experienced by the World Bank, which experienced a major change, in its 1999 performance appraisal rating

- Measures such as those used by HP Consulting, which has developed an evaluation of consultants

Balance a common framework with local control

This is a variation of "think globally, act locally." Not all business processes, nor all elements of a given process, will survive implementation in a localized setting. The probability of adoption at the local level is greatly facilitated by local input and responsibility for the implementation.

Continue the journey

There are some important lessons learned that contribute to the healthy, long-term development of KM in the enterprise:

- Stage 5 requires adoption of KM as enabling the organization strategy or mission

- The organization structure will change to fit the new way of working

- KM is not a "way we work" until it is part of the performance appraisal system

- Stage 5 is a journey, not a destination

7.3   The Microsoft technology-enabling framework

In most respects the KM technology framework that has been developed by Microsoft is more advanced than the framework that has been developed for business intelligence and data mining. This is because KM is more encompassing and touches upon all but the most routine and highly automated enterprise processes. In the development of their approach to KM, Microsoft product managers have proposed an evolutionary process, which is described in Figure 7.10.

A shown in the figure, KM is conceived of as rising through a series of capabilities as follows:

- Messaging and collaboration

- Development of a complete intranet

- Development of subscription and notification services

- Real-time collaboration

- Development of a metadata-driven repository

- Document management

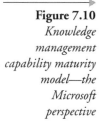

Figure 7.10
Knowledge management capability maturity model—the Microsoft perspective

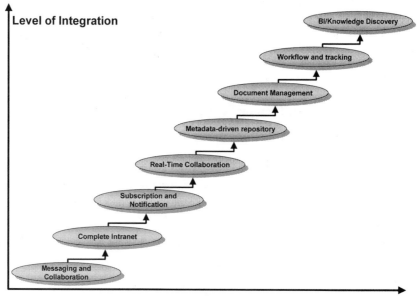

- Workflow and tracking
- Business intelligence and knowledge discovery

The capability maturity model approach suggests that each of the steps are necessary conditions to the development of a technological support infrastructure for KM. The model suggests a logical order of technological introduction so that as more capability is introduced it builds on earlier steps. Full capability is attained with successive levels of integration of associated components.

As shown in Figure 7.11, the infrastructure components that are provided by Microsoft may be grouped into three levels consisting of:

1. *Desktop services.* The desktop services are supported by technologies such as Windows 9x, NT, and 2000. Such products as Office 2000 and Outlook 2000 may be included here as well.

2. *Development services.* Development services include SQL Server, Site Server, Exchange Server, Internet Information Server, Index Server, Search Server as well as Visual Studio and Microsoft Back Office. Back Office contains facilities to set up an Intranet Publishing Server and Intranet Collaboration Server and a Branch Office Server.

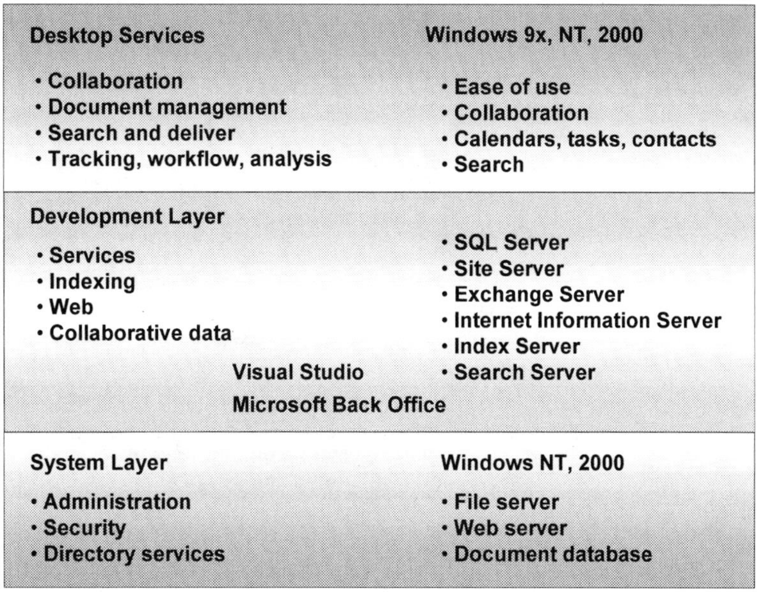

Figure 7.11
Layers in the Microsoft knowledge management technology infrastructure

Desktop Services	Windows 9x, NT, 2000
• Collaboration • Document management • Search and deliver • Tracking, workflow, analysis	• Ease of use • Collaboration • Calendars, tasks, contacts • Search
Development Layer	
• Services • Indexing • Web • Collaborative data Visual Studio Microsoft Back Office	• SQL Server • Site Server • Exchange Server • Internet Information Server • Index Server • Search Server
System Layer	**Windows NT, 2000**
• Administration • Security • Directory services	• File server • Web server • Document database

3. *Systems layer.* The System layer provides access to system level services, such as those performed by Windows NT and 2000.

Intranet Publishing Server provides a complete intranet site as a departmental solution to enable communication among workers, the publishing of documents (in Customizable Document Libraries), the creation of Team Workspaces. This facility can run full text searches against the documents and can be used to build an intranet directory.

The Intranet Collaboration Server extends the Intranet Publishing Server with further collaborative functions like threaded discussions and team and events calendars. It also enables enterprisewide collaboration.

The Branch Office Server connects the Microsoft BackOffice Server to a corporate network and enables central administration and intranet/Internet access for its network client.

7.3.1 Critical functions and enablers

Effective technological support for KM includes facilitators to create and access knowledge. These facilitators are grouped by Microsoft into eight categories, as shown in Figure 7.12.

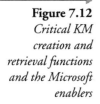

Figure 7.12
*Critical KM
creation and
retrieval functions
and the Microsoft
enablers*

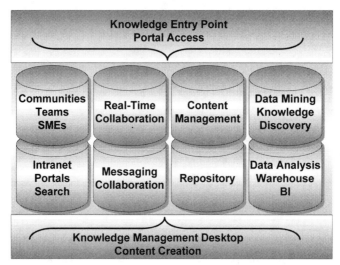

Portals and search

Portals and search facilities provide the means of accessing potentially large collections of KM objects. Typical portal objects include:

- Important enterprise and team links

- Team applications links

- Incoming mail notifications and headers

- Personal tasks

- Enterprise search

- Integration with BI data

    The requirements of an effective portal and search system include:

- Personalization systems that allow customization

- Web browsers with personalization systems that include access to Desktop services like e-mail, collaboration data and BI tools

- Catalog and search services

- Services to build a virtual single storage that combines all catalogs

- Notification services

- Database replication and transformation services

Messaging and collaboration

Messaging and collaboration enables the sharing of thoughts, ideas, and documents coupled with efficient search and retrieval techniques to find this information. Typical components of messaging and collaboration include:

- Productivity suites

- E-mail systems

- Web browsers

- Simple search

- Collaboration services and databases

- Web access to documented knowledge

- Indexing services for full text search

- Organized, central storage of file, Web, and document databases

KM technologies for real-time collaboration and multimedia content include:

- Chat services with transcript functionality for distance discussions

- Video conferencing for virtual meetings

- Screen sharing services for sharing of the document creation process, virtual whiteboards, and application sharing

- Streaming media services for recording virtual meetings and video meeting on domain services

- Event and meeting databases for organizing the virtual event center

Communities, teams, and experts

Support for communities, teams and experts enables the sharing of knowledge developed through collaboration and document-based knowledge sources and contributes to building to higher levels of access and integration, often through successive levels of input from a wide audience. Communities are interest driven and teams are task driven. Subject matter experts (SMEs) are functional or domain experts.

Requirements of technologies in this area include:

- Establish directory and membership services that support the building of communities through grouping people together into expert teams working on the same set of information or having the same needs and interests in specific information

- Use forum services to create workspaces for communities and teams that contain all interest-related data

- Provide self-subscription services to specific matters of interest for dependent information delivery and subscribing

- Provide services to assign specific roles to knowledge workers

- Provide workflow services for automating processes based on roles and subject matter experts (SMEs)

- Provide dynamic e-mail distribution list services for automated subscription services

- Provide e-mail services for automating notification, routing, and simple workflow services

- Ensure enterprise databases integration; for example, ensure the integration of people skills and the human resources databases in order to facilitate community, team and experts information (as well as to search for this information)

- Provide home pages on Web servers for each community, team, or expert to speed up the access to knowledge sources

The repository

Microsoft's repository efforts have typically been concentrated in the activities of the Meta Data Coalition (MDC). The coalition was established to ally software vendors and users with a common purpose of driving forward the definition, implementation and ongoing evolution of a metadata interchange format standard and its support mechanisms.

As stated on the Web page (http://www.mdcinfo.com/), "… the need for such standards arises as metadata, or the information about the enterprise data emerges as a critical element in effective data … and knowledge *(author insert)* … management. Different tools, including data warehousing, distributed client/server computing, databases (relational, OLAP, OLTP, …), integrated enterprisewide applications, etc. … must be able to cooperate and make use of metadata generated by each other."

In September 2000 the MDC and the Object Management Group (OMG), two industry organizations with competing data warehousing standards, jointly announced that the MDC will merge into the OMG. As a result, the MDC discontinued independent operations and work will continue in the OMG to integrate the two standards. This development laid the groundwork for the development of a common set of standards and metadata approaches to record, capture, organize, and deliver knowledge in metadata format through such repository devices as the Meta Object Facility (MOF).

Microsoft repository technologies include:

- Microsoft Office 2000, FrontPage, Visual InterDev, and XML Notepad for the creation of XML-based documents and data, or to extend existing documents with XML tags

- Microsoft Internet Explorer or XML parser to process XML-based data

- Microsoft Site Server Tag Tool to apply tags to HTML document to categorize them. Site Server Search will use these tags to gather and catalog these documents

- Site Server can also be used to integrate analysis services in the knowledge management system

- Site server analysis functions can be used for analyzing both the usage and content of the KM system

- Site Server voting components can be used to track the quality of the KM information

Content management

Content management enables the consolidation of information from various sources into a well-organized knowledge base. Typically this component consists of a knowledge framework, which in turn is based on a flexible knowledge taxonomy, that is grounded in a metadata framework that is held in the repository.

The required operations of a content management capability include:

- Retrievals from heterogeneous sources

- Listing and browsing

- Sorting

- Grouping

- Filtering

- Searching

- Publishing of information to the knowledge base

Table 7.3　*Content Store Technology/Function Capabilities*

	Publishing Based on Metadata	Rich Views–Based Metadata	Subscription and Notification Services	Approval and Workflow Processes	Check In/Check Out Mechanisms	Versioning Mechanism
Windows File System	strong	weak	medium	weak	none	none
Exchange Server	strong	very strong	strong	medium	medium	weak
SQL Server	weak	strong	strong	very strong	medium	weak

Document content stores may be found in the Windows File System, Exchange Server, SQL Server and in external sources accessible through DTS.

Functions of content management may include:

- Publishing based on metadata

- Rich views based metadata

- Subscription and notification services

- Approval and workflow processes

- Check in/check out mechanisms

- Versioning mechanism

Table 7.3 outlines the level of capability in the current Microsoft content management environment.

Putting it all together: an example application

The rich KM infrastructure that has been described here is capable of supporting a wide range of KM implementations. Indeed, Appendix F, "Summary of KM Case Studies," presents about 100 case study descriptions that describe a range of applications—from collaboration, to knowledge base access, to e-business—in a range of industries spanning manufacturing, pharmaceuticals, communications and finance.

Figure 7.13 provides a brief example that demonstrates how the technology roadmap outlined here can be used to build a KM application.

The task of this example is to extend the knowledge base descriptions of enterprise people skills and publish this indexed and searchable information on the enterprise knowledge base. The process begins by starting up Microsoft Exchange Server. Scan the Global Address List looking for

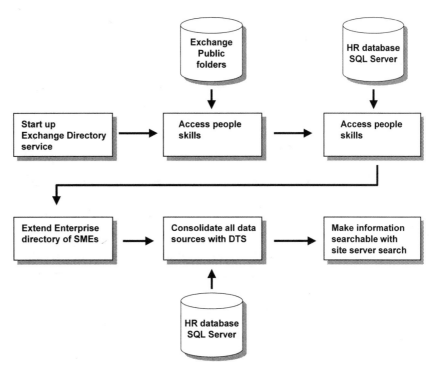

Figure 7.13
Example process description of a knowledge management application

expert's information that matches Outlook Contacts Forms with descriptions of people skills data. The retrieved features can be used to create new, enriched expert descriptions in the Exchange Public folders. Alternatively, use the Human Resources database in SQL Server form, for example.

From here, use SQL Server Data Transformation Services to consolidate the existing people skills data in Exchange Public Folders or, alternatively, in a consolidated SQL Server database of skills information. Microsoft Site Server Search can be used to make this information searchable in either the Exchange Public Folder form or in SQL Server form.

Other examples are provided in a number of documents that are available from the Microsoft Web Site and Microsoft TechNet. These documents include:

- A Way to KM Solutions

- Every Intranet Project Starts Somewhere and the Best Ones Never End (from *CIO Magazine*)

- Implementing Search in the Enterprise—Large and Small

- Integrating Microsoft Site Server Search with Microsoft Exchange

- Getting the Most Out of Site Server Knowledge Manager
- Site Server Personalization and Membership Tutorial
- Microsoft Site Server Deployment Guide
- Microsoft BackOffice Integration with Microsoft Office 2000
- Extending Microsoft Office 2000
- Microsoft Office 97 and the Intranet
- Microsoft Office 2000 Product Enhancements Guide
- Accessing Heterogeneous Data with SQL Server 7.0
- Developing with Microsoft English Query with SQL Server 7.0
- Building and Managing Document-Based Intranets
- Using Microsoft FrontPage to Create and Manage an Intranet
- Microsoft FrontPage 2000
- Using NetMeeting 2.1 on Intranet Web Pages
- Microsoft NetShow Provides Key Intranet Solutions
- Hosting Multiple User Communities with a Membership Directory

7.4   Summary

The Microsoft Technological components for a KM framework are obviously comprehensive and multifaceted. Figure 7.14 presents a summary overview of the various KM functions with an indication of the dependence on Microsoft technologies, as indicated in the figure.

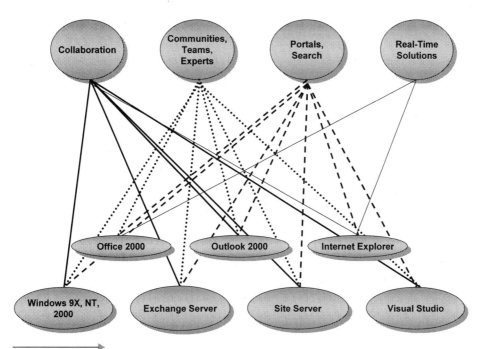

Figure 7.14 *A roadmap of knowledge management functions and associated Microsoft technologies*

A detailed description of the connections between the various functions and the associated Microsoft technology is contained in Table 7.4.

Table 7.4　*Detailed Knowledge Management Function—Microsoft Enabling Technology Cross-Referenece*

Component or Subcomponent	Collaboration	Communities, Teams, Experts	Portals and Search	Real-Time KM Solutions
Office 2000		Server extensions for notification services based on subscription to Office documents	Web folders. Access through HTTP/WebDAV	
PowerPoint				Presentation broadcasts
NetMeeting				For video conferencing, document, and application services and whiteboard functionality
Outlook 2000	Calendars, tasks, discussions	Team activity tracking		
View control			Portal search with dynamic data	
Web components	Coworkers can store all Office documents on Web servers		Portal search with dynamic data	Integration with Net-meeting conferencing software and NetShow
Windows 9X, NT, 2000 Desktop	Heterogeneous data access via IE			
Windows NT, 2000 Server		Database of skills		
DTS		Use DTS to consolidated skills and HR information from relationship databases and deliver to Exchange Public folders or SQL Server database	Build central repository for information related to specific business tasks	

Table 7.4 *Detailed Knowledge Management Function—Microsoft Enabling Technology Cross-Referenece (continued)*

Component or Subcomponent	Collaboration	Communities, Teams, Experts	Portals and Search	Real-Time KM Solutions
Internet Information Server/ HTTP	Document file system URL, directory services, file servers, home pages Use ASPs and com to access common data sources over the Web	Access to skills database	Use ASP to access roles and responsibility data	
Index Server	Full-text search			
Exchange Server	Exchange Directory Service to build enterprise directory (skills, resources)	Team activity tracking	E-mail notification	
	Exchange Public folders IMAP/NNTP/HTTP Multipurpose database	Assign discussion moderators Use DTC and CDO to access forum data in Exchange Public folders		
Chat Services			Chat services and tran-scripts	
Internet Explorer	Information Broker		Dynamic HTML (DHTML) for portal interfaces	
Microsoft Site Server				
Site Server Search	SQL database/Exchange folder search		Build full-text retrieval system	

Table 7.4 *Detailed Knowledge Management Function—Microsoft Enabling Technology Cross-Referenece (continued)*

Component or Subcomponent	Collaboration	Communities, Teams, Experts	Portals and Search	Real-Time KM Solutions
Personalization services		Build communities, Site Server search, knowledge briefs, notification	Personalization (e.g., KM portal)	
Knowledge Manager			Build shared knowledge briefs (searches against Site Server 3.0 catalogs) Make accessible on the KM Portal	
Microsoft NetShow Server and Content Editing Tools				Recording, broadcasting, and multicasting of online events and meta-data content tagging tools
Visual Studio	HTML and ASPs (use Design Time controls) Use Active Directory Service (ADSI) to access Exchange Directory (alternative to LDAP APIs)	Build forum webs	Development of easy access to directory data	
Visual Interdev		Develop directory, forums and people skills data	Rich portals; search based on catalogs	
Microsoft FrontPage	Build home pages		Rich portals; search based on catalogs	

Glossary

ADO (active data objects) A set of programmable interfaces that Microsoft SQL Server communicates with.

Best practices According to the U.S. GSA Office of Government, best practices are good practices that have worked well elsewhere. They are proven and have produced successful results. The GSA has also developed a set of best practice principles and ways to identify, evaluate, and distribute best practices.

Business intelligence This is a term coined in 1994 by Howard Dresner, an analyst at the Gartner Group, to distinguish a form of analytical software that would cease to be the domain of specialized analysts but, rather, would be oriented to support the daily information processing functions of all business analysis and managerial users.

C5.0 A decision tree algorithm that uses an information gain statistic to provide a set a rules that describe the decisions. Developed by J. Ross Quinlan, it is a successor to the C4.5 and ID3 (Interactive Dichotimizer) algorithms.

CART (Classification and Regression Trees) An approach to developing decision trees. The approach results in binary trees with two branches or nodes at every decision point.

CHAID (Chi-Squared Automatic Interaction Detection) An approach to building decision trees whereby the branches of a node are determined through the application of the Chi-Squared text of significance. CHAID trees included both binary and multinode branches.

Classical statistics For example, multiple regression and logistic regression, these are statistical approaches that have been developed as a way of making sense out of observation made about the world, generally in the name of natural science or political science. Descriptive statistics give general information about observations—what are the average and median values, what are the observed errors, what is the distribution of values. Regression analysis refers to techniques used to interpolate and extrapolate these observations.

Classification models   Microsoft's term for outcome models.

Cluster detection   The automatic assignment of objects into similar groups.

Correlation   A statistical measure or the association (or co-relation) between two fields of data.

Customer relationship management   CRM is a strategy and set of associated processes and technological enablers to support effective optimization of the business to customer relationship throughout the entire customer life cycle of identification, recruitment, cultivation, and retirement.

Decision trees   A decision tree consists of nodes and branches, starting from a single root node. Each node represents a test or decision. Depending on the outcome of a decision, given by examining the branch attributes, a class assignment (or prediction) can be made.

Deming   Dr. W. Edwards Deming was a statistician and a student of Dr. Shewhart. His early career was spent teaching the application of statistical concepts and tools within industry. Later he developed a theory of management and profound knowledge. Deming was well known to the Japanese and their national award for quality management was named for him. He remained largely unknown in his native United States until he was "discovered" by the media in 1981. He continued to write and to deliver his four-day seminar (with the famous "red bead" experiment) until his death in 1990.

DTS (Data Transformation Services)   This is the major way that Microsoft SQL Server imports or exports data.

DTD   Document type definitions are structured formats that are used to describe SGML and XML documents.

EIPs (Enterprise information portals)   Or B2E systems, as they are sometimes known, provide relevant information and applications to the desktop staff inside the enterprise.

Genetic algorithms   This is a class of machine learning algorithms that is based on the theory of evolution.

HTML (Hypertext Markup Language) The language that has traditionally been used to create a Web page. It is used to format text in the document, to specify links to other documents and to describe the structure of the Web page. HTML may be used to display video, image, and sound.

ISV (Information System Vendors) Typically, an ISV takes a manufacturer's product as a building block to develop application- or industry-specific solutions.

Knowledge worker A term coined by Peter F. Drucker in a November 1994 article in Atlantic Monthly. In the article Drucker outlines the emerging role of knowledge and the knowledge worker in the creation of social and economic wealth and in the direction of policy.

Lift A number used to describe the increase in response from a target marketing application using a predictive model over the response rate that would be achieved if no model were used.

Link analysis Link analysis follows relationships between records to develop models based on patterns in the relationships.

Market basket analysis A form of clustering used for finding groups of items that tend to occur together in a transaction (or market basket).

Memory-based reasoning This is a directed data mining technique that uses known instances as a model to make predictions about unknown instances.

Model A general term to describe a conceptual representation of some phenomenon typically consisting of symbolic terms, factors, or constructs that may be rendered in language, pictures, or mathematical notation.

Moore's law The observation made in 1965 by Gordon Moore, co-founder of Intel, that the number of transistors per square inch on integrated circuits had doubled every year since the integrated circuit was invented. Moore predicted that this trend would continue for the foreseeable future. In subsequent years, the pace slowed down a bit, but data density has doubled approximately every 18 months, and this is the current definition of Moore's law, which Moore himself has blessed. Most experts, including Moore himself, expect Moore's law to hold for at least another two decades. Moore's second law is that the cost of production would double every generation.

Neural networks Learning algorithms that consist of multiple nodes that communicate through their connecting synapses. Neural networks imitate the structure of biological nervous systems.

OLAP (On-Line Analytical Processing)   This originally referred to the ability to analyze data in real time for decision making. The term now implies multidimensional reporting based on dimensional cubes.

Outcome models   A model with a target or outcome field or variable that is shown to be a function of one or more input or predictor fields or variables. Outcomes may be categorical (buy/no buy) or continuous (dollars spent, time spent). With categorical outcomes the models are called classification models and with continuous outcomes they are typically called regression models.

Outer join   A type of link between tables that returns every row of data from the tables that are associated with the link.

Over fitting   This is a situation where the pattern that is extracted from the data is specific or unique to that particular data set, and will not generalize well to novel data sets. The typical approach to guard against over fitting to split the pattern detection task into two phases: learn (or train) and test (or validate). In this fashion, any patterns that are identified in the first phase are confirmed, or validated, with a new data set so as to ensure that the pattern does not reflect specific idiosyncrasies of the training data set used in the first phase.

Pattern   A set of relationships between fields of data typically derived through statistical methods such as correlation analysis to show the associations in the set of relationships.

PMML (Predictive Model Markup Language)   An XML-based language that provides a quick and easy way for companies to define predictive models and share models between compliant vendors' applications. A PMML document provides a nonprocedural definition of fully trained or parameterized analytic models with sufficient information for an application to deploy them. By parsing the PMML using any standard XML parser the application can determine the types of data input to and output from the models, the detailed forms of the models, and how, in terms of standard data mining terminology, to interpret their results. Version 1.0 of the standard provides a small set of DTDs that specify the entities and attributes for documenting decision tree and multinomial logistic regression models. This is by no means a comprehensive set, and the expectation is that this standard will evolve very rapidly to cover a robust collection of model types. The purpose of publishing this limited set is to demonstrate the fundamentals of PMML with a realistic and useful initial value of what will emerge as a comprehensive and rich collection of modeling capabilities. Version 1.0

DTDs follow a common pattern of combining a data dictionary with one or more model definitions to which that dictionary immediately applies.

Predictive model   See outcome models, classification models.

Query   An SQL statement that serves to retrieve data from one or more tables and that typically includes the SELECT statement.

RDBMS (Relational Database Management Systems)   These are database programs that store data in tables that relate to one another.

SGML (Standard Generalized Markup Language)   A standard format under the auspices of the International Organization for Standardization (ISO). Its formal, full name is ISO 8879 Information processing—Text and office systems—(SGML). SGML is a format used in publishing printed documents and multimedia CD-ROMS and has been extended as a generalized method of describing, documenting, and controlling the format of SGML documents (including XML documents).

SQL (Structured Query Language)   The standard language used by all relational databases, including SQL Server.

Structure.   In Microsoft terms the product of a data mining task is a display of the structure of the data as revealed through patterns. This structure may be conceived of as a model

Total Quality Management   TQM is a management philosophy based on a set of principles and supported by a set of proven methodologies and tools. The underlying principles may seem like common sense, but they are certainly not common practice. They include:

- Focusing the organization on satisfying customers needs

- Developing and tapping the full human potential of all employees

- Involving everyone in efforts to "find better ways"

- Managing business processes, not just functions or departments

- Managing by fact, using reliable data and information

- Adding value to society, as well as achieving financial goals

Transact-SQL   The version of SQL that Microsoft SQL Server uses. It contains some specific keywords, statements, and constructs that only Microsoft SQL can execute.

URL (Uniform Resource Locator)   The user-readable address associated with a Web page.

XML (Extensible Mark Up Language)   Based on SGML, XML is used to describe the format, presentation and control of content of documents that are based on this language. The Extensible Markup Language (XML) is descriptively identified in the XML 1.0 W3C Recommendation as an extremely simple dialect, or subset, of SGML the goal of which is to enable generic SGML to be served, received, and processed on the Web in the way that is now possible with HTML, for which reason XML has been designed for ease of implementation, and for interoperability with both SGML and HTML.

B

References

Pieter Adriaans and Dolf Zantinge. *Data Mining*. Addison-Wesley, 1996.

Michael J. A. Berry and Gordon Linoff. *Data Mining Techniques for Marketing, Sales, and Customer Support*. John Wiley & Sons, 1997.

W. A. Belson. "A technique for studying the effects of a television broadcast," *Applied Statistics*, 5, 1956, 195.

Michael J. A. Berry and Gordon S. Linoff. *Mastering Data Mining: The Art and Science of Customer Relationship Management*. John Wiley & Sons, 2000.

Alex Berson, Stephen Smith, and Kurt Thearling. *Building Data Mining Applications for CRM*. McGraw-Hill, 2000.

David Biggs, B. de Ville, and E. Suen, "A method of choosing multiway partitions for classification and decision trees," *Journal of Applied Statistics*, 18, 1, 1991, 49–62.

Leo Breiman, J. H. Friedman, R. A. Olshen, and C. J. Stone. *Classification and Regression Trees*, Wadsworth, 1984.

Barry de Ville, "Applying statistical knowledge to database analysis and knowledge base construction," *Proceedings of the Sixth IEEE Conference on Artificial Intelligence Applications*, IEEE Computer Society, Washington, 30–36, March 1990.

N. M. Dixon. *Common Knowledge: How Companies Thrive by Sharing What They Know*, Harvard Business School Press, 2000.

H. J. Einhorn. "Alchemy in the behavioral sciences," *Public Opinion Quarterly*, 36, 1972, 367–378.

Usama M. Fayyad, Gregory Piatetsky-Shapiro, Padhraic Smyth, and Ramasamy Uthurusamy. *Advances in Knowledge Discovery and Data Mining*, AAAI Press, The MIT Press, 1996.

Morten T. Hansen, Nitin Nohria, and Thomas Tierney. "What's Your Strategy for Managing Knowledge?" *Harvard Business Review*, 77, 2, 1999, 106–16. (Available: http://www.hbsp.harvard.edu/products/hbr/marapr99/99206.html)

E. Hunt, J. Marin, and P. Stone. *Experiments in Induction*, Academic Press, 1966.

Bill Inmon. *Managing the Data Warehouse*, John Wiley & Sons, 1996.

Robert S. Kaplan and David P. Norton. *The Balanced Scorecard: Translating Strategy into Action*, Harvard Business School Press, 1996.

Olivia Parr Rud. *Data Mining Cookbook*. John Wiley & Sons, 2001.

Abraham Kaplan. *The Conduct of Inquiry: Methodology for Behavioral Science*. Chandler Publishing Company, 1964.

G. V. Kass. "Significance testing in automatic interaction detection," *Applied Statistics*, 24, 2, 1976, 178–189.

G. V. Kass. "An exploratory technique for investigating large quantities of categorical data," *Applied Statistics*, 29, 2, 1980, 119–127.

Thomas Kuhn. *The Structure of Scientific Revolutions*, Third Edition. University of Chicago Press, 1996.

Jesus Mena. *Data Mining Your Website*. Butterworth–Heinemann, 1999.

D. Michie. "Methodologies from Machine Learning in Data Analysis and Software," *The Computer Journal*, 34, 6, 1991, 559–565.

Shigeru Mizuno. *Management for Quality Improvement: The Seven New QC Tools*, Productivity Press, 1979.

J. N. Morgan and J. A. Sonquist. "Problems in the Analysis of Survey Data, and a Proposal," *Journal of the American Statistical Association*, 58, June 1963, 415.

C. O'Dell, F. Hasanali, C. Hubert, K. Lopez, and C. Raybourn. *Stages of Implementation: A Guide for Your Journey to Knowledge Management Best Practices*. APQC's Passport to Success Series, Houston, Texas, 2000.

L. W. Payne and S. Elliot. "Knowledge sharing at Texas Instruments: Turning best practices inside out," *Knowledge Management in Practice*, 6, 1997.

Dorian Pyle. *Data Preparation for Data Mining*. Morgan Kaufmann, 1999.

R. Quinlan. "Discovering rules by induction from large collections of examples," *Expert Systems in the Micro-electronic Age*, D. Michie (ed), Edinburgh, 1979, 168–201.

Reid G. Smith and Adam Farquhar. "The road ahead for knowledge management: an AI perspective, *AI Magazine*, 21, 4, Winter 2000, 17–40.

J. A. Sonquist, E. Baker, and J. Morgan. *Searching for Structure*, Institute for Social Research, University of Michigan, Ann Arbor, Michigan, 1973.

Thomas A. Stewart. *Intellectual Capital, The New Wealth of Organizations*, Doubleday-Currency, 1997.

Jake Sturm. *Data Warehousing with Microsoft® SQL Server™ 7.0 Technical Reference*, Microsoft Press, 1998

Ian Whitten and Eibe Frank. *Data Mining: Practical Machine Learning Tools and Techniques with Java Implementations*, Morgan Kaufmann, 2000.

C

Web Sites

http://www.dmg.org/   The Data Mining Group is a consortium of industry and academics formed to facilitate the creation of useful standards for the data mining community. The site is hosted by the National Center fro Data Mining at the University of Illinois at Chicago (UIC). The site provides a member area (for members only), a software repository and provides news and announcements.

http://www.kdnuggets.com/   KD Nuggets is a leading electronic newsletter on data mining and Web mining. Its monthly release provides up-to-date news items on developments in data mining and knowledge discovery.

http://www.oasis-open.org/   Organization for the Advancement of Structured Information Standards (OASIS) is a nonprofit international consortium that creates interoperable industry specifications based on public standards such as XML and SGML. OASIS members include organizations and individuals who provide, use and specialize in implementing the technologies that make these standards work in practice. Provides information on such emerging standards as Predictive Model Markup Language (PMML) in the separate XML Cover Pages site http://www.oasis-open.org/cover/.

http://www.xml.org   A credible, independent resource for news, education, and information about the application of XML in industrial and commercial settings. Hosted by OASIS and funded by organizations that are committed to product-independent data exchange, XML.ORG offers valuable tools, such as the XML.ORG Catalog, to help you make critical decisions about whether and how to employ XML in your business. For businesspeople and technologists alike, XML.ORG offers a uniquely independent view of what's happening in the XML industry.

http://www.microsoft.com/sql/index.htm   This is the home page for Microsoft SQL Server. This particular URL provides a list of Microsoft white papers related to SQL Server. The general site provides news and information about SQL Server and future releases.

http://www.microsoft.com/data/   This Microsoft Web site provides information on current and evolving Microsoft data access products, documentation (including standards documents), technical materials, and downloads. Here you will find the OLE DB for Data Mining and OLE DB for OLAP specifications and such evolving developments as the XML for Analysis Specification.

http://www.msdn.microsoft.com/downloads/   MSDN Online Downloads offers you one place to find and download all developer-related tools and add-ons, service packs, product updates, and beta and preview releases.

http://msdn.microsoft.com/library/default.asp   The MSDN Library is an essential resource for developers using Microsoft tools, products, and technologies. It contains a bounty of technical programming information, including sample code, documentation, technical articles, and reference guides.

http://backoffice.microsoft.com   This site provides information about any of the Microsoft back office products. Many of Microsoft's back office products integrate with SQL Server.

http://www.mssqlserver.com/   Technical reviews, frequently asked questions (FAQs), and all-around information resource for SQL Server issues and operations.

http://www.microsoft.com/solutions/km/DigitalDashboard.htm/
A Microsoft site that describes how to implement a digital dashboard.

http://www.microsoft.com/business/   The Microsoft Business Web site provides news, information, and executive perspectives from Microsoft about the technologies that can provide an edge in the digital age. This site provides a glimpse into Microsoft's vision for the future of technology, and how to use it to grow your business.

Sections include:

- *Microsoft's vision.* Learn about the Microsoft .NET platform and how it changes how business interacts with customers, employees and suppliers.

- *Business strategy.* In Measuring Business Value, use a tool Microsoft calls Rapid Economic Justification. It can help you quantify the business value of strategic technology investments to your management team. In e-commerce, find resources to help you start or grow your online business. Get details about how to get real-time access to your most powerful data in business intelligence, how to manage your business partnerships more effectively in customer relationship management, or how to share information within your organization through knowledge management. Or read how companies plan to use wireless and other mobile technologies in mobility.

- *Industries.* Get specifics on how other companies in the retail, healthcare, financial services, manufacturing, hospitality, and engineering industries are using solutions from Microsoft and its partners to grow their businesses.

- *Find a solution.* Find listings in various industries or regions for independent software vendors (ISVs) who build solutions for businesses in the solution directory.

http://www.mlnet.org/ This site is dedicated to the field of machine learning, knowledge discovery, case-based reasoning, knowledge acquisition, and data mining. This site provides information about research groups and persons within the community. Browse through the list of software and data sets, and check out our events page for the latest calls for papers. Alternatively, have a look at the list of job offerings if you are looking for a new opportunity within the field. And of course, they greatly appreciate any kind of feedback, so send us your comments and suggestions.

www.mdcinfo.com/ This site provides information on the Meta Data Coalition, an organization originally set up by Microsoft to provide meta data solutions in data warehousing, business intelligence and data mining.

http://www.icpsr.umich.edu/DDI/Resources.html The Data Documentation Initiative (DDI) is an effort to establish an international criterion and methodology for the content, presentation, transport, and preservation of metadata (data about data) about data sets in the social and behavioral sciences. Metadata constitute the information that enables the effective, efficient, and accurate use of those data sets. The site is hosted by the ICPSR (Inter-university Consortium for Political and Social Research) at the University of Michigan.

http://www.dhutton.com/ David Hutton Associates are consultants in quality management. They are specialists in Baldridge-style business excellence assessment as a tool to drive organizational change and improvement.

http://www.salford-systems.com/ Salford Systems are developers of CART and MARS data mining decision tree and regression modeling products. The site contains information about these products, white papers, and other technical reports.

http://research.swisslife.ch/kdd-sisyphus/   This is a site for a workgroup devoted to data preparation, preprocessing, and reasoning for real-world data mining applications. This workgroup is designed to bring together developers of algorithms who want to think about the reprocessing steps necessary to apply their algorithms to the data in a real-world database, as well as people who are interested in building tools that integrate various data mining algorithms as possible core phases for KDD applications.

The workgroup is especially interested in the following topics:

- Identify neccessary and useful preprocessing operations and tools (i.e., get the application know-how from the algorithm developer).

- Examine ways of how these preprocessing operations can be represented (e.g., for documentation and reuse) as well as executed efficiently on large data sets.

- Compare the different data mining approaches with respect to their input requirements.

- Compare different (logical) representations of the problem and discuss their advantages/disadvantages. Examine the need for multirelational representations to cover all the 1:N and N:M relations between the different entities of this KDD-Sisyphus problem.

- Establish usability criteria for various data mining approaches; for example:

  - scalability—number of records, number of attributes, multiple relations versus learning time and space requirements
  - robustness—handling of missing values, missing related tuples, noise-tolerance, nominal attributes with many different values, etc.
  - learning goal—classification, clustering, rule learning, etc.
  - understandability—size und presentation of mining results.
  - parameter-settings of the data mining algorithm and their impact on the mining result

The KDD-Sisyphus Workgroup provides the Sisyphus I package which is based on data extracted from a real-world insurance business application. As such it shows typical properties like fragmentation, varying data quality, irregular data value codings, and so on, which makes the application of data mining or machine learning algorithms a real challenge and usually requires sophisticated preprocessing methods.

The work package of KDD-Sisyphus I contains

- A data set consisting of 10 relations with 5 to 50 attributes and around 200,000 data tuples in ASCII format

- A rough schema description explaining the data types and their semantic relationships

- Three data mining task descriptions (two classification and one clustering task)

Data Mining and Knowledge Discovery Data Sets in the Public Domain

D.1   Statlog data sets

http://www.ncc.up.pt/liacc/ML/statlog/datasets.html

Statlog was a European project that assessed machine learning methods.

The Statlog data sets are as follows:

- Australian (Australian credit)
- Diabetes (diabetes of Pima Indians)
- DNA (DNA sequence)
- German (German credit)
- Heart (heart disease)
- Letter (letter recognition)
- Segment (image segmentation)
- Shuttle (shuttle control)
- Satimage (Landsat satellite image)
- Vehicle (vehicle recognition using silhouettes)

D.2   Machine learning databases

http://kdd.ics.uci.edu/

The UCI Knowledge Discovery in Databases Archive is an online repository of large data sets that encompasses a wide variety of data types, analysis tasks, and application areas. The primary role of this repository is to enable researchers in knowledge discovery and data mining to scale existing and future data analysis algorithms to very large and complex data sets.

This repository is currently under construction and is still in a preliminary form. This work is supported by a grant from the Information and Data Management Program at the National Science Foundation and is intended to extend the current UCI Machine Learning Database Repository by several orders of magnitude.

In addition to storing data and description files, the repository also archives task files that describe a specific analysis, such as clustering or regression, for the data sets stored. The call for data sets lists typical data types and tasks of interest.

D.2.1   Discrete sequence data

UNIX user data

This file contains nine sets of sanitized user data drawn from the command histories of eight UNIX computer users at Purdue over the course of up to two years.

D.2.2   Customer preference and recommendation data

Entree Chicago recommendation data

This data contains a record of user interactions with the Entree Chicago restaurant recommendation system. This is an interactive system that recommends restaurants to the user based on factors such as cuisine, price, style, atmosphere, and so on or based on similarity to a restaurant in another city (e.g., "find me a restaurant similar to the Patina in Los Angeles"). The user can then provide feedback such as find a nicer or less expensive restaurant.

D.2.3   Image data

CMU face images

This data consists of 640 black-and-white face images of people taken with varying pose (straight, left, right, up), expression (neutral, happy, sad, angry), eyes (wearing glasses or not), and size.

Volcanoes on Venus

The JARtool project was a pioneering effort to develop an automatic system for cataloging small volcanoes in the large set of Venus images returned by the Magellan spacecraft. This package contains a variety of data to enable researchers to evaluate algorithms over the same images as used for the JARtool experiments

D.2.4 Multivariate data

Census-income database

This data set contains unweighted PUMS census data from the Los Angeles and Long Beach areas for the years 1970, 1980, and 1990. The coding schemes have been standardized (by the IPUMS project) to be consistent across years.

COIL data

This data set is from the 1999 Computational Intelligence and Learning (COIL) competition. The data contains measurements of river chemical concentrations and algae densities

Corel image features

This data set contains image features extracted from a Corel image collection. Four sets of features are available based on the color histogram, color histogram layout, color moments, and co-occurence texture.

Forest CoverType

The forest cover type for 30 × 30 meter cells obtained from US Forest Service (USFS) Region 2 Resource Information System (RIS) data.

The insurance company benchmark (COIL 2000)

This data set used in the COIL 2000 Challenge contains information on customers of an insurance company. The data consists of 86 variables and includes product usage data and socio-demographic data derived from zip area codes. The data was collected to answer the following question: Can you predict who would be interested in buying a caravan insurance policy and give an explanation why?

Internet usage data

This data contains general demographic information on internet users in 1997.

IPUMS census data

This data set contains unweighted PUMS census data from the Los Angeles and Long Beach areas for the years 1970, 1980, and 1990. The coding schemes have been standardized (by the IPUMS project) to be consistent across years.

KDD CUP 1998 data

This is the data set used for The Second International Knowledge Discovery and Data Mining Tools Competition, which was held in conjunction with KDD-98 The Fourth International Conference on Knowledge Discovery and Data Mining. The competition task is a regression problem where the goal is to estimate the return from a direct mailing in order to maximize donation profits.

KDD CUP 1999 data

This is the data set used for The Third International Knowledge Discovery and Data Mining Tools Competition, which was held in conjunction with KDD-99 The Fifth International Conference on Knowledge Discovery and Data Mining. The competition task was to build a network intrusion detector, a predictive model capable of distinguishing between "bad" connections, called intrusions or attacks, and "good" normal connections. This database contains a standard set of data to be audited, which includes a wide variety of intrusions simulated in a military network environment.

D.2.5   Relational data

Movies

This data set contains a list of more than 10,000 films including many older, odd, and cult films. There is information on actors, casts, directors, producers, studios, and so on. The material also includes some social information, as "lived with" and "married to."

D.2.6   Spatio-temporal data

El Niño data

The data set contains oceanographic and surface meteorological readings taken from a series of buoys positioned throughout the equatorial Pacific. The data is expected to aid in the understanding and prediction of El Niño/Southern Oscillation (ENSO) cycles.

D.2.7   Text

20 newsgroups data

This data set consists of 20,000 messages taken from 20 Usenet newsgroups.

Reuters-21578 text categorization collection

This is a collection of documents that appeared on Reuters newswire in 1987. The documents were assembled and indexed with categories.

D.2.8 Time series

Australian sign language data

This data consists of sample of Auslan (Australian Sign Language) signs. Examples of 95 signs were collected from five signers with a total of 6,650 sign samples

EEG data

This data arises from a large study to examine EEG correlates of genetic predisposition to alcoholism. It contains measurements from 64 electrodes placed on the scalp sampled at 256 Hz (3.9-msec epoch) for 1 second.

Japanese vowels

This data set records 640 time series of 12 LPC cepstrum coefficients taken from nine male speakers.

Pioneer-1 mobile robot data

This data set contains time series sensor readings of the Pioneer-1 mobile robot. The data is broken into "experiences" in which the robot takes action for some period of time and experiences a controlled interaction with its environment (i.e., bumping into a garbage can).

Pseudo periodic synthetic time series

This data set is designed for testing indexing schemes in time series databases. The data appears highly periodic, but never exactly repeats itself. This feature is designed to challenge the indexing tasks.

Robot execution failures

This data set contains force and torque measurements on a robot after failure detection. Each failure is characterized by 15 force/torque samples collected at regular time intervals starting immediately after failure detection.

Synthetic control chart time series

This data consists of synthetically generated control charts.

D.2.9 Web data

Microsoft anonymous Web data

This data set records which areas (Vroots) of www.microsoft.com each user visited in a one-week timeframe in February 1998.

Syskill Webert Web data

This database contains the HTML source of web pages plus the ratings of a single user on these pages. The Web pages are on four separate subjects (bands, or recording artists; goats; sheep; and biomedical.)

D.3   MLnet online information service

http://www.mlnet.org/

The MLnet Online Information Service is dedicated to the field of machine learning, knowledge discovery, case-based reasoning, knowledge acquisition, and data mining. The site provides information on research groups and persons in the community. You can browse through the list of software and data sets, and check out the events page for the latest calls for papers. The site also provides lists of job offerings if you are looking for a new opportunity within the field.

D.4   KDD Sisyphus

http://research.swisslife.ch/kdd-sisyphus/

This site provides a large, unpreprocessed, multirelational, and partially documented database extract. This data is intended for use in research on preprocessing techniques for real world data. "The KDD-Sisyphus Workgroup provides the Sisyphus I package, which is based on data extracted from a real-world insurance business application. As such it shows typical properties like fragmentation, varying data quality, irregular data value codings, etc. which makes the application of data mining or machine learning algorithms a real challenge and usually requires sophisticated preprocessing methods."

D.5   StatLib—data sets archive

http://lib.stat.cmu.edu/datasets/

Statlib is a data mining and knowledge discovery data set resource that is hosted by Carnegie Mellon University (CMU).

If you have an interesting data set or collection of data from a book, please consider submitting the data.

The data sets archive currently contains the following data sets.

D.5.1   NIST statistical reference data sets (StRD)

A pointer to a NIST site that contains reference data sets for the objective evaluation of the computational accuracy of statistical software. Both users and developers of statistical software can use these data sets to ensure and improve software accuracy.

D.5.2   agresti

Contains data from *An Introduction to Categorical Data Analysis*, by Alan Agresti (John Wiley & Sons, 1996), plus SAS code for various analyses. aa@stat.ufl.edu (28/Feb/96, 12k)

D.5.3   alr

This file contains data from *Applied Linear Regression*, 2nd edition, by Sanford Weisberg (John Wiley & Sons, 1985). sandy@umnstat.stat.umn.edu (36808 bytes)

D.5.4   andrews

This data for the book *Data*, by Andrews and Herzberg. Available by FTP, gopher, and Web, but not by e-mail.

D.5.5   arsenic

This datafile contains measurements of drinking water and toenail levels of arsenic, as well as related covariates, for 21 individuals with private wells in New Hampshire. *Source:* M. R. Karagas, J. S. Morris, J. E. Weiss, V, Spate,

C. Baskett, and E. R. Greenberg. "Toenail Samples as an Indicator of Drinking Water Arsenic Exposure," *Cancer Epidemiology, Biomarkers, and Prevention* 5, 1996, 849–852. Therese.A.Stukel@Dartmouth.EDU (MS Word format, 21/Jul/98 ,5 kbytes.

D.5.6 backache

This file contains the "backache in pregnancy" data analyzed in Exercise D.2 of *Problem-Solving: A Statistician's Guide*, 2nd edition, by C. Chatfield (Chapman and Hall, 1995). cc@maths.bath.ac.uk (2/Oct/95, 16 kbytes)

D.5.7 balloon

A data set consisting of 2001 observations of radiation, taken from a balloon. The data contain a trend and outliers. *Source:* Laurie Davies (mata00@de0hrz1a.BITNET). (43k, 5/Feb/93)

D.5.8 baseball

Data on the salaries of North American major league baseball players. The data set has performance and salary information on players during the 1986 season. This was the 1988 ASA Graphics Section Poster Session data set, organized by Lorraine Denby. There are two files to retrieve:

- baseball.data, which consists of a shar archive of the data, and helpful information including a description of the data, pitcher, hitter, and team statistics. (54448 bytes)

- baseball.corr, which is a set of differences from the published data set (in UNIX diff format).

    baseball.hoaglin-velleman is another set of differences from the published data set (in UNIX diff format). See Hoaglin and Velleman, *The American Statistican*, August 1994, 227–285.

D.5.9 biomed

I was able to find the old 1982 "biomedical data set" generated by Larry Cox. It consists of two groups. These give observation number, blood id number, age, date, and four blood measurements. I don't really remember the instructions for analysis, although I seem to recall that the idea was to figure out if some of the blood measurements that were less difficult to obtain were as good at distinguishing carriers from normals as the more difficult measurements. Unfortunately, I don't remember which measurement is which. There are two files to retrieve:

- biomed.desc, which is a short description of the data and a reference. (1457 bytes)

- biomed.data, which is a shar archive of containing the data for carriers and normals. (7843 bytes)

D.5.10 bodyfat

Lists estimates of the percentage of body fat determined by underwater weighing and various body circumference measurements for 252 men. Submitted by Roger Johnson (rwjohnso@silver.sdsmt.edu). (2/Oct/95, 35 kbytes)

D.5.11 bolts

Data from an experiment on the affects of machine adjustments on the time to count bolts. Data appear as the STATS (Issue 10) Challenge. Submitted by W. Robert Stephenson (wrstephe@iastate.edu). (8/Nov/93, 5k)

D.5.12 boston

The Boston house-price data of D. Harrison and D. L. Rubinfeld, "Hedonic prices and the demand for clean air," *J. Environ. Economics & Management* 5, 1978, 81–102. Used in Belsley, Kuh, and Welsch, *Regression Diagnostics* (John Wiley & Sons, 1980). (51256 bytes)

D.5.13 boston_corrected

This consists of the Boston house price data of Harrison and Rubinfeld (1978) JEEM with corrections and augmentation of the data with the latitude and longitude of each observation. Submitted by Kelley Pace (kpace@unix1.sncc.lsu.edu). (11/Oct/99, 62136 bytes)

D.5.14 business

Link to data from two case study books: *Basic Business Statistics* and *Business Analysis Using Regression*, by Foster, Stine, and Waterman (Springer-Verlag, 1998).

D.5.15   cars

This was the 1983 ASA Data Exposition data set. The data set was collected by Ernesto Ramos and David Donoho and dealt with automobiles. I don't remember the instructions for analysis. Data on mpg, cylinders, displacement, etc. (eight variables) for 406 different cars. The data set includes the names of the cars. The data are in one file:

- cars.data, a shar archive containing files with a description of the car data, names of the cars, and the car data itself. (33438 bytes)

- cars.desc, the original instructions for this exposition. (6206 bytes)

D.5.16   cloud

These data are those collected in a cloud-seeding experiment in Tasmania. The rainfalls are period rainfalls in inches. TE and TW are the east and west target areas, respectively, while NC, SC, and NWC are the corresponding rainfalls in the north, south and northwest control areas, respectively. S = seeded, U = unseeded. Submitted by Alan Miller (alan@dms-melb.mel.dms.CSIRO.AU). (4/May/94, 7 kbytes)

D.5.17   chscase

A collection of the data sets used in the book *A Casebook for a First Course in Statistics and Data Analysis* by Samprit Chatterjee, Mark S. Handcock, and Jeffrey S. Simonoff (John Wiley & Sons, 1995). Submitted by Samprit Chatterjee (schatterjee@stern.nyu.edu), Mark Handcock (mhandcock@stern.nyu.edu), and Jeff Simonoff (jsimonoff@stern.nyu.edu). (updated 1/Dec/95, 325 kbytes)

D.5.18   christensen

Contains the data from *Analysis of Variance, Design, and Regression: Applied Statistical Methods* by Ronald Christensen (Chapman and Hall, 1996). Ronald Christensen (fletcher@math.unm.edu). (22/Oct/96, 57k)

D.5.19   christensen-llm

Contains data from *Log-Linear Models and Logistic Regression*, 2nd edition, by Ronald Christensen (Springer Verlag, 1997). Ronald Christensen (fletcher@stat.unm.edu) (24/Mar/97, 33k)

D.5.20 cjs.sept95.case

Data on tree growth used in the case study published in the September 1995 issue of the *Canadian Journal of Statistics*. Nancy Reid (reid@utstat.utstat.toronto.edu) (4/Oct/95, 141k)

D.5.21 colleges

1995 Data Analysis Exposition sponsored by the Statistical Graphics Section of the American Statistical Association. The U.S. news data contains information on tuition, and so on for more than 1,300 schools, while the AAUP data includes average salary, and so on. Robin Lock (rlock@vm.stlawu.edu)

D.5.22 confidence

This file contains the monthly frequencies for six consumer confidence items collected by the Conference Board and the University of Michigan in 1992. reference in *Sociological Methodology*. Submitted by Gordon Bechtel (bechtel@nervm.nerdc.ufl.edu). (22/Oct/96, 6k)

D.5.23 CPS_85_Wages

These data consist of a random sample of 534 persons from the CPS, with information on wages and other characteristics of the workers, including sex, number of years of education, years of work experience, occupational status, region of residence, and union membership. *Source:* Berndt, ER. *The Practice of Econometrics* (Addison-Wesley, 1991). (Therese.A.Stukel@Dartmouth.EDU) (MS Word format, 21/Jul/98, 23 kbytes)

D.5.24 csb

See the separate csb collection for data from the book *Case Studies in Biometry.*

D.5.25 detroit

Data on annual homicides in Detroit, 1961–73, from Gunst and Mason, *Regression Analysis and its Application* (Marcel Dekker). Contains data on 14 relevant variables collected by J. C. Fisher. (alan@dmsmelb.mel.dms.csiro.au) (10/Feb/92, 3357 bytes)

D.5.26 diggle

Data sets from P. J. Diggle. *Time Series: A Biostatistical Introduction* (Oxford University Press, 1990). Submitted by Peter Diggle (maa026@central1.lancaster.ac.uk). (35800 bytes)

D.5.27 disclosure

Data sets from S. E. Fienberg, U. E. Makov, and A. P. Sanil. "A Bayesian Approach to Data Disclosure: Optimal Intruder Behavior for Continuous Data," (1994). Submitted by S. E. Fienberg (fienberg@stat.cmu.edu). (4/Jun/98, 111 kbytes)

D.5.28 djdc0093

Dow-Jones Industrial Average (DJIA) closing values from 1900 to 1993. See also spdc2693. Submitted by Eduardo Ley (edley@eco.uc3m.es). (13/Mar/96, 383 kbytes)

D.5.29 fienberg

The data from Fienberg's "The Analysis of Cross-Classified Data," in a form that can easily be read into Glim (or easily read by a human). (mikem@stat.cmu.edu) (25/Sept/91, 14398 bytes)

D.5.30 fraser-river

Time series of monthly flows for the Fraser River at Hope, B.C. A. Ian McLeod (aim@julian.uwo.ca) (26/April/93, 10 kbytes)

D.5.31 hip

This is the hip measurement data from Table B.13 in Chatfield's *Problem Solving*, 2nd edition (Chapman and Hall, 1995). It is given in eight columns. First four columns are for control group. Last four columns are for treatment group. (Note there is no pairing. Patient 1 in control group is *not* patient 1 in treatment Group). (cc@maths.bath.ac.uk) (28/Feb/96, 2k)

D.5.32 houses.zip

These spatial data contain 20,640 observations on housing prices with nine economic covariates. It appeared in Pace and Barry, "Sparse Spatial Autoregressions," *Statistics and Probability Letters* (1997). Submitted by Kelley Pace (kpace@unix1.sncc.lsu.edu). (9/Nov/99, 536 kbytes)

D.5.33 humandevel

United Nations Development Program, Human Development Index. A nation's HDI is composed of life expectancy, adult literacy, and Gross National Product per capita. Information on 130 countries plus documentation. Tim Arnold (arnold@stat.ncsu.edu) (31/Oct/91, 10031 bytes)

D.5.34 hutsof99

Data from *The Multivariate Social Scientist: Introductory Statistics Using Generalized Linear Models* by Graeme D. Hutcheson and Nick Sofroniou (SAGE Publications, 1999), plus GLIM 4 code for various analyses. Submitted by Nick Sofroniou (nso@gcal.ac.uk). (12/Jul/99, 56k)

D.5.35 iq_brain_size

This datafile contains 20 observations (10 pairs of twins) on 9 variables. This data set can be used to demonstrate simple linear regression and correlation. *Source:* M. J. Tramo, W.C. Loftus, R. L. Green, T. A. Stukel, J. B. Weaver, and M. S. Gazzaniga, "Brain Size, Head Size, and IQ in Monozygotic Twins." *Neurology* 1998 (in press). (Therese.A.Stukel@Dartmouth.EDU) (MS Word format, 21/Jul/98, 5 kbytes)

D.5.36 irish.ed

Longtitudinal educational transition data set for a sample of 500 Irish students, with four independent variables (sex, verbal reasoning score, father's occupation, type of school). Submitted by Adrian E. Raftery (raftery@stat.washington.edu). (20/Dec/93, 13 kbytes)

D.5.37 kidney

Data from McGilchrist and Aisbett, *Biometrics* 47, 1991, 461–66. Times to infection, from the point of insertion of the catheter, for kidney patients using portable dialysis equipment. There are two observations on each of 38 patients. The data has been used to illustrate random effects (frailty) models for survival data. Submitted by Terry Therneau (therneau@Mayo.EDU). (10/Jun/99, (4kbytes)

D.5.38   lmpavw

Time series used in "Long-Memory Processes, the Allan Variance and Wavelets" by D. B. Percival and P. Guttorp, a chapter in *Wavelets in Geophysics*, edited by E. Foufoula-Georgiou and P. Kumar (Academic Press, 1994). This time series was collected by Mike Gregg, Applied Physics Laboratory, University of Washington, and is a measurement of vertical shear (in units of 1/second) versus depth (in units of meters) in the ocean. The role of time in this series is thus played by depth. Permission has been obtained to redistribute this data. Questions concerning this series should be sent to Don Percival (dbp@apl.washington.edu). (6/Feb/94, 62 kbytes)

D.5.39   longley

The infamous Longley data, "An appraisal of least-squares programs from the point of view of the user," *JASA* 62, 1967, 819–841. (therneau@mayo.edu) (1301 bytes)

D.5.40   lupus

Eighty-seven persons with lupus nephritis. Followed up 15+ years. 35 deaths. Var = duration of disease. Over 40 baseline variables available from authors. Submitted by Todd Mackenzie (tmacke@po-box.mcgill.ca). (4k)

D.5.41   hipel-mcleod

McLeod Hipel time series data sets collection. The shar file, mhsets.shar, contains more than 300 time series data sets taken from various case studies. These data sets are suitable for model building exercises such as are discussed in the textbook, *Time Series Modeling of Water Resources and Environmental Systems* by K. W. Hipel and A. I. McLeod (Elsevier, 1994). For PC users there is also a zip file, mhsets.zip. The shar file and the zip files are about 1.7 Mb and 0.5 Mb, respectively. Ian McLeod (aim@fisher.stats.uwo.ca) (1/Mar/95)

D.5.42   mu284

This file contains the data in "The MU284 Population" from Appendix B of the book *Model Assisted Survey Sampling* by Sarndal, Swensson, and Wretman (Springer-Verlag, 1992). The data set contains 284 observations on 11 variables, plus a line with variable names. Please consult Appendix B for more information about this data set. Esbjorn Ohlsson (esbj@matematik.su.se) (24/Mar/97, 16k)

D.5.43 newton_hema

Data on fluctuating proportions of marked cells in marrow from heterozygous Safari cats from a study of early hematopoiesis. Michael Newton (newton@stat.wisc.edu) (8/Nov/93, 5k)

D.5.44 nflpass

Lists all-time NFL passers through 1994 by the NFL passing efficiency rating. Associated passing statistics from which this rating is computed are included. Roger W. Johnson (rjohnso@silver.sdsmt.edu) (28/Feb/96, 8k)

D.5.45 nonlin

The data sets from Bates and Watts, *Nonlinear Regression Analysis and Its Applications* (John Wiley & Sons, 1988). They are in S dump format as data frames. (If you don't know what a data frame is, don't worry. Just consider them to be lists. Data frames are described in *Statistical Modeling in S*. (bates@stat.wisc.edu) (7/Feb/90, 19851 bytes)

D.5.46 papir

This file contains two multivariate regression data sets from paper industry, described in M. Aldrin, "Moderate projection pursuit regression for multivariate response data," *Computational Statistics and Data Analysis*, 21, 1996, 501–531. Submitted by Magne Aldrin (magne.aldrin@nr.no). (14/Apr/99, 17916 bytes)

D.5.47 pbc

The data set found in Appendix D of Fleming and Harrington, *Counting Processes and Survival Analysis* (John Wiley & Sons, 1991). Submitted by Terry Therneau (therneau@Mayo.EDU). (25/Jul/94, 36 kbytes)

D.5.48 pbcseq

A follow-up to the PBC data set, this contains the data for both the baseline and subsequent visits at 6 months, 1 year, and annually thereafter. There are

1945 observations on 312 subjects. Submitted by Terry Therneau (therneau@Mayo.EDU). (10/Jun/99, 160 kbytes)

D.5.49   places

Data taken from the Places Rated Almanac, giving the ratings on 9 composite variables of 329 locations. (From an ASA data exposition, 1986) The data are in one file, places.data, which is a shar archive of three files which document the data, present the data itself, and provide a key to the actual places used. (27720 byes)

D.5.50   plasma_retinol

This datafile (N=315) investigates the relationship between personal characteristics and dietary factors, and plasma concentrations of retinol, beta-carotene, and other carotenoids. *Source:* D. W. Nierenberg, T. A. Stukel, M. R. Karagas. and the Micronutrient Study Group. The effects of dietary factors and personal characteristics on plasma concentrations of retinol, alpha-tocopherol and five carotenoids. submitted. (Therese.A.Stukel@Dartmouth.EDU) (MS Word format, 21/Jul/98, 26 kbytes)

D.5.51   pollen

Synthetic data set about the geometric features of pollen grains. There are 3,848 observations on 5 variables. From the 1986 ASA Data Exposition data set, made up by David Coleman of RCA Labs. The data are in one file:

- pollen.data, a shar archive of 9 files. The first file gives a short description of the data, then there are 8 data files, each with 481 observations. (205954 bytes)

- pollen.extra, some extra comments about the data. Look here for hints.

D.5.52   pollution

This is the pollution data so loved by writers of papers on ridge regression. *Source:* G. C. McDonald and R. C. Schwing, "Instabilities of regression estimates relating air pollution to mortality," *Technometrics* 15, 1973, 463–482. (8540 bytes)

D.5.53 profb

Scores and point spreads for all NFL games in the 1989–91 seasons. Contributed by Robin Lock (rlock@stlawu.bitnet). (15/Sept/92, 27733 bytes)

D.5.54 prnn

This shar archive contains the data sets used in *Pattern Recognition and Neural Networks* by B. D. Ripley (Cambridge University Press, 1996). (ripley@stats.ox.ac.uk) (1/Dec/95, 101 kbytes)

D.5.55 rabe

This file contains data from *Regression Analysis By Example*, 2nd edition, by Samprit Chatterjee and Bertram Price (John Wiley & Sons, 1991). (schatter@stern.nyu.edu) (6/Feb/92, 40309 bytes)

D.5.56 rir

This file contains data from *Residuals and Influence in Regression*, R. Dennis Cook and Sanford Weisberg (Chapman and Hall, 1982). (sandy@umnstat.stat.umn.edu) (Updated 25/May/93, 5206 bytes)

D.5.57 riverflow

Data sets mentioned in "Parsimony, Model Adequacy and Periodic Correlation in Time Series Forecasting," *ISI Review*, A. I. McLeod (1992, to appear). Submitted by A. Ian McLeod (aim@stats.uwo.ca). Time series data. A shar archive. (22/Jan/92, 294052 bytes)

D.5.58 sapa

Time series used in *Spectral Analysis for Physical Applications* by D. B. Percival and A. T. Walden (Cambridge University Press, 1993). (dbp@apl.washington.edu) (4/Nov/92, 50788 bytes)

D.5.59 saubts

Two ocean wave time series used in "Spectral Analysis of Univariate and Bivariate Time Series," by D. B. Percival; Chapter 11 of *Statistical Methods for Physical Science*, edited by J. L. Stanford and S. B. Vardeman (Academic Press, 1993). (dbp@apl.washington.edu) (14/Apr/93, 47 kbytes)

D.5.60 schizo

"Schizophrenic Eye-Tracking Data," by Rubin and Wu, *Biometrics*, 1997. Yingnian Wu (wu@hustat.harvard.edu) (14/Oct/97, 21k)

D.5.61 sensory

Data for the sensory evaluation experiment in C. J. Brien and R. W. Payne, Tiers, structure formulae and the analysis of complicated experiments (1996, submitted for publication). Chris Brien (matcjb@ntx.city.unisa.edu.au) (22/Oct/96, 19k)

D.5.62 ships

Ship damage data, from *Generalized Linear Models* by McCullagh and Nelder, section 6.3.2, p. 137. (therneau@mayo.edu) (1709 bytes)

D.5.63 sleuth

Contains 110 data sets from the book *The Statistical Sleuth* by Fred Ramsey and Dan Schafer (Duxbury Press, 1997). (schafer@stat.orst.edu) (14/Oct/97, 172k)

D.5.64 sleep

Data from which conclusions were drawn in the article "Sleep in Mammals: Ecological and Constitutional Correlates," by T. Allison and D. Cicchetti, *Science* 194 (November 12, 1976) 732–734. Includes brain and body weight, life span, gestation time, time sleeping, and predation and danger indices for 62 mammals. Submitted by Roger Johnson (rwjohnso@silver.sdsmt.edu). (27/Jul/94, (8k)

D.5.65 smoothmeth

A collection of the data sets used in the book *Smoothing Methods in Statistics*, by Jeffrey S. Simonoff (Springer-Verlag, 1996). Submitted by Jeff Simonoff (jsimonoff@stern.nyu.edu). (13/Mar/96, 242kbytes)

D.5.66 socmob

Social Mobility (United States, 1973). Two four-way 17x17x2x2 contingency tables: father's occupation, son's occupation (first and current), family structure, race. Submitted by Timothy J. Biblarz (biblarz@uscvm.bitnet). (corrected 25/Jan/93)

D.5.67 space_ga

Election data including spatial coordinates on 3,107 United States counties. Used in Pace and Barry, *Geographical Analysis* 29, 1997, 232–247. Submitted by Kelley Pace (kpace@unix1.sncc.lsu.edu). (3/Nov/99, 548 kbytes)

D.5.68 spdc2693

Standard and Poor's 500 index closing values from 1926 to 1993. See also djdc0093. Submitted by Eduardo Ley (edley@eco.uc3m.es). (13/Mar/96, 333 kbytes)

D.5.69 stanford

Two versions of the Stanford heart transplant data: "The Statistical Analysis of Failure Time Data," by Kalbfleisch and Prentice, Appendix I, pages 230–232; and from the original paper by Crowley and Hu. (therneau@mayo.edu) (corrected 8/Mar/93, 15003 bytes)

D.5.70 stanford.diff

The differences between the two Stanford data sets.

D.5.71 strikes

Data on industrial disputes and their covariates in 18 OECD countries, 1951–1985. Prepared by Bruce Western (western@datacomm.iue.it). (2/Oct/95, 44k)

D.5.72 tecator

The task is to predict the fat content of a meat sample on the basis of its near-infrared absorbance spectrum. Regression. Submitted by Hans Henrik Thodberg (thodberg@nn.meatre.dk). (23/Jan/95, 302 kbytes)

D.5.73   transplant

Data on deaths within 30 days of heart transplant surgery at 131 U.S. hospitals. See *Bayesian Biostatistics*, D. Berry and D. Stangl, eds (Marcel Dekker, 1996). Cindy L. Christiansen and Carl N. Morris (22/Oct/96, 3k)

D.5.74   tsa

Software and Data Sets for *Time Series Analysis and Its Applications* by R. H. Shumway and D. S. Stoffer (Springer-Verlag, 2000). Submitted by David Stoffer (stoffer@stat.pitt.edu)[10/Mar/00)

D.5.75   tumor

Tumor Recurrence data for patients with bladder cancer taken from Wei, Lin, and Weissfeld, *JASA* 1989, p. 1067. From Terry Therneau (therneau@mayo.edu). (23/Mar/93, 5/Jun/96, 3k)

D.5.76   veteran

Veteran's Administration lung cancer trial, taken from Kalbfleisch and Prentice, pp. 223–224. (therneau@mayo.edu) (8249 bytes)

D.5.77   visualizing.data

This shar file contains 25 data sets from the book *Visualizing Data* published by Hobart Press (books@hobart.com) and written by William S. Cleveland (wsc@research.att.com). There is also a README file so there are 26 files in all. Each of the 25 files has the data in an ASCII table format. The name of each data file is the name of the data set used in the book. To find the description of the data set in the book look under the entry "data, name" in the index. For example, one data set is barley. To find the description of barley, look in the index under the entry "data, barley." The S archive of Statlib has a file created by S that contains the data sets in a format that makes it easy to read them into S. (12/Nov/93, 17/Oct/94, 23/Oct/97)

D.5.78   wind

Daily average wind speeds for 1961–1978 at 12 synoptic meteorological stations in the Republic of Ireland (Haslett and Raftery, *Applied Statistics*

1989). There is a large amount of data. Please be sure you want it before you ask for it! There are two entries to obtain:

- wind.desc, a short desciption of the data. (815 bytes)
- wind.data, the data. (532494 bytes)

D.5.79 wind.correlations

Estimated correlations between daily 3 p.m. wind measurements during September and October 1997 for a network of 45 stations in the Sydney region. From Nott and Dunsmuir, *Analysis of Spatial Covariance Structure from Monitoring Data*, Technical Report, Department of Statistics, University of New South Wales. Submitted by David Nott (djn@maths.unsw.edu.au). (8/Mar/00, 13 kbytes)

D.5.80 witmer

A shar archive of data from the book *Data Analysis: An Introduction* by Jeff Witmer (Prentice Hall, 1992). Submitted by Jeff Witmer (fwitmer@ocvaxa.cc.oberlin.edu). (28/Jun/94, 29 kbytes)

D.5.81 wseries

These data tell whether or not the home team won for each game played in all World Series prior to 1994. The data appear as the STATS Challenge for Issue 11. Submitted by Jeff Witmer (fwitmer@ocvaxa.cc.oberlin.edu). (20/Mar/94, 3 kbytes)

D.5.82 Vinnie.Johnson

Data on the shooting of Vinnie Johnson of the Detroit Pistons during the 1985–1986 through 1988–1989 seasons. Source was the New York Times. Submitted by Rob Kass (kass@stat.cmu.edu). (18/Aug/95, 26 kbytes)

D.5.83 submissions

Information on how to submit data to this archive.

D.6   Other Sources

D.6.1   Time series data library

Rob Hyndman's collection of more than 500 time series organized by subject.

D.6.2   EconData

Several hundred thousand economic time series, produced by the U.S. government and distributed by the government in a variety of formats and media, have been put into a standard, highly efficient, easy-to- use form for personal computers.

D.6.3   Oceanographic and earth science data

From Scripps Institution of Oceanography Library.

D.6.4   The data zoo

California coastal data collection.

Journal of Statistics Education Information Service also has some data.

D.7   Delve data sets

http://www.cs.toronto.edu/~delve/data/datasets.html

This is a collection of data, hosted by the University of Toronto, for developing, evaluating, and comparing learning methods.

The Delve data sets and families are available from this page. Every data set (or family) has a brief overview page and many also have detailed documentation. You can download gzipped-tar files of the data sets, but you will require the delve software environment to get maximum benefit from them. Data sets are categorized as primarily assessment, development or historical according to their recommended use. Within each category we have distinguished data sets as regression or classification according to how their proto-tasks have been created. Details on how to install the downloaded data sets follow.

There is also a summary table of the data sets.

D.7.1 Assessment data sets

We recommend that data sets from this section be used when reporting results for your learning method. You should run your method once on each task and report the results from that run. That is, you should not use results from the testing data to modify your method and then rerun it.

Regression data sets

1. abalone. Download abalone.tar.gz

    Predict the age of abaolone from physical measurements. From the UCI repository of machine learning databases.

2. bank. Download bank-family

    A family of data sets synthetically generated from a simulation of how bank customers choose their banks. Tasks are based on predicting the fraction of bank customers who leave the bank because of full queues.

3. census-house. Download census-house.tar.gz

    Predicting median house prices from 1990 US census data.

4. comp-activ. Download comp-activ.tar.gz

    Predict a computer system activity from system performance measures.

5. pumadyn family of data sets. Download pumadyn-family

    This is a family of data sets synthetically generated from a realistic simulation of the dynamics of a Unimation Puma 560 robot arm.

Classification data sets

1. adult. Download adult.tar.gz

    Predict if an individual's annual income exceeds $50,000 based on census data. From the UCI repository of machine learning databases.

2. splice. Download splice.tar.gz

    Recognize two classes of splice junctions in a DNA sequence. From the UCI repository of machine learning databases.

3. titanic. Download titanic.tar.gz

    Information on passengers of the Titanic and whether they survived

D.7.2 Development data sets

We recommend that you use data sets from this section while developing a new learning method, or fine-tuning parameters. That is, you can rerun your method several times on a data set until you obtain the desired performance. If you do use a data set in this manner, you should not use it when reporting your method's performance; you should use data sets from the assessment section.

Regression data sets

1.   boston. Download boston.tar.gz

      Housing in the Boston Massachusetts area. From the UCI repository of machine learning databases.

2.   demo. Download demo.tar.gz

      The demo data set was invented to serve as an example for the Delve manual and as a test case for Delve software and for software that applies a learning procedure to Delve data sets.

3.   kin family of data sets. Download kin-family

      This is a family of data sets synthetically generated from a realistic simulation of the forward kinematics of an eight-link all-revolute robot arm.

Classification data sets

1.   image-seg. Download image-seg.tar.gz

      Predict the object class of a 3×3 patch from an image of an outdoor scence. From the UCI repository of machine learning databases.

2.   letter. Download letter.tar.gz

      Classify an image as one of 26 upper case letters. The inputs are simple statistical features derived from the pixels in the image. From the UCI repository of machine learning databases.

3.   The mushrooms data set. Download mushrooms.tar.gz

      Classify hypothetical samples of gilled mushrooms in the Agaricus and Lepiota family as edible or poisonous. From the UCI repository of machine learning databases.

D.7.3 Historical data sets

Data sets from this section have been included because they are established in the literature. We have attempted to reproduce the original usage as closely as possible to facilitate comparisons.

Regression data sets

1.   add10. Download add10.tar.gz

     A synthetic function suggested by Jerome Friedman in his "Multivariate Adaptive Regression Splines" paper.

2.   hwang. Download hwang.tar.gz

     Five real-valued functions of two variables used by Jenq-Neng Hwang, et al. and others to test nonparametric regression methods. Both noisy and noise-free prototasks are defined based on these functions.

Classification data sets

1.   ringnorm. Download ringnorm.tar.gz

     Leo Breiman's ringnorm example. Classify cases as coming from one of two overlapping normal distributions.

2.   twonorm. Download twonorm.tar.gz

     Leo Breiman's two normal example. Classify a case as coming from one of two normal distribution, one distribution lies within the other.

Microsoft Solution Providers

The Solutions Directory contains listings for independent software vendors (ISVs) and Web service providers that build customized products, services, and knowledge management solutions with Microsoft technologies. Companies are represented for the following vertical industries: retail, healthcare, financial services, government, manufacturing, engineering, digital media, hospitality, legal, energy, real estate, construction, an utilities. Available solutions include: business intelligence, collaboration, commerce, customer relationship management, data center, document managment, ERP and accounting knowledge managment, and supply chain managment.

Company Name	Product Name	E-mail/Web	Phone Number
12:34 MicroTechnologies	Customized ASP document management and search system	www.1234micro.com	717-396-0600
ABT	PowerCAMPUS	www.abtcampus.com	800-220-2281
Accelerated Technloghy Laboratories	SampleMaster	www.atlab.com	800-565-5467
Accelerex Ltd.	AxCims 1.0	sales@accelerex.com	44 (0)1753 578833
AccessWare Inc.	OnCue	rkot@alarmware.com	713-681-7977
account 4.com	Professional Services Automation software	www.account4.com	617-964-1633
Acenter	Tracker Office for Projects	www.acentre.com	520-882-9287
ACI Worldwide	WinStoredValue	scottm@tsainc.com	727-530-1555 ext. 236
ACS Software	AutoEDMS	www.acssoftware.com	310-325-3055

Company Name	Product Name	E-mail/Web	Phone Number
Action Technologies	Action Works Metro	www.actiontech.com	510-521-6190
ActionaPoint, Inc.	Actionapoint Interaction Management System	www.actionpoint.com	800-371-3783
Active Computer	Ospreyr Silver 5.2	postoffice@activecomputer.com	410-280-0714
Active Solutions	Business, contact management and voice data integration	www.asolution.co.uk	012-00-440409
Actuate Software Corporation	Actuate Reporting System 3.2	info@actuate.com	650-638-2000
Acuity Corporation	Acuity WebCenter 2.0	info@acuity.com	512-425-2200
Adaytum Software	Adaytum e.Planning 1.0	sales@adaytum-msp.com	612-858-8585
Adaytum Software	Web-based business planning	www.adaytum.com	612-858-8585
Adlan Datenverarveitung GmgH	CTAP-Server	www.adlon.de	0049 (0) 751-76070
Advanced Information Technologies, Inc.	DataPipe Data Mart Software Suite 1.2	sales@aitinc.com	256-766-0248
Advanced Production Systems, Inc. (A.P.S)	QMAPS	info@teamaps.com	502-423-0882
Advox AB	e-mail and messaging solutions	www.advox.se	011-46-8-54490900
AEIT	Knowledge Management	www.alpha-eng.com	503-452-8003
AFD Software Ltd	AFD Postcode 4.1	sales@afd.co.uk	44 1624 811711
Again Technologies, Inc.	CompSense	info@againtech.com	650-401-8800 ext. 107
Agresso Group ASA	Admininistrative management, control and reporting	www.agresso.com	47 22 58 85 00
AKSIS	Knowledge Management	www.aksis.com.tr	90 212 270 73 90
Alacrity Inc.	Alacrity Results Management 7	mchung@alacrity.com	416-362-5099

Company Name	Product Name	E-mail/Web	Phone Number
ALH Group, Incorporated	WinCMS Data Warehouse & OLAP Manager Anvil	Sales@alh.com	805-541-8739
Alliance Software Corporation	Dynamic Membership 4.2	aspeno@alliance-software.com	315-472-9730
Allin Consulting	Knowledge Management	www.alin.com	888-404-9800
AllPoints Systems Inc.	e-Fulfillment	www.allpoints.com	781-501-2600
AlphaBlox Corporation	Web-based analysis	www.alphablox.com	650-526-1700
Alternate Computer Services, Inc.	ClubPac 2.0	acs@altcomser.com	847-726-1992
AltiGen Communications, Inc.	AltiWare 3.51	info@altigen.com	510-252-9712
Altris Software	eB IDM product suite	www.altris.com	858-625-3000
AM1 Link S.A.	Digital Dashboard products	www.am1-link.com	511 2225177
American Management Systems	CaseFlow COM and DCOM components	www.amsinc.com	800-682-0028
Angoss Software	Angoss KnowledgeSTUDIO Angoss KnowledgeSEEKER	www.angoss.com	416-593-2416
ANT USA Inc.	Buyer's SKUTrack 2.0	marketing@antusa.com	978-635-0877
Anvil Technology Limited	ABSOLUTE 2.1	anvil@anvtech.co.uk	44(0)1707393 099
Apex Systems	WINit 1.6	winit@apexsystems.com	44(0)1455234 011
Applied Business Services, Inc.	ClientAccess 3.0	maureenw@clientaccess.com	301-417-2999
Applix, Inc.	Applix Helpdesk 7.0;	info@applix.com	508-870-0330
AppsCo Software	Analytic and BI development tools	www.appsco.com	425-451-9777
Appsmart	Appsmart 2.0	webmaster@appmart.com	408-777-4422
Appsource Corporation	Wired for OLAP 4.0	info@appsource.com	407-888-8050
Apropos Technology	Call Link 3.5	info@apropos.com	630-472-9600

Company Name	Product Name	E-mail/Web	Phone Number
Archer Enterprise Systems Inc.	Archer Enterprise for ACT! 3.0	info@archerent.com	416-292-5751
Archicentro CDS, c.a.	Document Management	www.archicentro.com.ve	58-2-251-2486
Archimedes Software	Bug Base 2.1	74012.1511@compuserve.com	425-828-4305
arcplan Information Services	inSight 2.40	info@arcplan.com	49 21130087
Ardent Software	Datasage data integration infrastructure	www.informix.com	508-366-3888
ARIS Software	NoetixDW 1.0	noetixsales@aris.com	425-372-2747
ARTech Consultores S.R.L.	Workflow solutions	www.genexus.com	(598 2) 402 20 82
ASD Corporation	Microsoft based accoutning, e-commerce and busines automtation software	www.advandedsoftware.com	800-859-6007
Aspect Telecommunications	Aspect WinSet for Windows 2.1	steve.bonbright@aspect.com	408-325-2200
Astea Internation	Service centric CRM and integrated eCRM software solutions	www.astea.com	215-682-2500
Astea Int'l., Inc.	AllianceMobile 4.0	info@astea.com	
Atec Group	network design and configruation	www.atecgroup.com	518-452-3700
Attachmate Corporation	Crosstalk Classic 3.1	support@attachmate.com	425-644-4010
Attar Software Limited	XpertRule Miner 2	info@attar.co.uk	441-942608844
Aurigen Sytems	Content driven software systems	www.aurigin.com	408-873-8400
AutoData Systems	Automated data collection software and imaging scanners	www.autodata.com	800-662-2192
Automated Concepts	Information technolgoy consuting fimr specializing in KM systems integratin	www.autocon.com	732-602-0200

Company Name	Product Name	E-mail/Web	Phone Number
Avance	CallTrak 5.20	swrdfghtr@worldnet.att.net	610-280-0694
Avensoft	Perfect Tracker 3.5	master@avensoft.com	714-606-5321
Avnet Applied computing	MCSE-cerified technical development managers	www.acs.avnet.com	626-307-6101
AVT corporation	Business to business communications solutions	www.avtc.com	425-825-3486
Axisoft	KM software	www.axisoft.com.hk	852-2603-6662
Axix Consulting	Consulting services related to the architecture, design and implementaiton of BI solutions	www.axisconsulting.com	908-508-0872
Axonet	Integrated workflow, dcoument management, digitial signature, encryption. E-forms, database access, threaded discussion and security access control	www.axonetinc.com	978-772-3590
Axtel Applied Technology	ScanImage tools for imaging systems	www.axtel.com	714-964-6686
AZMY Thinkware, Inc.	SuperQuery Office Edition 1.20	mail@azmy.com	201-947-1881
Baan	Baan Company is a leading provider of enterprise business software	www.bann.com	703-234-6000
Baan Company	BaanBIS Decision Manager 1.3	abogert@baan.nl	+31 342 477664
BackWeb Tedchnologies	e-business solutions that enable companies to communicate time sensitive, business-critical information	www.backweb.com	408-933-1739
Bamboo Solutions	Infotrak is an enterpreise information control software	www.bamboosolutions.com	877-BAMBOO2

Company Name	Product Name	E-mail/Web	Phone Number
BCTS	Pre-packaged solutin for BI	www.bcts.com.pe	511-441-7273
BEKESANTOS Group	Manuals for policies, norms and procedures	www.bekesantgos.com	582-761.60.82
Bendata Inc.	HEAT (Helpdesk Expert Automation Tool) 4.1	moreinfo@bendata.com	719-531-5007
Bennelong Software International	Professional Knowledge Manager 1.0	sales@bennelong.com.au	+ 61 2 9929 5711
Best Pratices LLC	IKM	www.kmexcellence.com	919-403-0251
Big Island Communication	YoYo Call Tracker for Windows 95/NT/98 1.1	info@big-island.com	650-237-0350
BI-Logix, Inc.	No Product Name Specified	info@bilogix.com	973-360-0750
Blackboard	Blackboard is the leading online education company	www.blackboard.com	202-463-4860
Blue Ocean Software	Track-It! Help Desk/ Inventory Software 3.0	info@blueocean.com	813-977-4553
Blueware Project Management Services	Project management	www.bluwtr.com	253-874-8884
BMC Software	BMC software provices systems and application management solutions for Microsoft Windows NT environments	www.bmc.com	800-841-2031
BNS Group	Office Email Merge 1.3	sales@bnsgroup.com	612 62851988
Borealis Technology Corporation	Arsenal 3.1	info@brls.com	702-888-3200
BORN Information Services	e-business and technology solutions	www.born.com	800-469-BORN
Brainware.CRM AG	Internet/Intranet	www.brainware.de	49-7525-92150
Breakaway International, Inc.	Breakaway Vision	gpeek@breakawaynet.com	817-788-8888
Brightware	eCustomer Assistance software for the Internet	www.brightware.com	800-532-2890

Company Name	Product Name	E-mail/Web	Phone Number
Brio Technology	BI, enterprise information portal, enterprise reporting, and analytic application solutions	www.brio.com	800-879-2746
Brio Technology Inc.	BrioQuery Designer 5.5	info@brio.com	650-856-8000
Broadbase Software	Analytic and operational applicaitonsw that enable e-business to get closer to their cuswtomers	www.broadbase.com	650-614-8300
BTRG, Inc.	Membership Management System 2.7	info@btrg.com	407-886-2533
Buchanan Associates	e-business, B2B and B2C applications	www.buchanan.com	888-730-2774
Bullseye Systems	Tracker I 1.1	sales@bullseyesystems.com	408-266-9226
Bullseye Systems	Helpdesk I 4.0	sales@bullseyesystems.com	408-266-9226
Business Architects International NV	Banking and insurance business solutions	www.bai.be	32-15-27-34-03
Business Engine Software	e-commerce solutions for global IT, R&D, and professional services organizations	www.businessengine.com	415-616-4000
Business Objects	e-business intelligence (e-BI) solutions	www.businessobjects.com	408-953-6000
BYM Epistem	Distributed networks and KM	www.epistem.com.tr	90-212-03-21
ByteQuest Technologies	e-mail management solutions	www.bytequest.com	613-728-5977
C&S Informatica e Multimidia	C&S JADE job scheduler	www.ces.com.br	55-21-722-3017
C.Halezle Associates	Printers, scanners, spares, repairs and consumables	www.chainc.com	949-251-9000
C2C	Active folders for exhange	www.C2C.com	44-1189-511-211
Cactus	KM and BI	www.cactus.ca	819-778-0313

Company Name	Product Name	E-mail/Web	Phone Number
CallWare Technologies, Inc	CallWare Voice Mail for Windows NT 5.2	sales@callware.com	801-984-1100
Captiva Software	Formware 3.0	www.captivasoftware.com	858-320-1000
Cardiac	IMATIS is a distributed information system	www.cardiac.no	47-35-93-06-00
CAS GmbH	CP Sales Suite	www.cas.com	49-6331/727-0
CAVU Corporation	Lumber Sales Automation System 1	sales@cavucorp.com	919-846-9275
CDP Communicarions	Bill presentment technology	www.cdpcom.com	416-865-9966
Centra Software	Software infrastructure and a B2B marketplace for live Internet collaboration	www.centra.com	781-861-7000
Chase Bobko	Plan, build, and manage services for Web-based applications and content management	www.chasebobko.com	206-547-4310
Cincom Systems	Complete multi-channel CRM selling solutions	www.cincom.com	513-612-2300
Cipher Systems	Knowledge.Works	h.hadfield@cipher-sys.com	410-349-0537
Cipher Systems	KM groupware application for competitive intelligence professionals	www.cipher-sys.com	410-349-0537
CIS	Package software for knowledge workers	www.cis.co.jp	81-3-3438-0531
Cizer software	e-reporting and OLAP	www.cizer.com	800-622-1240
Clarify, Inc.	ClearSupport (r)	info@clarify.com	408-573-3000
Click2learn.com	e-learning applications	www.click2learn.com	425-462-0501
ClickService Software	Web and intranet solutions	www.clickservice.com	408-377-6088
Coeur Business Int'l	VARoffice 2.0	info@coeurbiz.com	913-888-5588
Cognos	End-to-end enterprise business intelligence	www.cognos.com	613-738-1440

Company Name	Product Name	E-mail/Web	Phone Number
Cogos	Andromedia2000 for Microsoft Outlook/ Exchange	www.cogos.com	978-448-6712
COM:ON Communication Systems GmbH	C3-Messenger 3.1	înfo@com-on.de	+49 40 23 658
COM2001.com	NTX Enterprise Communications Server 1.0	sales@COM2001.com	619-314-2001
Comintell	Solutions, portals and applications for KM and competitive intelligence	www.comintell.com	617-867-0282
Command Software Systems	Command AntiVirus	www.commandcom.com	561-575-3200
Commercial Banking Applications	IBAS International Banking Automation Systems	www.cba.no	47-22-80-00
Compsys Australia Pty Ltd	IntrDesk 4.0	info@compsysaus.com.au	612 99225055
CompuDoc, Inc	Chamber of Commerce Membership Program CH2	rmajors@compudoc-inc.com	501-812-4030
CompuEx	CompuEx Easy Accounting	anass@compu-ex.com	
Computer Aided Marketing, Inc.	CAM Frequent Diner 2.0	sales@caminc.com	919-932-5566
Computer Associates International, Inc.	Unicenter TNG Advanced Help Desk Option	cainfo@cai.com	516-342-5224
Computer Research Group	Information management applications	www.crginfo.com	760-510-9800
Computer Research Group, Inc.	i-SITE Sales Manager 2.0	CRG@crginfo.com	760-510-9800
Computer Science Innovations, Inc.	Visualizer Workstation 1.0	info@csihq.com	407-676-2923

Company Name	Product Name	E-mail/Web	Phone Number
Computer Solutions Group	Enterprise consulting, solution design, development and integration, technical and end user training and support services	www.tcsc.com	804-794-3491
Computing Solutions Limited	Linkway 6.x	Sales@CSLLink.com	441 906000000
CompuTrac	LFMS Firm Management System	www.computrac.com	972-234-4241
Comshare	MPC Management Planning and Control		734-994-4800
ComSquared Systems	Turnkey solutions for high-volume business applications	www.comsquared.com	770-734-5300
Conform Systems	Conference and event management	www.consys.com	44-1730-302930
Connectivity Software Systems	Directory Monitor to copy files and programs over a network link	www.csusa.com	520-885-5200
Context Co., Ltd.	DALSolution 4.0	context@context.ru	+007-095-124 2566
Coral Sea Software	Barracuda 1.2	sales@coralsea.com.au	617 54434050
Coral Sea Software	SysMan 3.3	sales@coralsea.com.au	617 54434050
Coresoft Technologies, Inc.	CenterPoint	info@coresoft.com	801-431-0070
Cornerstone Management Systems	CMS TextMap 1.0	info@cmshome.com	405-238-4144
Corporate Workflow Solutions	Workflow development, business process re-engineering, system integration migration, cross-platform connectivity, document management, KM and collaboration management	www.corp-workflow.com	561-747-0808

Company Name	Product Name	E-mail/Web	Phone Number
Correlate Tedchnologies Inc.	B2B and enterprise information exchange	www.correlate.com	650-827-8888
CorVu Corporation	CorPortfolio	amissroon@corvu.com	770-329-8749
CosmoCom, Inc.	CosmoCall Universe	info@cosmocom.com	631-940-4200
CoSORT (Innovative Routines Int'l, Inc.)	CoSORT Parallel Sorting 7.00	info@iri.com	407-952-9400
CrossRoads Software	CrossRoads Customer Management	info@crossroads-software.com	650-685-9966
CubeNet Internet Services, Inc.	E-Commerce Solutions for MAS 90		949-766-0831
CurrentView	Imaging and dcoument management technologies	www.currentviewinc.com	800-920-0728
Cyberscience Corporation	CQ/A – Cyberquery Accelerator 7.00	info@cyberscience.com	+44 (0) 1992441111
Cybertech Solutions	@Path 2000 Workflow System	www.cybertechx.com	852-2856 3801
Cycos Ag	MRS – Message Routing System	www.cycos.com	49-2402-901
Cypress	Integrated document and Knowedge server	www.cypressdelivers.com	248-852-0066
D2K Incorporated	D2K-Tapestry 2.0	sales@d2k.com	408-451-2010
D2K Incorporated	D2K-Tapestry 2.0	sales@d2k.com	408-451-2010
Dart Communications	Power TCP 1.0	info@dart.com	315-431-1024
Dart Communications	Power TCP 1.0	info@dart.com	315-431-1024
Data Junction Corporation	Data Junction 6.5		512-459-1308
Datacap	Data and document capture applications	www.datacap.com	914-366-0100
Dataflight Software, Inc.	Concordance Information Retrieval System 6.60		310-471-3414
DataFlux Corporation	Blue Fusion	info@dataflux.com	919-846-9000

Company Name	Product Name	E-mail/Web	Phone Number
Datalink	Networked storage systems for open system computing environments	www.datalink.com	800-448-6314
Datamax Technologies	VisiFlow Suite	www.dtmx.com	310-645-4199
Datametrics Systems	ViewPoint—for the analysis of system performance of system, database, storage, Intenet and e-mail servers	www.datametrics.com	703-385-7700
DataMirror	Transformation Server 4.1	info@datamirror.com	905-415-0310
Datasweep	Web centric suypply chain manufacturing solutions	www.datasweep.com	408-275-1400
Datatrade	Digital report management system	www.datatrade.com	417-882-1576
Datawatch Corporation	Monarch Data Pump 1.00	sales@datawatch.com	(978)988-9700
Datum Inc.	TymServe 2100-GPS	sales@datum.com	408-578-4161
Decision Support Panel	Data warehouse client in Microsoft Outlookand Digital Dashboards	www.dspanel.com	46-8-457-56-70
Decision Support Systems	Business Intelligence	www.decision.ie	003-1-661-9530
Decisioneering, Inc.	Crystal Ball 4.0		303-534-1515
Decisionism	e-business information reporting and analysys solutions	www.decisionism.com	303-938-8805
Definitive Software Inc.	Definitive Scenario 2.0	jteigen@definitivesoftware.com	303-460-0100
Definitive Software Inc.	Definitive Scenario 2.0	jteigen@definitivesoftware.com	303-460-0100
DEK Software International	SysMan 3.3		800-335-5595
DeLani Technologies, LLC	SwiftKnowledge	info@delani.com	888-643-1986
Delano Technology	e-business interaction suite	www.delanotech.com	905-764-5499

Company Name	Product Name	E-mail/Web	Phone Number
Delfin Systems	Collaborative business solutions	www.delfinsyhstems.com	703-449-7600
DeltaPro	Market Analysis Matrix(TM)		425-672-1407
Dendronic Decisions Limited	No Product Name Specified	info@dendronic.com	780-421-0800
Digital Lava Inc.	ASP—Application Services Provider	www.digitallava.com	310-577-0200
DocuCorp	Communications	www.docucorp.com	800-735-6620
Docunet AG	DocuWare document management system	www.docunet.com	49-89-894433-0
Domain Knowledge Inc.	ProCarta document and process knowledge maps	www.domainknowledge.com	416-597-2733
DST Systems	Automated work distributor	www.dstsystems.com	888-DST-INFO
ease, Global Insurance	Analytical and management information	www.ease-corp.com	582-234-4601
Eastman Kodak	Document Imaging	www.kodak.com	800-243-8811
eB Networks	Consulting, design, development, and infrastructure	www.ebnetworks.com	973-428-9600
eCertain	Internet service company	www.eCertain.com	512-477-1892
Eclipsys	Healthcare	www.eclipsys.com	561-243-1440
ECMS	Enterprise communications and messaging solutions	www.ecms.net	803-978-5600
EDGE Software	WorkDraw	www.workdraw.com	925-462-0543
EDM International	Data capture and Information Processing	www.edmi.com	915-225-2580
eGroup	Computer systems design, installation and support	www.eGroup-us.com	843-722-6360
eLabor.com	Labor resource planning	www.elabor.com	805-383-8500
ELAN GMK	Internet based publishing solution	www.elan-gmk.com	805-577-0288

Company Name	Product Name	E-mail/Web	Phone Number
Elind Systems	K-Space (Knowledge Space) for KM	www.eelind-india.com	91-080-532-1255
Eloquent	Web-based rich media business communications	www.eloquent.com	650-294-6500
Engenia Software	XML based Digtal Dashboard	www.engenia.com	703-234-1400
e-office bv	KM in e-Commerce with groupware	www.e-office.com	31-30-693-05-50
EOS International	Library information management and access	www.eosintl.com	800-876-5484
Epicor Software	Performance solutions	www.epicor.com	44-1344-468-468
EPM Technology	Express Data Manager	www.epmtech.jotne.com	47-23-17-17-00
EPS Software	Budget 2000 3.1	slawson@epssoftware.com	905-279-8711
Equisys	Fax server software	www.zetafax.com	770-772-7201
eRoom Technology	Digital workplace	www.eroom.com	888-593-7666
Esker	Fax automation	www.esker.com	405-624-8000
eTEK International	Open database, web-enabled client/server accounting	www.etek.net	303-627-4737
European Management Systems	ActiveAnalyst 1.0	dpmlee@euroman.co.uk	
Evolutionary Technologies Inc. (ETI)	ETI*EXTTRACT FX 4.0	information@eti.com	512-327-6994
Evolutionary Technologies International	Enterprise data integration management	www.eti.com	512-383-3000
Excalibur Technologies	Intelligent search solutions	www.excalib.com	703-761-3700
eXcelon	B2B commerce	www.exceloncorp.com	781-674-5000
ExecuSys, Inc	Graphical Enterprise Management Solution	info@execusys.com	407-253-0077
Executive Focus Group	EM&S (Enterprise Marketing and Sales)	robbinh@efgstl.com	314-878-6900

Company Name	Product Name	E-mail/Web	Phone Number
Executive Technologies	Search Express document imaging	www.searchexpress.com	205-933-5494
Exocom	Integrateed e-business strategy and technology implementation	www.exocom.com	613-237-0257
ExperVision	Typereader Professional scanner	www.expervision.com	800-732-3897
Explorer Software Inc.	Explorer Contract Manager.cs	sales@explorer-software.com	800-665-8966
Extreme Logic	e-services consultancy	www.extremlogic.com	800-682-4099
FAILSAFE	Med E Tools		916-624-7678
FDP	Contact Partner	pattif@fdpcorp.com	305-858-8200
Fenestrae	Knowledge Management	www.fenestraw.com	31-70-3015-100
Fieldscope	Measurement and reporting solutions	www.fieldscope.com	203-637-1922
FileLink Corporation	FileLink Medical Archive Software 4.5	info@filelink.com	612-883-3280
FileNET	Web content management	www.FileNET.com	714-327-3400
FinancialCAD Corporation	FinancialCAD for Excel / PLUS 3.05	info@fincad.com	604-572-3682
Firstlogic, Inc.	No Product Name Specified	information@firstlogic.com	608-782-5000
Firstwave Technologies, Inc.	TakeControl	info@firstwave.net	770-431-1200
Fiserv	CRM systems	www.fiserv.com	800-872-7882
Flatiron Solutions, Inc.	Mainframe Data Engine 2000 7	info@flatironsolutions.com	212-645-3838
FLEXSTOR.net	Digital content and asset management	www.flexstornet.com	612-829-0300
FMR Systems, Inc.	The Relationship Management System	sales@fmr-systems.com	847-934-5566
FrontZone Corporation	GoldSupport 1.1	sales@frontzone.com	408-615 0110

Company Name	Product Name	E-mail/Web	Phone Number
F-Secure	Security solutions	www.F-Secure.com	408-938-6700
FutureNext Consulting	e-business and supply chain management solutions	www.futurenext.com	877-847-1600
Geppetto's Workshop	AntQuery 1.2	geppetto@geppetto.com	630-986-8700
GHS Global Inc.	G4 System	anne.marie.fields@ghsglobal.net	415-289-1118
Global Village Communication	FaxWorks Server 2.0	sales@globalvillage.com	408-523-1000
GlobeNet Software	Interact BizCast 4.1	sales@globenetsoftware.com	480-718-7000
Glossary Inc	Production Assistant 1.3	sales@glossaryinc.com	734 697-4970
Gnossos Software, Inc	Keep In Touch: Grassroots	info@gnossos.com	202-463-1200
GoldMine Software	Account management, sales force automation and marketing automation	www.goldmine.com	310-454-6800
GoldMine Software Corporation	GoldMine Standard Edition 4.0		310-454-6800
gov24.com	Government empowerment	www.gov24.com	877-MYGOV24
Graycorp Pty Ltd	Gcorp 2000	byron@graycorp.com.au	+61 8 8365 6822
GroupLink	Help Desk / Support Center Module 2.0	info@GroupLink.net	801-298-9888
Handley Computer Corp	HCC Conference Registration System V1.25	bruceh@csn.net	303-494-6035
Harbor Technology Group	Affinity Sales Support 3.0	joegreco@dnai.com	510-523-6623
Harmony Software Inc.	Harmony Software Solution	vhuntzinger@harmony.com	650-696-9580
helpIT systems ltd	matchIT 4.0	sales@helpit.co.uk	
Highlander Business Solutions	LawOffice 2000 Corporate Manager		416-971-7460 ext. 234

Company Name	Product Name	E-mail/Web	Phone Number
HiSoftware	Web sites, Knowledge management	www.hisoftware.com	603-229-3055
Hogia Säljsystem AB	Hogia Open 990304	tommy.wiberg@hogia.se	
House-on-the-Hill Software Ltd.	SupportDesk 6.00	info@houseonthehill.com	0161 449 7057
Hummingbird Communications	Enterprise software solutions		416-496-2200
ibhar Software	Enterprise relationship management	www.ibhar.com	91-44-621750
ICL	Legacy integration and SQL Server, Internet and COM+ technologies	www.ICL.com	44-28-904-74200
iCommunicate	iCommunicate.NET	ally.sharad@icommunicate.net	888-484-4401
icomxpress	Keyflow Commerce	cindym@icomxpress.com	603-883-3800
Idea Integration	Knowledge warehouse	www.consultinpartners.com	972-386-7858
IDS Scheer	ARIS Toolset	www.ids-scheer.com	610-558-7600
if...	if...Synchrony 3.0	info@iftime.com	510-864-3480
IFCA Consulting Group	IFCA Construction & Project Information System		603-705-3838
iManage	B2B collaboration networks	www.imanage.com	650-356-1166
Imecom Group, Inc.	Fax Resource Connector for MS Exchange 4.1		603-569-0600
Imparto Software Corp.	Imparto Web Marketing Suite 1.5	sales@imparto.com	650-567-5700
IMR	Knowledge sharing portals	www.imrgold.com	303-689-0022
Incendo	Dedal	denisf@incendo.hr	+385 1 4804888
Inference	Personalized e-service and support solutions	www.inference.com	415-893-7200
Influence Software	Aperio 2.0	info@influencesw.com	408-617-0400
Info Directions, Inc.	CostGuard 2.0	sales@infodir.com	716-924-4110

Company Name	Product Name	E-mail/Web	Phone Number
InfoActiv, Inc.	ProActiv Design Reporter 1.1	sales@infoactiv.com	610-692-6292
Infocorp	Corporate Information Portal	www.infocorp.com.uy	5982-707-5155
InfoImage	Decision portal software	www.infoimage.com	602-234-6900
InfoKinetics	Custom software development	www.infokinetics.com	970-223-9248
Informatica	eCRM Analytics	www.informatica.com	650-687-8200
Informatica Corporation	Informatica PowerCenter 1.0	sales@infodir.com	415-462-8900
Information Advantage	MyEureka! 6.0		0181 867 4600
Information Builders	Data integration and business intelligence	jon.drakes@infoadvan.co.uk	212-736-4433
Information Discovery	Data mining oriented decision support	www.datamining.com	310-937-3600
Infosquare.com	Information portals	www.infosquare.com	408-556-0590
Infozech – Innovative software Solutions	Billing and customer care solutions 3.0	market@infozech.com	
Innovations Media	KM systems	www.innovationsmedia.com	905-949-0049
InsignIO	Enterprise infrastructure Business Software	www.insignio.com	631-444-5389
Integra Business Systems	Enterprise Report Management (COLD)	www.ibsimage.com	727-725-4507
Integral Solutions Limited	Clementine V4.0	isl@isl.co.uk	
Integration Technologies Group, Inc.	Folders for ACT! Solution Framework 2.2	info@itgonline.com	703-698-8282
IntegrationWare	Enterprise search, knowledge repository and portal capabilities	www.integrationware.com	847-777-2323
Integrator Software Internacional	Integrator Windows 2.0	company@integrator.es	

Company Name	Product Name	E-mail/Web	Phone Number
Interact Commerce Corporation—formerly SalesLogix	SalesLogix2000 for Sales		480-368-3835
Interactive Intelligence	Communications software	www.inter-intelli.com	317-872-3000
Interactive Intelligence, Inc.	Interaction Director 1.0		317-872-3000
InterActive WorkPlace, Inc.	InterActive WorkPlace 1.0	info@activework.com	781-238-1500
Interface Software, Inc.	InterAction 4.0	sales@interfacesoftware.com	630-572-1400
International Software Group, Inc.	ISG Navigator 1.6	info@isgsoft.com	781-221-1450
Internet Software Sciences	Web+Center Free Version 1.5		650 949-0942
Intersis, S. A.	VoiXX – Voice for Microsoft Exchange 1.0	marketing@voixx.com	770-980-6615
IntraNet Solutions	Web content management	www.intranetsolutions.com	952-903-2000
Intraspect Software	Business to business collaborative solutions	www.intraspect.com	650-943-6000
Inxight Software	Knowledge extraction and informatin visualization in support of EIPs	www.inxight.com	877-INXIGHT
IQ Software Corporation	IQ/Objects 6.0		770-446-8880
ISI Infortext	Infortel NT 3.10	sales@isi-info.com	847-995-0002
ISI Infortext	Infortel for Windows 3	sales@isi-info.com	847-995-0002
ISYS/Odyssey Development	Search and Index engines	www.isysusa.com	303-689-9998
IT Resources Inc.	SPIN Retail Data Analysis System		856-761-4006
IXOS Software	Internet document portal	www.ixos.com	650-294-5800
JAMLogic Software, Inc.	Healthcare Counselor	aev@jamlogic.com	303-690-8113
Janna Systems	Enterprise Relationship Management		416-483-7711

Company Name	Product Name	E-mail/Web	Phone Number
Janus Technologies, Inc.	Argis 5.0		
Jetform	Knowledge management workflow and tracking	www.jetform.com	613-230-3676
KCI Computing Inc.	CONTROL 7.1	Sales@KCIcorp.com	310-643-0222
KM Technologies	KMSuite	www.kmtechnologies.com	514-495-4201
KML Systems	SharpShooter 2.0	grant.wattie@clear.net.nz	64 4 5650903
Knosys	Proclarity analytical platform	sales@knosysinc.com	208-344-1630
Knowledge Junction Systems Inc.	ConciseTarget 1.0		604-939-4170
Knowledge Management Software	Knowledge management systems	www.kmspic.com	888-355-4098
Knowledge Systems Design	Knowledge-based systems	www.knowledgesys.com	949-723-2944
Knowledge Technologies International	Knowledge-based applications	www.ktiworld.com	01926-438100
KnowledgeTrack	Enterprise portal platform	www.knowledgetrack.com	925-738-1000
KPI Technologies Inc	KPI Manager 3.5	sales@kpi-tech.com	770-590-5001
KPMG Consulting LLC	Web-centric, knowledge management services	www.kpmgconsulting.com	410-295-9555
Kuster Computers	The Courier Solution 3.0	kuster@gate.net	305-513-0655
LeadingWay Corporation	KM Learning System	paulk@leadingway.com	949-453-1112
Legacy Systems Research	Cost$Benefit Analysis Tool 3.1	legasys@aol.com	208-522-5401
Leigh Business Enterprises Ltd.	LBE Web Helpdesk 1.02	sales@lbehelpdesk.com	+44 (0)2380 871465
Lingo Computer Design Inc	Fiscal	lingo@rogerswave.ca	416-593-5334
Lucent Technologies	CRM Central 2000	www.lucent.com	877-FOR-CRM1
Magic Solutions International, Inc.	SupportMagic//WEB 4.0	info@magicrx.com	201-587-1515

Company Name	Product Name	E-mail/Web	Phone Number
Magic Solutions International, Inc.	SupportMagic Enterprise Edition 4.0	info@magicrx.com	201-587-1515
Main Sequence Technology	PCRecruiter 3.90.399	martin@mainsequence.net	440-209-8301
Mainstream Software, Inc.	Mainstream Service System 4.0	sales@mainstreams.com	330-963-0103
Mallorn Information Systems Innovators	Enterprise Infonet System (EIS) 1.8	sales@misi.ca	613-591-7644
MathSoft Inc., Data Analysis Products Di	StatServer 2.0	sales-info@mathsoft.com	206-283-8802
Maximal	Easy-to-use BI software	www.maxsw.com	703-925-5959
Maximal Corporation	Max™ business intelligence software	info@maxsw.com	703-925 5959
Maximal Corporation	Max™ for ProClarity®	info@maxsw.com	703-925 5959
Media Consulting	Web Replicator Light 1.0		
MEI Group	UniverSell 2.2	infomei@mei.ca	514-384-6411
Menhir Ltd.	Rapport 2.9	info@menhir.com	
Mesa Systems Guild	Product development portal	www.mesavista.com	888-637-2797
Mesonic International	WINLine SupportNET 1.1	info@mesonic.com	
Meta4	Knownet provides active management of individuals and their knowledge	www.meta4.com	404-760-4300
Metastorm	eBusiness software for medium- and large- sized enterprises	www.metastorm.com	410-647-9691
Methodus	InsuranceReady for insurance customer relationship management	www.methodus.com	351-214228870
Metro One	Business Category Thesaurus 2.0	info@db-one.com	716-377-0580
Metz Software	Enterprise contact and relationship management	www.metz.com	425-641-4525

Company Name	Product Name	E-mail/Web	Phone Number
METZ Software, Inc.	METZ Phones Pro Small Business Edition 8.0	metz@metz.com	425-641-4525
Micro Consulting SA	Office Maker Addresses 3.1	info@microconsulting.ch	
MineShare	ASP—Application Services Provider	www.mineshare.com	310-396-6463
MIS	MIS Alea 3.7		
Moding Ltd.	BizDoc	sales@moding.com	(972)-9-8851110
MoneySoft, Inc.	Coporate Valuation 1.0	mbray@moneysoft.com	619-689-8341
Montauk Technology Co. LLC	Montauk Sales Automation 1.1	sales@montauktechnology.com	201-368-0462
Moss Software, Inc.	ActiveSales 3.2	sales@mosssoftware.com	949-260-0300
Motiva	eBusiness solutions for collaborative change management	www.motica.com	858-481-4822
Multiactive Software	Maximizer 97is	info@multiactive.com	604-601-8000
Mustang Software, Inc.	Internet Message Center – Business 2.4	sales@mustang.com	661-873-2500
mydocuments.com	Document management	www.myudocuments.com	631-567-9409
NCR	Windows 2000-based Teradata Active Warehouse	www.ncr.com	937-445-5000
NetMagic Systems, Inc.	NetMagic-Pro HelpDesk 4.0	jharris@netmagicinc.com	914-739-4579
NetManage, Inc.	eDemo 1.1		408-973-7171
NetManage, Inc.	SupportNow 2.3	et-sales@netmanage.com	408-973-7171
NetPower	DocManager – CRM		51958000
Network Associates Inc.	McAfee HelpDesk 3.5		408-988-3832
Newmarket International, Inc.	Global SFA 7.1.2a	salesinfo@newsoft.com	603-436-7500
Nextwave Media Inc.	AV Imaginet	ccarman@nextwavemedia.com	215-860-9597
NovaStor Corporation	NovaNet 7 7.0	sales@novastor.com	805-579-6700

Company Name	Product Name	E-mail/Web	Phone Number
Numerical Algorithms Group	NAG Library		630-971-2337
OLAP@Work Inc	OLAP@Work for Excel 1.2	sales@olapatwork.com	613-271-7199
Omtool	Fax Sr.	asksales@omtool.com	603-898-8900
ON!contact Software Corporation	Client Management Software (CMS) 4.0	info@oncontact.com	262.375.6555
Onyx Software	Front Office 2000 enterprise-wide, customer-centric eBusiness solutions	www.onyx.com	888-ASK-ONYX
ONYX Software Corporation	ONYX Customer Center 3.5		425-451-8060
Open Universal Software	No Product Name Specified	sdurand@universal.com	514-344-6040
OpenPlus International	OpenPlus Sales Order Management		512-328-1231
OpenText	Intranet, extranet and eBusiness applications	www.opentext.com	800-499-6544
Optas, Inc.	Optas Direct 2.1	info@optas.com	781-729-3332
Optika	Process and content delivery over the web	www.optika.com	719-548-9800
Optima Technologies, Inc.	Opti-InSight		770-951-1161
OPTIUM Digital Solutions	Disease Self Management Network	acole@optium.com	416-485-1100
Orbital Software	Expert-based community software and services	www.orbitalsw.com	508-485-4007
Orbital Software Inc	Organik V3.1	Robert@orbitalsw.com	508-663-2000
Pacific Edge Software	Project knowledge management solutions	www.pacificedge.com	425-897-8800
PakNetX Corporation	PNX(tm)ACD 1.0	sales@paknetx.com	603-890-6616
Paradigm Technologies Corp.	RouteMan 2.0	thendric@paradigmtechcorp.com	905-828-4197

Company Name	Product Name	E-mail/Web	Phone Number
ParkerSoft	FastCast Time Series Forecaster 1.0	info@parkersoft.com	203-552-9230
Pegasystems Inc.	PegaSystem 97.1	info@pegasystems.com	617-374-9600
Pena Systems, Inc.	Gabriel 1.00	mestabro@penasys.com	303-684-6711
Peregrine Systems, Inc.	AssetCenter 3.0		619-481-5000
Persoft, Inc.	Persona Entry 2.0	sales@persoft.com	608-273-6000
Persoft, Inc.	Persona Insight 2.0	sales@persoft.com	608-273-6000
Pilot Software Inc.	Pilot Decision Support Suite		617-374-9400
Pipestream Technologies, Inc.	Sales Continuum	jandrews@ipctech.com	804-285-9300
Pivotal Software, USA	Pivotal Relationship 99	info@pivotal.com	604-988-9982
Platinum Technology	Platinum InfoPump		630-620-5000
Portera	Web-hosted, subscription based applications and business services	www.portera.com	408-364-3600
Portola Dimensional Systems	Coronado 1.0	sales@portolasystems.com	415-836-6710
PowerCerv	PowerCerv Sales Force Automation 7.0		813-226-2600
Powerway	Document management	www.powerway.com	800-964-9004
Pragmatech Software	The RFP Machine 3.0	rfpinfo@rfpmachine.com	603-672-8941
Pragmatech Software	No Product Name Specified	rfpinfo@rfpmachine.com	603-672-8941
Prairie Development Inc.	EmpACT Advanced Office Automation System 6.0	salesinfo@prairiedev.com	612-854-3050
PricewarehouseCoopers	SUMMIT Ascendant	www.summitcoe.com	610-993-5381
Primera Technologies, Inc.	PrimEnterprise 1.0	rbl@primeratech.com	508-485-8880
Primus	eCRM sofware and services	www.primus.com	206-292-1000
Prism Solutions	Prism Executive Suite 2.0	info@prismsolutions.com	408-752-1888

Company Name	Product Name	E-mail/Web	Phone Number
Productivity Systems	Optionfind.com		860-927-1236
Profit Solutions, Inc.	Profit Solutions e-CRM 5.0	info@profitsolutions.com	612-893-2388
Prolog Business Solutions Ltd	SalesNet 1.15	snetsales@prolog.co.uk	44 (0) 1246 439400
ProVantage Software, Inc.	ProVantage 4.0	sales@provantagesoftware.com	425-455-3507 ext. 214
Ptech	eEnterprise Architectures	www.ptechinc.com	800-955-9345
Qiva Sdn. Bhd.	IQship	ian_k_grant@qiva.com	603-2164-5800
Quintus	Electronic CRM	www.quintus.com	510-770-2800
Quintus Corporation	eContact Suite 5.0	sales@quintus.com	510-624-2800
Quintus Corporation	No Product Name Specified	sales@quintus.com	510-624-2800
Radiant Systems, Inc.	Wave	kmildenburger@radiantsystems.com	770-576-6573
Raft International	Reusable COM business components	www.raftinternational.com	44-20-7847-0400
Rational Concepts	Web browser for performance measurement	www.rationalconcepts.com	760-632-0444
Red Brick Systems, Inc.	Red Brick Warehouse for Windows NT 5.1	info@redbrick.com	408-399-3200
Remedy Corporation	Action Request System	info@remedy.com	415-903-5200
Report2Web	Report portal	www.report2web.com	919-787-5464
Resource Company	Business operations and KM	www.resourcecompany.com	540-372-9290
RODOPI Software	RODOPI Billing Software 4.02	sales@rodopi.com	619-558-8522
RoweCom	Acquisition of knowledge resources (magazines, newspapers, journals and books)	www.rowe.com	800-ROWECOM
royalblue technlogies	royalblue HelpDesk 5.0	frontoffice@royalblue.com	44 (0) 1483 744400

Company Name	Product Name	E-mail/Web	Phone Number
Saba	Internet-based B2B learning networks	www.saba.com	877-saba-101
Saba Software, Inc.	Saba Education Management System (EMS) 2.1.3	info@sabasoftware.com	650-696-3840
Sagemaker	EIP solutions	www.sagemaker.com	704-973-3766
SalesLogix	Sales and support automation software	www.saleslogix.com	800-176-193
Saratoga Systems	Enterprise customer relationship management software	www.saratogasystems.com	408-558-9600
SAS Institute	Open OLAP server, BI, and data mining solutions	www.sas.com	919-677-8000
sbasoft, Inc	Datastatistics Service	redenzon@sbasoft.com	818-505-6409 ext. 140
Seagate Software	Access, analyze, report and share organizational data	www.seagatesoftware.com	604-681-3435
Securit-e-Doc, Inc.	Securit-e-Doc	dhoskins@securit-e-doc.com	800-497-1670
Selligent	CRM software	www.selligent.com	32-2-7-14-5420
Semeron	Products, services and technology solutions	www.semeron.com	206-686-1360
SenseNet	Document and information sharing	www.sensenet.com	212-824-5000
Sension Ltd	No Product Name Specified	sales@sension.com	01606 723000
Sequoia Software	XML Portal Server (XPS)	www.sequoiasoftware.com	410-715-0206
SER MacroSoft	Document management	www.sermacrosoft.com	248-853-5353
ServicePlus Corporation	ServicePlus Enterprise	info@serviceplus.com	819-770-4000
ServiceSoft	Knowledge-driven e-service solutions	www.servicesoft.com	508-853-4000
ServiceSoft Corporation	Web Advisor 3.0	sales@servicesoft.com	617-449-0049
ServiceWare	e-service solutions	www.serviceware.com	800-572-5748

Company Name	Product Name	E-mail/Web	Phone Number
Shoreline Communications	IP voice communications	www.shorelineteleworks.com	408-331-3300
Siebel Systems, Inc.	Siebel Sales Enterprise 5.0	ahsu@siebel.com	650-295-5000
Silknet Software, Inc.	No Product Name Specified	mcentrella@silknet.com	603-625-0070
Silvon Software	Customizable BI solutions	www.silvon.com	800-874-5866
Silvon Software, Inc.	DataTracker 2.1	info@silvon.com	630-655-3313
Simbient Pty	Strategic consulting and systems integration	www.tsg.com.au	61-2-9965-1888
Sirius Software, Inc.	Sirius GT Accounting for Windows 6.1	sales@siriusgt.com	937-228-4849
SiteScape	Web-based, asynochronous team collaboration software	www.sitescape.com	910-256-5038
Skillset Software	Enterprise workforce management	www.skillset.com	925-201-7200
SMARTech Corporation	Staff Ware 1.1	Info@SMARTechCorp.com	423-265-1892
Smartforce	eLearning applications	www.smartforce.com	650-817-5900
SmartSales	Opportunity Management and Sales Forecasting software	www.smartsales.com	416-410-3256
SmartSales Inc	OutSmart	nsleeth@smartsales.com	905-948-1709
SME Corporation	Web-based project portfolio management	www.smecorporation.com	415-381-9639
Smead Software Solutions	Smeadlink Integration Document Management Software	www.smead.com	800-216-3832
Soffront Software, Inc.	TRACKWeb SFA 6.0	sales@soffront.com	510-413-9000
SoftCell Communications	Real-View v2.2 – Real-Time Monitoring for Microsoft Exchange	info@scell.com	573-256-5550
Softgen	CIMNet 1.2	sales@softgenintl.com	214-880-0866

Company Name	Product Name	E-mail/Web	Phone Number
SoftPro	Manager 2000	arian@softpro.hr	(+385) 1 4848896
Software Artistry, Inc.	SA-Expertise for CRM 3.5	info@softart.com	317-843-1663
Software Innovation Inc.	Enterprise SalesMaker 5.5	helpdesk@softinn.com	416-368-3000
SOLARIUM SOFTWARE SYSTEMS, LLC	Glass-2000 2.1	marketing@solariumsoftware.com	909-766-6221
Sopheon	Knowledge solutions	www.sopheon.com	303-456-8246
SpartaCom	Web-based groupware applications	www.spartacom.com	770-622-2820
Spectria	e-business services	www.spectria.com	562-590-8090
Speedware Corporation Inc.	Esperant 4.0 4.0	moreinfo@speedware.com	925-867-3300
Speedware Corporation Inc.	Customer Service Analyzer (CSA) 1.0	moreinfo@speedware.com	925-867-3300
SQL Power Group Inc.	Power*Loader Suite 2.04	info@sqlpowergroup.com	416-218-5551
Sqribe Technologies	InSQRIBE 1.0	info@sqribe.com	650-298-9400
SRA International	Web KM templates for law, etc.	www.knowledge4m.sra.com	703-803-1971
Staffware	Enterprise workflow solution	www.staffware.com	781-271-0003
Statware Inc.	Statit e-QC 5.1	sales@statware.com	541-753-5382
Stellcom	e-business integration solutions	www.stellcom.com	888-554-2024
STEPS: Tools Software	STEPS: Tools Service Desk 3.0	info@stepstools.com	416-481-5047
Sterling International Consulting Group	TabMaint v1.0	webadmin@sterling-consulting.com	704-664-8400
Sterling Management Consulting Inc.	TradeBI	info@sterlingmgt.com	609-452-9300
Sterling Software, IMD	VISION:Clearaccess 6.1	vision@sterling.com	818-716-1616

Company Name	Product Name	E-mail/Web	Phone Number
Structural Dynamics Research Corporation	eBusiness collaboration solutions	www.sdrc.com	513-576-2400
Success Technology	ST Synergy – Digital Nervous System 2.5.11	sales@success.com.au	+ 61 8 93452677
Synaptec Software	KM solutions	www.lawbase.com	800-569-3377
Synchrologic, Inc.	SyncKit 2.0		404-876-3209
Syncsort Inc.	SyncSort for Windows NT 1.0	info@syncsort.com	201-930-8200
Syspro Impact Software	IMPACT Encore	sales@sysprousa.com	800-369-8642
Systems Farm Software	KM, B2B, workflow and document management	www.systemsfarm.com	604-760-9119
Systems Farm Software Inc.	No Product Name Specified	info@systemsfarm.com	604-760-9119
T4G	Business Intelligence and data warehousing	www.t4g.com	800-399-5370
T4G Limited	T4G marketplace 1.5	info@t4g.com	416-462-4200
Tailer Market Media Group	CRM software	www.taylormmg.com	303-832-9388
Talisma Corporation	Talisma Enterprise	sales@talisma.com	425-897-2900
TARGIT A/S	TARGIT Analysis	joanne_i@targit.net	(+45) 96 23 19 00
Taurus Software	DataBridge 2.05	sales@taurus.com	650-961-1323
Taylor Market Media Group	Sales Management Plus 3.8	sales@taylormmg.com	303-832-9388
TeamScope	Outlook Extensions Library	phils@teamscope.com	818-876-0776 ext. 102
TeamScope	TeamWork Workflow	phils@teamscope.com	818-876-0776 ext. 102
Telekol Corporation	IntegraX Unified Messaging System 5.0	info@telekol.com	781-487-7100
Teltech Resource Network	KM consulting services	www.teltech.com	952-851-7500
Telution, LLC	The Communication Exchange 1.8	sbrown@telution.com	312-935-3408

Company Name	Product Name	E-mail/Web	Phone Number
Tenrox	Web based project, time and expense management	www.tenrox.com	514-336-4567
Tenuteq International	e-solutions	www.tenuteq.com	01295 279955-272787
Tesseract	Service Centre 4.1	sales@tesseract.co.uk	01494 465066
The Electric Mail Company	Global internet e-mail	www.electricmail.com	800-419-7463
The Haaverson Corporation	SmartDL 1.2	sales@haav.com	877-684-3837
The Haaverson Corporation	WebDIR 1.2	sales@haav.com	877-684-3837
The Loki Group, Inc.	MetaSuite 6.0.1	dave@loki.com	773-761-4654
The Loki Group, Inc.	RJ Gescom32 1.0	dave@loki.com	773-761-4654
The Solution Foundry	EMSolution	mpierle@solutionfoundry.com	7.71E+09
The Sutherland Group	Monaco 1.0	bob_moline@suth.com	800-388-4620
Three-Entity Sdn Bhd	ProcureFlow	tck@3ntity.com	603-7957 6355
TIS Worldwide	e-business solutions integrator	www.tisworldwide.com	212-962-1550
TopTier Software	TopTier Entrprise Integration Portal 2.0	sales@toptiersw.com	408-360-1700
TopTier Software	Web navigation, BI and Enterprise Application Integration (EAI)	www.toptier.com	408-360-1700
Touchtone Software International	Wintouch 3	info@wintouch.com	714-470-1122
Tower Technology	No Product Name Specified	inquiry@towertech.com	617-236-5500
Tower Technology	Integrated document management	www.towertech.com	617-236-5500
Trackit Software, Inc.	Service Central Pro	info@trackit.com	770-522-8550
Transcom Software	KM solutions	www.transcomsoft.com	415-292-0160

Company Name	Product Name	E-mail/Web	Phone Number
Transform Research	Web and e-mail response software built on Exchange and Outlook	www.transformResponse.com	613-238-1363
Transform Research Inc.	Transform Response 5.0	info@transres.com	613-238-1363
Trensic Corporation, Inc.	Health Care Workflow (Name to be determined)	al@trensiccorp.com	303-457-8100
Trilogy Development Group	Selling Chain	info@trilogy.com	512-794-5900
TRT, Inc.	CommPoint for NT 1.1	trtsales@trt.com	916-784-7777
Tympani Development	Intranet extranet information management applications	www.tympani.com	408-735-9555
Ultimus	Workflow Suite software to automate business processes	www.workflowzone.com	919-678-0900
Ultragenda nv/sa	Ultragenda Pro	marcv@ultragenda.com	
Uniplex Software	Document Repository	www.uniplex.com	800-255-4499
Unipress Software	Knowledge base builder for self or collaboration	www.unipress.com	800-222-0550
UniPress Software, Inc.	Footprints Helpdesk 1.142	info@unipress.com	732-287-2100
Uniscape	Web-based ASP platform	www.uniscape.com	888-464-4186
Unisys	Electronic business solutions	www.unisys.com	800-874-8647
Universal Document Management Systems	Step2000 B2B eBusiness	www.udms.com	513-583-5680
Univest	Enterprise!	kim@univest.com	501-223-8184 ext. 504
UpDate Marketing Inc.	Marketing Manager 3.5	sales@updatemarketing.com	650-631-2550
UpShot Corporation	UpShot Sales 1.0	sales@upshot.com	650-426-2200
Vality Technology	Data standardization and matching software	www.vality.com	617-338-0300
Vendor Managed Technologies (VMT)	No Product Name Specified	jbeckett@ezedi.com	

Company Name	Product Name	E-mail/Web	Phone Number
Venturini & Associates	Complaint Master 1.0	sales@venturiniassoc.com	949-720-7433
Verano	Secure supply chain management	www.verano.com	650-237-0200
Verbatim	Data Storage	www.verbatimcorp.com	704-547-6500
Verix Software	Verix eSales 1.1	sales@verix.com	213-743-4226
Vidya Technologies	Knowledge intensive framework for strategic planning, problem solving	www.vidyainc.com	617-244-6394
Vineyardsoft	KnowledgeSync real time alerts for front and back office management	www.vineyardsoft.com	508-696-6495
Vision 4 Ltd	Gemini 4	sales@vision4.co.uk	
Visual Insights	Data visualization software	www.visualinsights.com	630-753-8600
Visual Software	docLibrarian	info@doclibrarian.com	215-493-8210
Vocalsoft Corporation	PCI	mharoon@vocalsoft.com	972-470-9744
VocalTec Communications Ltd.	Internet Phone 5.0	info@vocaltec.com	201-768-9400
VocalTec Communications Ltd.	Telephony Gateway 3.0 3.0	info@vocaltec.com	201-768-9400
Wall Data Incorporated	Cyberprise DBApp Developer, Pro Ed. 2.5	sales@walldata.com	425-814-9255
Ward Systems Group, Inc.	NeuroShell Predictor 2.0	wardsystems@msn.com	301-662-7950
WebGecko Software	Active Page Generator 2.0	jimv@webgecko.com	206-709-0732
Webridge	Enterprise eCommerce	www.webridge.com	503-219-8500
Wildridge Technolgies Sdn. Bhd.	Kube.NET	funj@wrt.po.my	603-254-0700
Wincite Systems	DBMS and Interface for developing KM, BI and CRM solutions	www.wincite.com	312-424-6420
WinSales,Inc	WinSales ClientVision 4.0	info@winsales.com	425-453-9050

Company Name	Product Name	E-mail/Web	Phone Number
Wizdom Systems	Business process portal	www.wizdom.com	630-357-3000
WizSoft Inc.	WizRule 3.0	info@wizsoft.com	516-393-5841
Wolcott Systems Group	Knowledge architecture	www.wolcottgroup.com	330-869-9500
Worldtrak	Browser based CRM		888-814-2880
Worldtrak Corporation	Worldtrak 4.2	www.worldtrak.com	612/814-3677
Xchange	eCRM for campaign management and enterprise marketing automation	www.xchangeinc.com	713-361-0020
xnet	Collaborative business solutions	www.xnetconsulting.com	617-956-5000
Yankee Group	Enterprise KM planning services	www.yankeegroup.com	

F

Summary of Knowledge Management Case Studies and Web Locations

http://www.microsoft.com/BUSINESS/km/resources/finish.asp

Business and technical solutions for IT professionals and business decision makers looking to solve business problems by with applications and technology built by ISVs on the Microsoft family of servers.

http://www.microsoft.com/BUSINESS/km/casestudies/
changepoint_dell.asp

ChangePoint and Dell—Knowledge Management Case Study. Dell Technology Consulting upgraded its business management software to Changepoint's PSA solution. Running on Microsoft Windows NT Server and the Microsoft SQL Server database, the solution integrates and manages vital service delivery processes.

http://www.microsoft.com/BUSINESS/km/resources/quiz.asp

Knowledge Management Software Advisor—Microsoft Business. Business and technical solutions for IT professionals and business decision makers looking to solve business problems by with applications and technology built by ISVs on the Microsoft family of servers.

http://www.microsoft.com/BUSINESS/km/casestudies/
kynetix_benfield.asp

Kynetix Technology Group and Benfield Greig Group plc—Knowledge Management Case Study. Benfield Grieg, with their Knowledge Management partner the Kynetix Technology Group, have installed an intranet that has streamlined many key administrative tasks and improved customer service levels.

http://www.microsoft.com/BUSINESS/km/casestudies/cinergy.asp

Cinergy—Knowledge Management Case Study. Cinergy built and deployed a system integration project to streamline work processes, make better use of data, and deliver high levels of customer service.

http://www.microsoft.com/BUSINESS/km/casestudies/fosterparents.asp

Foster Parents Plan of Canada—Knowledge Management Case Study. Foster Parents Plan uses a Microsoft-based data warehouse to obtain the relevant information that helps it more effectively market its programs, communicate with partners, and manage resources.

http://www.microsoft.com/BUSINESS/km/resources/overview.asp

Microsoft's Vision and Strategies for Knowledge Management. Business and technical solutions for IT professionals and business decision makers looking to solve business problems by with applications and technology built by ISVs on the Microsoft family of servers.

http://www.microsoft.com/BUSINESS/km/casestudies/
ecms_snapper.asp

Enterprise Communication and Messaging Solutions (ECMS) and Snapper Power Equipment Company—Knowledge Management Case Study. Read how Snapper built a sales-force automation system based on Microsoft products to enhance knowledge sharing and effectively address customers and competition.

http://www.microsoft.com/BUSINESS/km/casestudies/
prism_soaustralia.asp

PRISM and the South Australian Government—Knowledge Management Case Study. The Education department uses a Microsoft product-based knowledge management application to track project details and share information.

http://www.microsoft.com/BUSINESS/km/casestudies/jdedward.asp

J.D. Edwards—Knowledge Management Case Study. Read how J. D. Edwards used Microsoft technologies to build a corporate-information network that improves knowledge sharing and manages the growing company.

http://www.microsoft.com/BUSINESS/km/casestudies/bp.asp

British Petroleum—Knowledge Management Case Study. BP implemented a Common Operating Environment, based on Microsoft technology, that allows them to communicate, collaborate, and share information more efficiently across the organization.

http://www.microsoft.com/BUSINESS/km/casestudies/casestudies.asp

Knowledge Management Case Studies on Microsoft Business. Knowledge Management case studies and business solutions using Microsoft applications and technology.

http://www.microsoft.com/BUSINESS/km/resources/snapperTDG.asp

The Snapper technical deployment guide discusses how they built a salesforce automation system based on Microsoft products, translating business requirements into a technological solution.

http://www.microsoft.com/BUSINESS/km/casestudies/leverent_motorola.asp

Motorola calls on knowledge management solution to build OneTeam, a knowledge management solution designed to provide customer information to every Motorola employee working on any aspect of that customer's business.

http://www.microsoft.com/BUSINESS/km/resources/welcomtdg.asp

The World Economic Forum developed an Internet-based videoconferencing and collaboration service using Microsoft technologies, allowing members to share knowledge easier and more efficiently.

http://www.microsoft.com/BUSINESS/km/casestudies/paconsulting.asp

One PA, a business philosophy, was created to bring together the knowledge and expertise the business has developed over 50 years but technology was critical in making it happen.

http://www.microsoft.com/BUSINESS/km/casestudies/microsoft_siemens.asp

Siemens created a unified knowledge management solution using Microsoft products to provide a centralized knowledge library that matches skills with projects, and access anytime and anywhere.

http://www.microsoft.com/BUSINESS/km/casestudies/8020_telstra.asp

Telstra Corporation Ltd. reduces on-the-job accidents and lowered medical claims with 80-20 Software Inc and Microsoft Exchange Server.

http://www.microsoft.com/BUSINESS/km/casestudies/directaccess.asp

Find out how Microsoft's technical information Web sites use Microsoft tools to create an easy-to-use, Web-based newsgroup service for the company's worldwide community of developers.

http://www.microsoft.com/BUSINESS/km/casestudies/ ecompanystore.asp

eCompanyStore.com created an end-to-end e-commerce solution to provide real-time access to product and delivery status and enhanced customer service.

http://www.microsoft.com/BUSINESS/km/casestudies/ entertainment.asp

We're Entertainment created an efficient business-intelligence solution that would minimize IT system management.

http://www.microsoft.com/BUSINESS/km/casestudies/harris.asp

Harris Microwave Communications created a business intelligence solution to consolidate and organize data from disparate manufacturing sites. Find out how they did it.

http://www.microsoft.com/BUSINESS/km/casestudies/ redwood_firstunion.asp

Following a period of corporate expansion, First Union Corporation found that it had acquired a myriad of disparate computer systems. The company needed a tool to bridge the information distribution gap. Report2Web, by Redwood Software proved to be the solution. Using the bank's intranet, or visiting the Web site, users can easily access reports they need.

http://www.microsoft.com/BUSINESS/km/resources/win2000km- article.asp

There are several key technologies that will impact the Knowledge Management Industry like no other operating system release to date and in this first article we'll take a look at one of the most exciting features of Windows 2000; the Active Directory.

http://www.microsoft.com/BUSINESS/km/resources/win2000km- pt2.asp

COM+ is designed to greatly simplify the creation and use of software components, which provides a runtime and services that are readily used from any programming language or tool, and enables extensive interoperability between components regardless of how they were deployed.

http://www.microsoft.com/BUSINESS/km/casestudies/ harperccollins.asp

Learn how HarperCollins switched to a Microsoft-based data warehouse to digitally track daily sales and distribute consistent, accurate sales data to key decision-makers.

http://www.microsoft.com/BUSINESS/km/resources/skillset-xscript- article.asp

Transcript of a conversation between Microsoft Knowledge Management Industry Manager, Jeffrey Kratz, and Skillset Software Founder, Dan White, regarding the HR market as it relates to the Microsoft KM strategy.

http://www.microsoft.com/BUSINESS/km/casestudies/ mii_connectaustria.asp

Connect Austria built a knowledge management solution based on Microsoft products to streamline internal communications and improve customer service through better information sharing.

http://www.microsoft.com/BUSINESS/km/default.asp

Business and technical solutions for IT professionals and business decision makers looking to solve business problems by with applications and technology built by ISVs on the Microsoft family of servers.

http://www.microsoft.com/BUSINESS/km/resources/kmpract.asp

Learn how to enhance knowledge management solutions by partnering technology with business processes, facilitating a better exchange of information. Find out more in this white paper.

http://www.microsoft.com/BUSINESS/km/resources/resources.asp

Business and technical solutions for IT professionals and business decision makers looking to solve business problems by with applications and technology built by ISVs on the Microsoft family of servers.

http://www.microsoft.com/BUSINESS/km/casestudies/kpmg.asp

KPMG turns knowledge into value with Kworld, a Web-based knowledge management solution that combines technology with business practices.

http://www.microsoft.com/BUSINESS/km/casestudies/ccentral.asp

Find out how Comedy Central created a corporate intranet in order to ensure fast and effective knowledge sharing.

http://www.microsoft.com/BUSINESS/km/casestudies/cotelligent_californiapizzakitchen.asp

CPK deployed a centralized data warehouse based on Microsoft products, to provide faster access to data, allowing managers to make faster, better decisions and improve customer service.

http://www.microsoft.com/BUSINESS/km/casestudies/filenet_bank-of-america.asp

Bank of America gained faster, easier, and more secure company-wide access to schedules, task force updates, collaborative documents, standards and specifications, with FileNET's integrated Panagon document management solution and Microsoft BackOffice.

http://www.microsoft.com/BUSINESS/km/casestudies/icomxpress_coastal.asp

A powerful yet intuitive process automation solution by icomXpress, formerly Keyfile, and Microsoft has enabled Coastal Banc to improve efficiency, reduce waste, and maximize its existing technology investment.

http://www.microsoft.com/BUSINESS/km/casestudies/icomxpress_university-illinois.asp

This major university created an electronic procurement bulletin system that links the campuses to their suppliers and to each other. The Web-based system, provided by icomXpress, formerly Keyfile, reduces administrative effort and overhead, and should lower costs by opening bidding to more competitors.

http://www.microsoft.com/BUSINESS/km/casestudies/lucent_arm-financial.asp

To stay competitive and grow its business, this leading financial service provider needed to automate its paper-based annuity sales process. With View-Star from Lucent Technologies, questions that took hours or days to answer are now handled in a matter of minutes.

http://www.microsoft.com/BUSINESS/km/casestudies/microsoft_utexas.asp

The University of Texas at Austin Graduate School of Business has standardized on Microsoft products to create a unified platform to lower costs and make administrative tasks easier.

http://www.microsoft.com/BUSINESS/km/casestudies/rim_paulhastings.asp

This international law firm uses cutting-edge messaging technology to give its clients constant access to attorneys, who use RIM BlackBerry to receive voice mail, faxes, and e-mail remotely and in real time.

http://www.microsoft.com/BUSINESS/km/casestudies/silverlake_hobbs.asp

Looking to promote their presence on the Web, this leading national insurance broker needed an intranet/extranet/Internet document management system with an intuitive user interface.

http://www.microsoft.com/BUSINESS/km/casestudies/usx.asp

US Steel developed a sophisticated intranet solution to replace their outdated business management systems using Microsoft Visual Basic and Visual Interdev.

http://www.microsoft.com/BUSINESS/km/casestudies/dandt.asp

Read this case study detailing how this digital dashboard solution helped Deloitte & Touche communicate internally and exceed client expectations.

http://www.microsoft.com/BUSINESS/km/casestudies/bpcl.asp

Find out how BPCL built a collaborative platform and intranet solution to enable information flow and facilitate faster decision-making in their company.

http://www.microsoft.com/BUSINESS/km/casestudies/microsoft_nabisco.asp

Learn how Nabisco created Journey, a Microsoft-based product-planning solution to facilitate successful development of products and profitable product research.

http://www.microsoft.com/BUSINESS/km/casestudies/
microsoft_partnershealthcare.asp

Learn how Partners HealthCare System created a telemedicine program to distribute presentations and educational materials on the Internet.

http://www.microsoft.com/BUSINESS/km/casestudies/
microsoft_toysrus.asp

Toys

http://www.microsoft.com/BUSINESS/km/casestudies/praxa_victoria-
election-commission.asp

Praxa manages VEC's mission-critical election IT network and internal systems, including 54 remote offices, a centralized production network, a temporary tally room, a Web site and result feeds to the political parties.

http://www.microsoft.com/BUSINESS/km/casestudies/
scg_prandium.asp

Prandium, Inc., known around the world for its El Torito, Chi-Chi's, Koo Koo Roo, Hamburger Hamlet, and Casa Gallardo restaurants, delivers powerful OLAP analysis and daily restaurant sales reports to nontechnical users.

http://www.microsoft.com/BUSINESS/digitaldashboard/casestudies/
microsoft_trooplaw.asp

Read how the Troop Law firm created a digital dashboard using Microsoft Windows and Microsoft Office that provided a solution for their knowledge management challenges.

http://www.microsoft.com/BUSINESS/km/casestudies/ims_snyder.asp

Snyder implemented Microsoft Windows CE-based handheld PCs with a custom sales-force automation application to automate its paper-based process, cut costs, and reduce errors.

http://www.microsoft.com/BUSINESS/km/casestudies/
microsoft_uofakron.asp

University of Akron built a state-of-the-art virtual campus network to give distance-learning students access to collaboration and conferencing tools. Find out how they did it.

http://www.microsoft.com/BUSINESS/km/resources/KMSols.asp

Build your own knowledge management solution using your existing technology and business practices. Learn more in this white paper.

http://www.microsoft.com/BUSINESS/digitaldashboard/projcen.asp

Business and technical solutions for IT professionals and business decision makers looking to solve business problems by with applications and technology built by ISVs on the Microsoft family of servers.

http://www.microsoft.com/BUSINESS/siteindex.asp

Find the information you are looking for on the Microsoft Business site in this comprehensive site index.

http://www.microsoft.com/BUSINESS/crm/resources/carpenter-dns-article.asp

A digital nervous system puts the customer at the center of business processes by using technology to deliver improved methods of customer service and help customers solve their own problems.

http://www.microsoft.com/BUSINESS/awards/isa/judging.asp

The Industry Solution Awards recognize the best solutions built on Microsoft technology that help organizations serve customers, manage information, and make informed, effective business decisions. Enter your winning solution today!

http://www.microsoft.com/BUSINESS/health/casestudies/partnershealthcare.asp

To lower costs, improve patient care, and expand its geographical reach, Partners is prescribing telemedicine with using Microsoft technology, including Microsoft SQL Server 7.0, Microsoft Windows Media Technologies, and Microsoft NetMeeting, to make telemedicine an effective reality.

http://www.microsoft.com/BUSINESS/bi/casestudies/andersen.asp

Andersen Consulting created Pocket Xchange, a custom application to provide consultants with offline access to its massive knowledge management system. This application is a 1999 Windows World Open winner in the Business Intelligence category.

http://www.microsoft.com/BUSINESS/digitaldashboard/casestudies/ddsoftwarespectrum.asp

Read how Software Spectrum created a digital dashboard using Microsoft Windows and Microsoft Office that provided a solution for their knowledge management challenges.

http://www.microsoft.com/BUSINESS/digitaldashboard/casestudies/uop.asp

Read how Buchanan Associates created a digital dashboard for UOP using Microsoft Windows and Microsoft Office that provided a solution for their knowledge management challenges.

http://www.microsoft.com/BUSINESS/finance/casestudies/casestudies.asp

Financial Services case studies and business solutions using Microsoft applications and technology.

http://www.microsoft.com/BUSINESS/finance/resources/overview.asp

Business and technical solutions for IT professionals and business decision makers looking to solve business problems by with applications and technology built by ISVs on the Microsoft family of servers.

http://www.microsoft.com/BUSINESS/health/casestudies/casestudies.asp

Real-world success stories and case studies using Microsoft applications and technology.

http://www.microsoft.com/BUSINESS/health/resources/overview.asp

Business and technical solutions for IT professionals and business decision makers looking to solve business problems by with applications and technology built by ISVs on the Microsoft family of servers.

http://www.microsoft.com/BUSINESS/bi/casestudies/comshare_ut.asp

The faculty at the University of Toledo wanted to develop an applied capstone course to give their students experience in how business intelligence software could be used in decision analysis. They chose Comshare, Inc.'s DecisionWeb and Microsoft SQL Server 7.0 as the best decision support solution for a course that offers students experience in analysis of real-life business situations.

http://www.microsoft.com/BUSINESS/finance/casestudies/
sullivan_generalife.asp

G. A. Sullivan and GeneraLife Company case study on an exciting solution using the latest technologies.

http://www.microsoft.com/BUSINESS/ecommerce/casestudies/
gasullivan_cass.asp

Cass Information Systems, Inc. has built a leading-edge Internet Business Intelligence/Data Warehousing and Business-to-Business (B2B) e-commerce Solution to provide their external customers with a secure online reporting tool for reviewing freight billing and payment data.

http://www.microsoft.com/BUSINESS/health/casestudies/
dyncorp0720.asp

In this healhcare industry case study, DynCorp Healthcare Information Technology Services (HITS) created MDeis which provides a secure extranet application for hospitals to access their own medical data in a rich data repository maintained by HITS.

http://www.microsoft.com/BUSINESS/hospitality/casestudies/
infogenesis_station.asp

Case study about technology by Infogenesis and Station Casinos in the hospitality industry for a solution using the latest technologies.

http://www.microsoft.com/BUSINESS/km/casestudies/
tmssequoia_oklahoma-county.asp

This county government needed a more efficient way to manage its millions of public records.

http://www.microsoft.com/BUSINESS/bi/casestudies/
gasullivan_acnielsen.asp

ACNielsen Market Decisions' outdated information system was costing the company too much turnaround time. G. A. Sullivan provided the best solution with MarketVu II, using Microsoft SQL Server and Microsoft Transaction Server. Now, special requests that once took several days can be filled in as little as an hour, and business is rolling in.

http://www.microsoft.com/BUSINESS/finance/casestudies/ hypermedia_inter_europabank.asp

Case study of Inter-Európa Bank and Hypermedia Systems for the banking industry describing the development of HyperBank, the core element of Inter-Európa Bank's BankoNet, which is Hungary's first Internet-based electronic banking system.

http://www.microsoft.com/BUSINESS/health/casestudies/ conchango_mimrx.asp

Online pharmacy migrates to scalable MS software solution to upgrade affinity group-oriented Web site.

http://www.microsoft.com/BUSINESS/ecommerce/casestudies/ microsoft_centra.asp

Cost-effective, easy-to-scale Microsoft Platform facilitates live e-learning and collaboration.

http://www.microsoft.com/BUSINESS/manufacturing/casestudies/ symix_american.asp

Improved system maintenance has freed up 60 to 70 hours each week so managers can better spend their time growing the business. Sales staff can manage their own catalogs and enjoy faster access to product data with the knowledge that the information they share with customers is always up-to-the-minute.

http://www.microsoft.com/BUSINESS/health/casestudies/ eds_textron.asp

The latest healthcare industry solution success stories and case studies about building powerful applications on the BackOffice family of servers, including Windows NT Server and SQL Server.

http://www.microsoft.com/BUSINESS/casestudies_subject.asp

An index of case studies segmented by subject.

Index

A